AF469143

JAMES WRIGHT'S
East Anglia

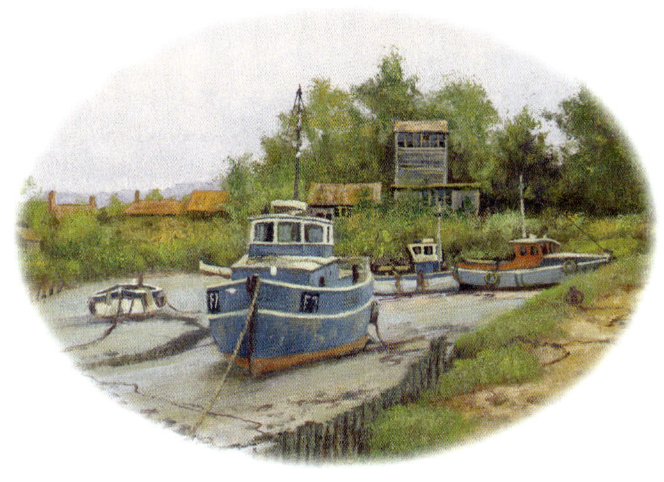

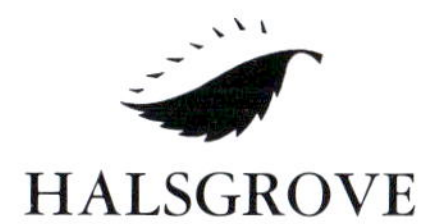

HALSGROVE

First published in Great Britain in 2006

British Library Cataloguing-in-Publication Data
A CIP record for this title is available from the British Library

ISBN 1 84114 522 X
ISBN 978 1 84114 522 8

HALSGROVE
Halsgrove House
Lower Moor Way
Tiverton, Devon EX16 6SS
Tel: 01884 243242
Fax: 01884 243325
email: sales@halsgrove.com
website: www.halsgrove.com

Printed and bound by D'Auria Industrie Grafiche Spa, Italy

Foreword

It gives me great pleasure to acknowledge the harmonious association that exists between James Wright and Picturecraft, for it has spanned nearly four decades and has involved three generations of the Hill family.

James made a very early decision that Picturecraft should be the only gallery in Norfolk to represent his work and his unswerving loyalty was to develop quickly into a special friendship which extends far beyond the confines of a normal business relationship. We continue to enjoy and cherish the close links made with James, and his wife Judy and their family, from the foundations of friendship that were made in those very early years.

Today, a fine selection of James Wright's paintings continue to feature at my son's award-winning gallery in Holt, the historic Georgian town in North Norfolk which has a fine reputation for its abundance of art galleries. Besides exhibiting annually, James also held two extremely successful major one-man exhibitions. The size of the gallery necessitates over eighty paintings being assembled in order to stage such an event, an exhausting and daunting task for any artist. However, James seized the challenge and produced some of his finest work – and the exhibitions continue to stimulate conversation to this day. Unsurprisingly, an appreciative audience has responded favourably over the years securing and maintaining his name as one of Picturecraft's most highly-respected professional artists.

Captivated by the wide, expansive open skies and gentleness of the Norfolk countryside, many paintings feature his love of my home county. He allows a viewer to share the beauty and mood of an English landscape at its best, the colours of all its seasons and in a style that unashamedly links back to a past era. James is a master of tradition, and his paintings reflect his close affinity with nature.

The pleasures James has given through his painting is beyond measure. But it is the human element of this sensitive, humble man, enormously blessed with a fine mix of great humour, that allows me to write with such a personal admiration and affection.

Michael Hill
Picturecraft of Holt

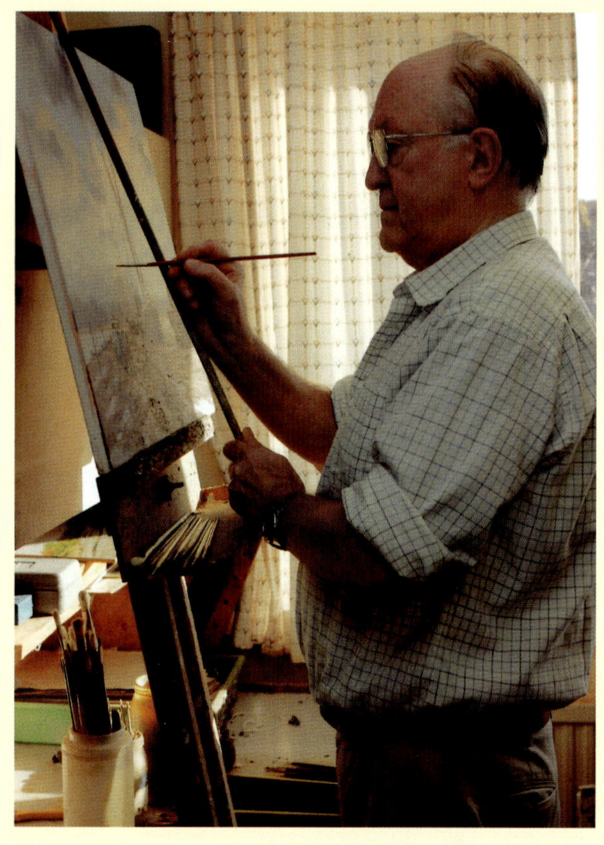

Introduction

Early Life

I was born on 13 January 1935. My parents originated from Retford in Nottinghamshire and Boston in Lincolnshire. They relocated to Peterborough to begin their married life, where my father George worked as a security guard for the local firm Frank Perkins Engineering. My mother Selina was content to be a housewife, the usual career for a married woman of that time. I was destined to be an only child, brought up during the austere years following the Second World War. Lacking the material comforts and computerised toys regarded as normal by the children of today, I thrived on such simple outdoor pursuits as exploring the surrounding countryside of Yaxley. I happily collected birds eggs (legal at that time) and fished in the local brick pits. In my teen years hobbies such as making model aeroplanes, playing the piano and helping my father grow flowers, kept me occupied and out of mischief.

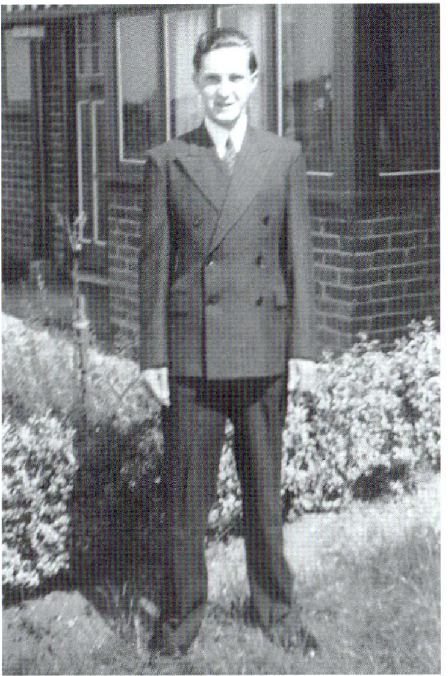

I attended the local primary school and then progressed to the nearby Fletton Grammar School where I can remember I was mortified to be the only boy without proper school uniform! My parents were blissfully unaware of the value of bonding and belonging! In those happy pre-Ofsted schooldays, life was mainly uneventful, and at the end my career choices much simpler. My parents had rarely visited the school, unlike today's anxious guardians of stressed, regularly tested offspring. Although they were aware that I had excelled artistically, they had already mapped out my career for me. No gap year for me then! Thus I dutifully followed their direction and found myself proudly enrolled as a very raw cadet into the Police Force. In their eyes, job security and a pension were much more important than any precarious experimentation with art!

A Variety of Jobs

National Service then reared its ugly head and I served my time as an R.A.F. policeman from 1953 until 1955. After this character-building period of my life I then naturally entered the Peterborough Police Force where I met and consequently married my first wife, Joyce. It didn't take long for me to realise that I had unwittingly been pushed into the wrong career. Therefore,

Above: *A teenager. Needless to say that we have had a good laugh at this photograph of me taken in the 1950s. Suited and booted all ready for a night on the town – note the Brylcreemed hair.*

much to my parents' obvious disappointment I bravely resigned from the service and went to work at the local Burdett's Nursery as a general dogsbody. There is nothing like working on the land in the middle of winter, toiling from early in the morning until late at night, to make one assess the meaning of life, and mine was definitely going nowhere.

Consequently I moved once again and worked for a box-making company where I gained experience performing general carpentry jobs. In my spare time I began to use my garden shed for personal cabinet-making projects. This in turn led me to consider the possibility of developing this hobby into a satisfying career. I was already taking the *Woodworking Magazine* and to this day I can remember the advertisement from Chambers College that caught my eye – 'Be a Handicraft teacher, no pass no fee.' So whilst still working long hours during the day I committed myself to the uphill task of furthering my education. In the evenings I studied for a City and Guilds Certificate in Woodwork. It took me four long years to achieve but it enabled me to change my life. In 1962 I enrolled as a proud mature student at Winchester Teacher Training College.

I thoroughly enjoyed this period of my life; the chance to make furniture and acquire new skills suited me down to the ground – I didn't have to be dragged to lectures! For the first time in my life I was experiencing job satisfaction and enjoying working with equally dedicated students. This year of creativity sped by and in 1963 I gained a distinction and left as a newly qualified teacher of woodwork and technical drawing. However the singlemindedness and dedication necessary in achieving this goal, whilst being the absent husband of Joyce and father to Deborah, had its downside. The many separations and pressures in the end caused the unhappy collapse of my marriage. Consequently I found myself alone once more, living in a flat in Spalding and embarking on the next stage of my life. I had been appointed as a teacher at the Gleed Boys' County Secondary School.

Exciting Beginnings

Little did I know of the challenging opportunities looming on the horizon. Having experienced the harsh reality of labouring manually for long hours for little wage and few holidays, the pleasures of a professional life were enthusiastically appreciated. I enjoyed my job which was then free from such horrors as the National Curriculum and frenzied testing. My colleagues Alec Booth and George Whittington proved to be real friends and we had time for chats and laughs during the day. Also the delights of teaching a ladies' adult evening class proved to be a very pleasing novelty.

Then the totally new experience of playing in an inter-school staff hockey match presented itself. I have to say at this point that I could never be described as athletic. Apart from the compulsory cross country school runs which I perversely enjoyed, sport is not for me. To my children's amusement this is where I met Judy who at that time was a physical education teacher at the adjoining Gleed Girls' School. In order to convince her that I was a worthwhile catch I even managed to make up foursomes to play badminton with our lifelong friends Pam and John Portas. However, after a year our relationship floundered, regretfully Judy had doubts. Indirectly she bears some responsibility for my eventual career, for it was at this point that I first began to experiment with oil painting, as for the first time in my life I had school holidays at my disposal and no one to share them with.

I read avidly to refresh and master the skills I had learnt long ago and eventually had the confidence to progress to painting on canvas. With time at my disposal I also joined a book club and quickly amassed a collection of inspiring illustrated volumes of my favourite artists. Then following an organised school trip to Austria I attempted enthusiastically to capture the characteristic chalets and woodland scenes. At this time I was experimenting with using a palette knife to give greater depth and texture. I think that there are still a few of these early crude attempts hanging in the houses of my family.

Carefree Days

Fortunately then Judy and I resumed our commitment to each other and, happily settled, my artistic career developed rapidly. Our holidays were spent visiting the traditional small fishing villages in Cornwall, Sussex and Kent. We happily explored these then-thriving harbours and boatyards and I have numerous sketch books filled with scenes of those nostalgic times. One of our most memorable holidays was spent in France, trawling round the many picturesque harbours in Brittany. My love of boats even resulted in us making a 16-foot cabin cruiser during one summer holiday. However, we later had to sell her as we were both too busy at that time to enjoy sailing her. Having both the opportunity to explore these fascinating places and the time to sketch and paint whenever I wanted to, led to an immediate upsurge in productivity. I painted whenever I wasn't at school. It became an all-consuming passion.

It came as no surprise to Judy that I had arranged our honeymoon to begin in Truro and then to explore once again the beautiful Cornish coastline, sketch books and camera for ever at the ready. Glorious sunny days muddy fishing boats, terrific views, a plentiful supply of fresh fish to eat, and Judy – what more could I wish for.

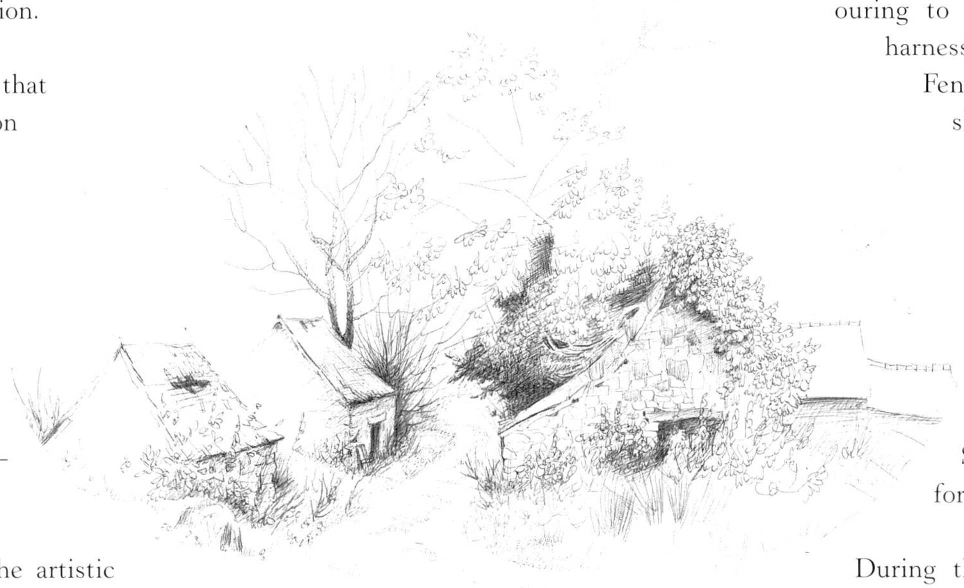

I absorbed wholeheartedly the artistic atmosphere of Cornwall. Luckily Judy was equally as fanatical. Every gallery, pavement artist and craft centre alternately gave me massive encouragement or the realisation that I was still very much a fledgling artist, with a long way to go. I was particularly impressed by the work of the popular artist Ben Maille and of course the legacy of the Newlyn School. On returning to the calm sleepiness of Lincolnshire I became engrossed with trying to capture the beauty of the places we had visited. Rewardingly, many of my works of that period have been reproduced in print.

Now that I had become reasonably adept at applying paint to canvas and had achieved some success with my portrayal of boats I turned to expanding my choice of subject. My first attempts at landscape had consisted of symbolic scenes containing a few trees silhouetted against glowing sunsets. I gradually gained confidence and progressed to challenging day time scenes. Then followed the problem of what to include as focus and meaning. Solution – what better than the traditional view of horses ploughing the fields. Unfortunately the majority of farmers by that time had been won over by the practicalities and convenience of tractor power to till their land, and so I traversed Lincolnshire in search of suitable subjects. We attended all the local ploughing matches to capture the scenes that I desired. Rarely have I felt under pressure when painting, but endeavouring to get all the finer details of harness tackle correct came near to it. Fen farmers eagerly spot the slightest error and show no hesitation in loudly proclaiming the mistake.

One of our favourite haunts is in Yorkshire, Holme on Spalding Moor, where still today the land is worked by magnificient Shire horses and exhibitions for enthusiasts are held regularly.

During this time we also enjoyed a holiday with Jean and George Hastings who owned a holiday home in Blakeney on the Norfolk coast. This was the beginning of many visits to this panoramic spacious harbour and a lifelong love for Norfolk.

After our marriage and the acquisition of a smart new house we both became dissatisfied at my use of a bedroom for my painting. Me because it wasn't large enough and Judy because of the permanent smell of paint! The next logical step was to build on a purpose-designed studio and workroom for me to make frames for the many canvases that I was now producing.

Above: *A sketch of the place we stayed in Brittany, called Tromarch.*

My Studio

This is where I have spent most of my working life. It measures 12 feet by 20 feet and has a large east-facing window. To compensate for not having the perfect northern light it is fitted with three large daylight double strip lights. I have a central desk which I custom built to hold all the paraphernalia necessary, fitted with a sturdy false top so that it doubles up as a another work surface for me to frame pictures. The studio is also now home for my Morso machine which has turned out to be one of the best investments that I have ever made. Way back in the 1960s it cost the exorbitant amount of £270 but it is now worth nearer £1500. I have another small desk near the window with a mini easel so that I can sit to paint my smaller pictures. The final luxury is a fitted carpet – we reasoned that if this was to be my creative home then I needed the support of physical comfort.

Expanding Horizons

Satisfyingly then my work became popular with friends and acquaintances and it soon became apparent that I needed more outlets for the volume of work that I was producing enthusiastically. Thus I was fortunate to discover John Hutton who owned a successful gallery in nearby Peterborough. I eagerly showed him samples of my work and to my delight he agreed to stage my first exhibition. It proved to be both a frightening and stimulating experience to see my paintings displayed. Previously the canvases had been propped against any available surface so to view them sensitively arranged and with the benefit of picture lights was a real pleasure. I fondly remember that to our amazement we spent a very happy and enjoyable evening socializing and celebrating, this being before the restrictions of drink driving.

Exhibition 1968

This was my very first exhibition held at the John Hutton Gallery in Peterborough. Just look at those frames – obviously made by me. I am staggered to see that I was smoking. I had smoked a pipe and enjoyed the puff of cigars before I met Judy but soon after our marriage I dutifully became a non smoker. Judy made her dress for this auspicious occasion, clearly dating the mini era. I cannot remember the location of the boat painting but I do recall that the mansion was somewhere in Brittany.

Any spare time that we had was spent travelling in Suffolk, with the dual purpose of discovering subject matter to paint and also suitable galleries that would be willing to exhibit the resulting pictures. Eventually we found the ideal place. With fear in our hearts and the courage of the innocent, without any prior arrangement or introduction, we approached Josephine and Derek Walpole who ran the popular Deben Gallery in Woodbridge. Fortunately they liked my style and so began my journey to become a real artist.

At this time I became engrossed with reading Ronald Blythe's book *Akenfield* which gives a fascinating insight into bygone country life in Suffolk. With renewed impetus I photographed and painted this beautiful countryside and in 1974 the resulting canvases were exhibited as 'Akenfield Revisited'. Rewardingly, the exhibition not only delighted the author but was a complete sell out. My career blossomed and flourished and I will always be grateful to the Walpoles for their guidance and friendship.

During a routine visit to the gallery we wandered down to the River Deben. Immediately I was captivated by the unique structure of the Tide Mill. The outer covering was of corrugated tin which had been painted with red lead. Luckily I was able to paint it in this original state and then later once again after it was renovated to its present form, resplendent with an outer coat of white boards.

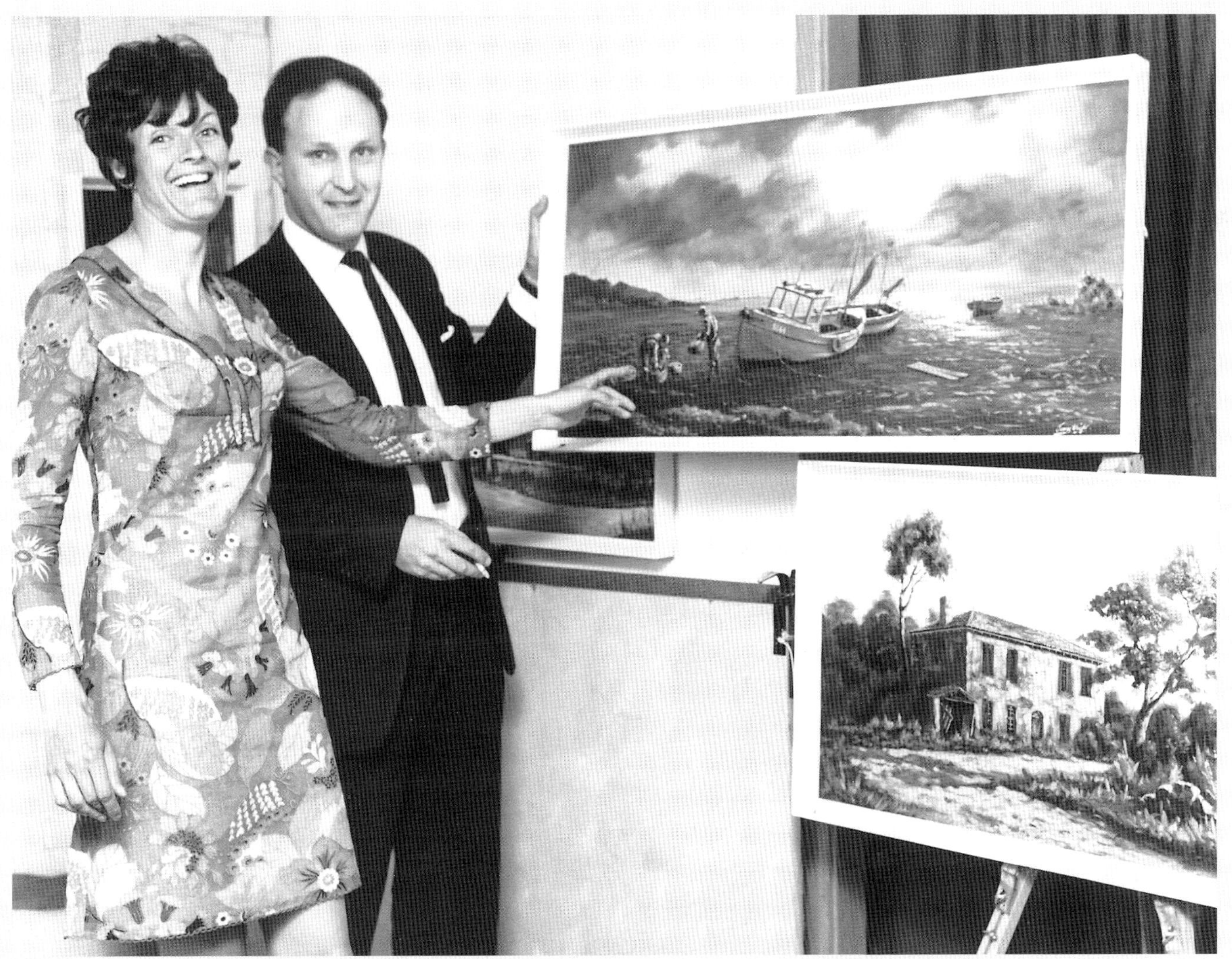

James and Judy enjoying James's first exhibition at the John Hutton Gallery.

Further Opportunities

One of the guiding principles in the development of my career has been to consider carefully where to show my work. Obviously, my orthodox fine art genre using oils would not prove popular in a gallery primarily known for contemporary work. Consideration also had to be given to the situation of suitable galleries as I feel it to be a mistake to exhibit in places near to each other. I much prefer to allow the chosen establishments generous catchment areas and I certainly don't wish to be the cause of any competition.

My outlet in Peterborough had been gently ticking over and consequently I was content for it to be the sole agent for that area. However, with the sad demise of John Hutton and the subsequent closing of his gallery it meant that I needed to explore other venues. Luckily I was able to exhibit in the Annakin Art Gallery in Peterborough which later relocated to Helpston. I knew Ann from when she worked with John, and many a pleasant day was spent discussing the state of the art trade with her partner Graehem Kinaird, while he continued with his framing.

The next step was for me to venture into my beloved Norfolk, so I set about investigating likely venues. Eventually, during a routine conversation with a representative of one of the framing companies I used, I was told of the success of the Picturecraft Gallery in Holt. It had acquired a reputation for supporting new artists, so responding to the truism nothing ventured nothing gained, I immediately made contact with the owner John Hill. This was to be the start of a successful working and friendly relationship that existed until his death. Far removed from the stereotyped formal austere establishment his gallery, like him, was friendly and welcoming. I have subsequently enjoyed working with his son Michael and the present owner, grandson Adrian.

Many happy days have been spent transporting paintings to the gallery and then meandering in a leisurely way around the wonderful Norfolk coastline. It is a great satisfaction to me that my work has sold regularly in the gallery for the past thirty years.

Interestingly my daughter Nicola now has her ceramic work on display in the gallery – a far cry from when she used to run around as a toddler.

At this time I also exhibited in the nearby popular Kelling Gallery, again successfully managed by John Hill. I felt sad when it was eventually closed, mainly due to the recession of that time, which indirectly caused a decline in the demand for luxury goods such as original paintings.

Farm at High Kelling

We first saw this farm when we were whizzing by travelling from Holt towards East Runton. It made such an impact that we turned round and went back to it. Conveniently there is a grassy lay-by, and a stony track to park off the main road, thus allowing time to peruse safely. The farm is a working farm and typifies bygone days. It has everything – irregular stone walls, tumbled outbuildings, sheds complete with cattle and free roaming chickens. I have painted it many times and we still continue to stop whenever we are passing.

Wider Afield

The next big milestone in my life was my introduction to the world of illustrative reproduction. In my wildest dreams I had never considered that this would become an option. Out of the blue we were invited by the prestigious company of Solomon and Whitehead Ltd to submit a few canvases, possibly to be considered suitable for printing. I recall that I managed to engineer a day off school in order to keep the appointment. We nervously set off from Moulton in our trusty Ford Anglia very early in the morning, our aim being to avoid the London rush hour traffic. We dutifully arrived outside the grand establishment at five o'clock in the morning! It proved to be a nerve wracking experience.

Our appointment was with a certain Miss Butcher who was extremely efficient and very professional. With a no-nonsense attitude and practical eye she quickly introduced us to the complexities and demands necessary to reach the required standard. Our confidence fell steadily during this initiation. Looking back I find it hard to believe that we ever had the courage to approach such a hallowed company. However, to my astonishment and immense relief, two canvases were selected initially and further contracts followed. So another feature of my career was safely accomplished.

Following this my work entitled 'Bringing in the Sheaves' was one of many limited editions reproduced by Felix Rosenstiels Widow and Son. At a later date in my career G.D.R. Marketing International also printed a limited series. It still continues to be exciting to see my work printed and my family take great delight in spotting 'my' greetings cards. My daughter thought that I had reached the pinnacle of success when as a student she discovered a print of mine displayed in Harrods. I can also remember Judy screaming with delight when she recognised a boat reproduction on the set of a B.B.C. play.

Popular Haunts

At this time my work was predominantly of scenes of my surrounding Lincolnshire. Glimpses of dilapidated barns, muddy ploughed fields with majestic trees standing proudly against the open skyline, overgrown ponds in the middle of nowhere and the appeal of rutted and water-filled cart tracks – these were the images that I enjoyed and endeavoured to capture. I was particular fascinated by the tumbledown farmyards which reminded me of my early childhood and of course the expanse and colour of the ever-changing Fenland sky.

Roaming in Norfolk

We also spent most of our leisure time exploring the wonders of the Norfolk coastal roads, beginning with the flat expanse of Old Hunstanton and continuing via Wells and Sherringham until we reached Cromer. We avidly researched Ordnance Survey maps in order to locate the windmills, ponds, rivers and churches in these areas. Thus our journeys were full of unexpected deviations and delights. Judy completed an enormous amount of crosswords while I happily trudged around in mud and water and walked along derelict farm tracks in order to capture the images of bygone days. I can confidentially say that there cannot be a boat, harbour, barn, church or pond that I haven't sketched or photographed.

Brancaster Staithe

This popular sailing and fishing village on the Norfolk coast is one place to which we are both happy to escape. I have painted it many times and never fail to be enthralled by its timeless beauty. The traditional Norfolk cottages provide a stunning background for the modern boats in the yacht club. When the tide is out the fishing boats are revealed beached along the numerous twisting creeks. The shingle provides a firm base for pottering but I have been known to venture too far into the mud in order to capture an elusive view.

A Chance Encounter

One of the favourite scenes that I have painted I discovered during one of the many journeys to Woodbridge. It was situated just outside Wisbech near the village of Salters Lode, and consisted of a derelict farm surrounded by a collection of tumbledown outbuildings. I have painted it many times, recording the relentless stages of decline and neglect. Eventually it sadly succumbed to the inevitable bulldozer and I missed it like a long lost friend. I did however have the pleasure of selling one of my paintings to the original owner of the once proud building.

Children

Then in 1972 we extended our family with the birth of Simon, half brother to Deborah. Steve arrived soon after and with the arrival of Nicola our happiness was complete. This then became one of the busiest and challenging times in my life. I was still teaching at the Gleed School and painting in every moment available to me. I guiltily recall that my one luxury occurred every Saturday when Judy obligingly transported the whole family to her parents Jack and Meg Blackburn for the whole day. She conveniently returned at the children's bedtime when I dutifully downed my paintbrushes and bathed the children while she recovered.

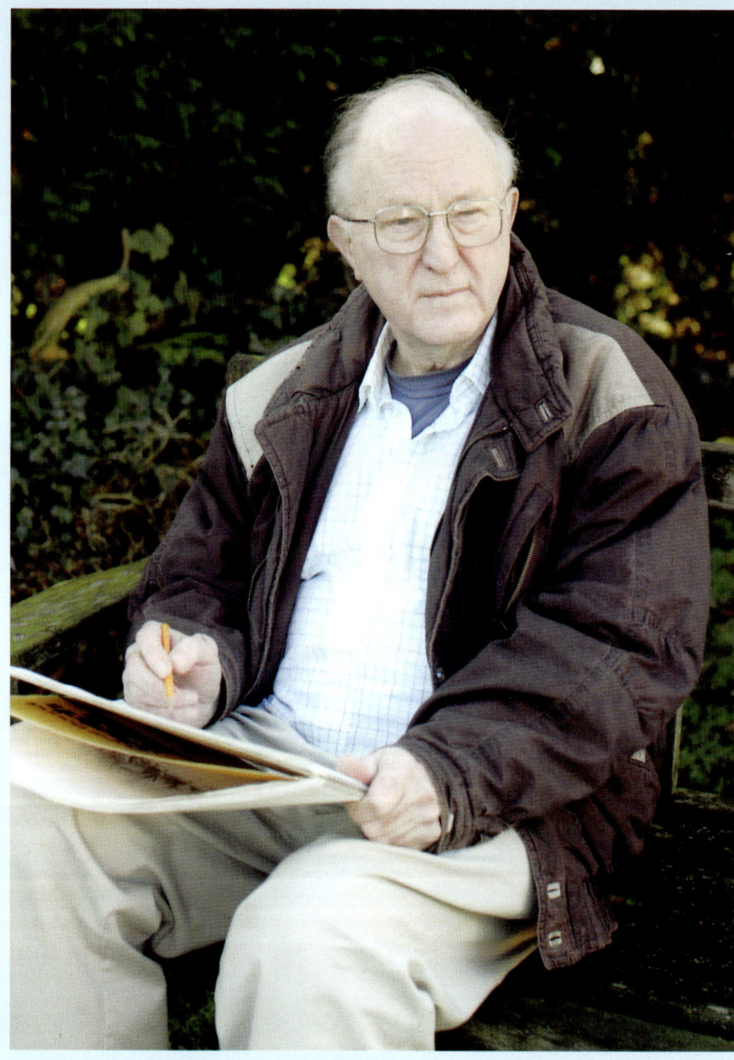

All in a day's work.

Hastings Beach

Needless to say that future family outings and holidays were planned to also accommodate their father's interests. One of our favourites was our visit to Hastings in Sussex. The children were happy playing on the beach, I was engrossed with the fishing boats and Judy, as always, was just happy that we were all content. The proud, workmanlike structure of the small sturdy boats, beached on the pebbled shore, readily appealed to me. The surrounding clutter of nets, chains, floats and posts added to the overall impression of the fishing life. We enjoyed similar experiences during a Cornish holiday based in Bude where I was able to record many snippets and scenes for future paintings.

West and East Runton

Another favourite holiday was spent at West Runton, again on the Norfolk coast. We rented a wooden bungalow situated in the middle of a small wood and it enabled us to unwind and have fun together. We travelled daily to the nearby village of East Runton where its now limited small fishing fleet and stony beach proved idyllic for us all. Still today one of our favourite outings is to walk from East Runton to Cromer along the water's edge and then treat ourselves to fish and chips before ambling back. However, the once wooden boats have now mainly been replaced by up-to-date fibreglass, but a few originals thankfully remain. I continue to photograph and sketch them from every possible angle.

Another delight was, and still is, to meander back along the winding coast road where the reedy and muddy marshes are a haven for many varieties of bird life. The sight of the sparse trees bent double from the force of the sea breeze is a powerful image. A convenient stopping place for tea and sandwiches was always Salhouse duck pond where we could admire the geese and swans before continuing on our way.

As I was so busy in my studio and Judy was a full time housewife and mother it also naturally fell upon her to be my link with the galleries as well. Luckily by this time we had an estate car large enough to transport three lively pre-school children, plus all the equipment required for their daily needs, and of course the all important canvases to Holt or Woodbridge. In those carefree days Judy would break her journey to Suffolk by stopping in Thetford Forest for the children to have toilet stops followed by a run around to let off steam. Once in the gallery they quickly learnt skills such as 'don't touch' and 'stand still' while she endeavoured to carry out the business transactions before they succumbed to mischief.

Going Professional

Life for us all became more and more hectic. The many demands of providing for and looking after a growing family, whilst in effect balancing two demanding careers, left me tired and dissatisfied. It was obvious that my main desire was to paint and it soon became apparent that a change of life style was necessary for the well being of us all. So in 1979 I made the brave decision to retire from teaching and to channel my energy into becoming a full time professional artist.

We reasoned that if it became a financial necessity Judy could be the one to return to teaching in order to boost our earnings. Thankfully it was never an issue, although she did resume her teaching career following the death of her mother, which coincided with our youngest child Nicola beginning school.

Daily Routine

This period of my life was the most productive artistically as I now had the freedom I desired and needed, to expand and develop. We settled into a well-oiled routine and I became a fashionable house husband, well before it became the norm. It was my responsibility to earn our living and to have a cooked meal ready at the end of the day. As ever a true Capricorn and creature of habit, I continued to work to school hours. I disciplined myself to be installed in my studio ready for action by 8.30a.m. and remained steadily working until my family returned home. Even today I still maintain this rigid structure although I have to confess that the starting time now varies.

After our evening meal and general-catch up time with family events I would either sneak back in or sketch and doodle whilst relaxing in front of the television. Again it fell upon Judy to ferry the children to their many sporting activities, although I do recall sitting in the car listening to the radio waiting for the boys to finish their training sessions.

Our children grew up thinking what a delightful life I had. The unseen pressures of working to deadlines completely passed them by. They only saw me happy to escape into my studio fortified with numerous cups of tea or taking the odd days off to go fishing! Indeed I only had one pressing concern – how to remain working in my studio, which I enjoyed, and at the same time spend valuable painting hours delivering my work to the galleries.

In the early days necessity forced me to overcome any reticence I felt about approaching prospective gallery proprietors, but I have never felt comfortable about promoting my work myself. I was very aware that in order to maintain my professional status I needed to expand my outlets further afield. Right on cue I received a telephone call that was to solve my dilemma.

New Contacts

The caller was Graham Reeve. He had seen my work and was interested in representing me. Thankfully, problem solved. This welcome development ensured that I could concentrate on my creative work and leave the promotion of my business to someone else. Thus began an association that continued until I semi-retired. He became my mediator and introduced my work to numerous galleries across the country. His own company has also reproduced many canvases of mine.

Occasionally I did venture out to explore outlets for myself and during one journey I came across the Frinton Gallery in Frinton on Sea in Essex. I introduced myself to the owner Stephen Corton who happily agreed to show my work. Again our association has flourished throughout my career.

Around this time I also made contact with Ian Davey and his daughter Anita who ran a thriving gallery in Yorkshire. Each room was tightly packed from floor to ceiling with an eclectic display of fine art. They possessed an uncanny sense for the type of work likely to be popular in their area and felt that my genre of rural country scenes with horses ploughing would fit in well. I found them to be both friendly and supportive and happily correct in their first assumption.

Lincoln

One of the concerns I had at that time was that although I was beginning to develop contacts in other areas I still lacked representation in my own county of Lincolnshire. This presented a real challenge as previously I had only relied on the customers who visited my studio to publicize my work, and the thought of having to trawl the vast area of my own county was not appealing.

Again the opportunity presented itself as a result of a telephone conversation with a friend and fellow artist, Trevor Parkin. In turn he had been contacted by Frank and Pamela Roberts who owned the Cassian Gallery situated in the prestigious area of Stoop Hill in Lincoln. Unfortunately for him he couldn't place his work with them as he was already under contract elsewhere. He generously suggested that I should make contact and – hey presto – another beneficial association was formed. This proved to be an ideal venue for my traditional landscapes and conveniently being only an hour away was easy to reach. Unfortunately due to the eventual lapsing of the lease on the property, and the retirement of Frank this popular gallery is now closed.

Hectic Times

My career was by now expanding in all directions and I found that I could just about keep all my own contacts supplied and happy. Graham visited me regularly and continued to distribute my work all over the country. My days were tightly structured and sometimes pressurised, but the joy of working for myself counteracted any negative feelings that occasionally surfaced.

Time for long holidays were few and far between but we managed to fit in a few snatched interludes. Our children were all heavily involved in a wide range of sporting activities, and with their success came the transporting of them to venues all over the country. I now appreciate how much time Judy spent acting as the main taxi service, leaving me with essential painting time.

Those frantic years juggling work and pleasure were full of enjoyable memories. As a family we all benefited from living and working closely together and then amazingly and far too soon we had reached the end of school and further education commitments. Consequently with the slight easing of the financial burden I felt able to relax and even take odd days off.

Relaxation

Then in the summer of 1997 during a visit to Devon, I made contact with Tony Crook, the owner of the Barle Gallery in Dulverton, Somerset. Graham had been supplying him with paintings over many years and I had been looking forward to meeting him in person. We spent an enjoyable time perusing his gallery and mulling over the state of the art world.

On returning home I was pleased to settle down to my well practised routine of painting, fishing and cooking – mostly in that order! Although I couldn't imagine my days without any painting at all, the attraction of moving into semi-retirement was beginning to have some appeal. The emerging idea of being able to paint for myself when I so desired, rather than the steady and relentless commitment to keep my galleries well stocked, was a pleasing one.

Consequently I made a half hearted attempt to minimise my output. However no sooner had I become engrossed with the technicalities of making model boats (a throwback to my missed opportunities as a child) than another must-do painting appeared on the scene. So it would be away with the blueprints and out with the brushes once again.

As an artist I find it impossible to work in fits and starts. I need to concentrate on the task in hand until it is finished, although I obviously work on a number of canvases at the same time to allow for the varying drying times of the oil paint. A professional painter cannot waste time waiting around and for this reason I like to work on differing surfaces. I can happily paint small pictures on boards until the larger canvases are ready for further attention.

Guiding Influences

I have always been attracted by the atmosphere and romance of the Norfolk and Suffolk countryside. I have a ready affinity with bygone days when horses ploughed the hedged fields and the trades of the blacksmith, miller, baker and fisherman flourished. It follows that I obviously appreciate and admire the work of the nineteenth-century Dutch and English landscape artists and particularly John Constable. Of course we have visited many of the places where he lived and painted his masterpieces and in my own way I have endeavoured to capture the beauty of the countryside he grew up in.

I have also been strongly influenced by the great East Anglian artist Edward Seago. His work appears so effortless that it immediately produces in me a challenge and incentive to develop these qualities in my own technique. Whenever I need a little motivation I only have to browse through one of his books in order to regain my enthusiasm.

At first glance the flat landscape of my own Lincolnshire would seem to lack inspiration for restless artists. However, I have found that what it lacks in hills and seashore is offset by its wonderful skies. They are vast in proportion and encompass infinite varieties of texture, form and colour. It is both rewarding and fascinating to record the many facets of mood, ranging from the extremes of violent storm, the ever-changing cloud formations and the vivid and many-layered sunsets.

Also although many of the hedgerows have disappeared to accommodate the demand for larger expanses of agricultural land, Lincolnshire has a beauty of its own. The trees, particularly, can be seen in all their glory against a seemingly empty background. I have always enjoyed depicting trees as they change colour and shape through the evolving seasons.

Technique

During my painting career I have been happiest working on canvas proportions measuring 16 inches by 24 inches, 20 by 30 inches and increasing to 24 by 36 inches. I have always used good quality Belgian canvas which I have stretched myself. For my smaller paintings such as 5 inches by 7 inches and upwards I have tended to work on boards, primed with a mixture of emulsion paint and plaster to create a gesso surface. I find that using a pink shade provides a warm undercoat for me to build upon.

Through trial and error I have devised a way to personalise good quality paint brushes to suit my style. Usually the normal round brushes tend to wear to a point during use and I prefer a straggly end to allow me to flick in undergrowth detail. To solve this problem I first remove the head from a large brush using a sharp chisel and then I split the hairs into five equal groups. I then retie each group on to the ends of old brush shafts and the desired result is achieved.

Incidentally, despite the vast volume of work that I have produced over the years I have never painted identical scenes. I have, however, enjoyed reproducing some of my favourite images in endless variations of seasons, weather and from differing angles. I have never grown tired of revisiting subjects.

Flowers

Only a few times have I been tempted to stray away from my usual landscapes. Inexplicably I felt a need to explore the challenge of painting flowers. To this end I enthusiastically gathered armfuls of gaillardias from the garden, hastily arranged them and set to work. Looking at the end result through rose-coloured spectacles I was really pleased and felt that I had acquitted myself well. Judy tactfully did her best to bring me down to earth. Obviously in her eyes yes, I had produced a fair image but one without atmosphere and soul.

Sufficient to say that the desire to deviate from the norm didn't last long and whenever I suggest such an adventure again Judy falls about laughing.

A Few Sticky Moments

One of the main factors that has ensured my life-long and continued love of painting landscape has been that I have always had the freedom to depict scenes that have attracted me. Fortunately my taste has appealed to a mass of like minded followers. But even today, the word commission causes palpatations and leads to unfamiliar stress. At a push I can cope with working to time deadlines but the pressure of doing justice to a much loved personal image is beyond me. Over the years I have succumbed a few times but only on the condition that the subject in question is still general enough to appeal to both me and others, just in case the original client is not happy with the end result.

Once I was approached to paint the treasured home of a gentleman who lived in Spain. I worked from the photographs he produced of the modern white-walled homestead that was his pride and joy. Despite being given a little artistic license to dirty it up (in my eyes to make it more visually acceptable) my heart wasn't in it and I was very disappointed with the result. I suspect that although he appeared to appreciate the finished canvas that he was as well.

I applaud those artists who delight in capturing such personal images, but I certainly am not one of them.

Woodland Scenes

One of the favourite and most satisfying scenes that I have painted has to be the splendour of small woods carpeted by bluebells. I particularly enjoyed visiting the idyllic Salhouse Broad in Norfolk with my grandchild Florence. The wood is small and hilly which adds to hidden depths and interest. The surrounding water is habitat for a wide variety of bird life and there is always the passing interest of the many small pleasure boats and the larger cruisers.

I have painted it from many angles and in differing seasons but the bluebell time has to rate as the most rewarding. I have no trouble with motivation – just looking at the array of colours before me, the textured trunks and twisted roots of the trees and the calmness of the water reflecting the blue sky above, pure heaven on earth. I have even been able to include my trademark pheasant to add further nostalgia.

The woods near Fotheringhay in Northamptonshire have a similar appeal, being small and compact with plenty of interesting undergrowth for me to incorporate the natural wildlife. My sister-in-law Susan keeps me well informed of the arrival of the bluebells.

Bourne Woods in Lincolnshire has to be another of my favourite haunts. Over the years we have enjoyed many rambles with the children and dogs exploring the long pathways cutting through the dense trees, home for the deer that are rarely seen. Although the terrain is obviously flat the woods have a timeless charm. Hidden in the middle is one of a pair of small overgrown ponds which I have painted many times. The rich profusion of the differing shades of green in the surrounding trees and the hidden depths of the still, water-lilied surface prove to be an irresistible attraction. Although we have seen the deer I haven't yet included one in my work.

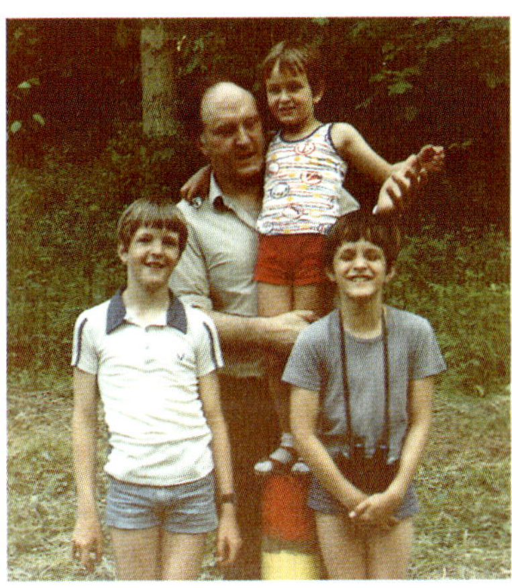

This photograph was taken early on in my life as a professional artist. Days wandering in these lovely woods were a treat for us all.

The Public

One of the most frequent questions I am asked is if I have favourite paintings. My answer is always no. I approach each canvas in the same way and my initial involvement and interest is all consuming. Once completed, however, I can let it go without any feeling of being emotionally attached. Of course there are some that I feel particularly happy with and Judy would definitely like to keep, but generally I just move on to the next objective.

Another popular question is usually asked by people who have never tried to paint at all. This concerns how long it takes for me to produce a picture. Especially if they happen to be watching me at work in the studio they appear to be mentally adding up the pounds earned as I apply each brushstroke. Again my answer is always the same – the time cannot be measured, size, drying time and unforeseen interruptions all play their part. The creative art involved does not figure in their calculations. I suppose because they are obviously appreciative of the end results they assume that it is always easy and without snags. I wish!

As a landscape artist I am also asked if I paint outside and again the reply is no, this romantic image is not for me. The reality of first finding a view and then transporting all the equipment necessary before the light or weather changes is difficult. Coupled with the time factor and the distraction of overhearing interested bystanders' whispered remarks, this venue is not for me. I much prefer to make quick working sketches noting details of colour, light and texture, thus providing me with a substantial image to develop at home. My camera is also an essential tool, particularly when spying a view in an inaccessible place.

Semi-retirement

With the approach of the 1990s I felt that I had achieved some measure of my goal to become established as an artist. The children were beginning to spread their wings, my work was selling steadily and had been circulated widely in print form. I was also pleased to discover that many canvases had homes in other countries as well.

The routine of my life was all that I could have hoped for. I found that I had time to rediscover my first love of cabinet making, even if it was mainly to provide my children with pieces to furnish their homes!

Family life then entered the next stage with the appearance of grandchildren and Judy and I were able to enjoy the arrival of Max, Florence, Ben, Eva and the twins Daphne and Maude. During this time Judy retired early from teaching – the love of our own little ones being a greater pull than looking after those of others. Also at a time when my work-load was decreasing by choice, hers was becoming increasingly pressured with frequent testing, inspections and parental imput. Witnessing her commitment and workload made me appreciate even more my daily life.

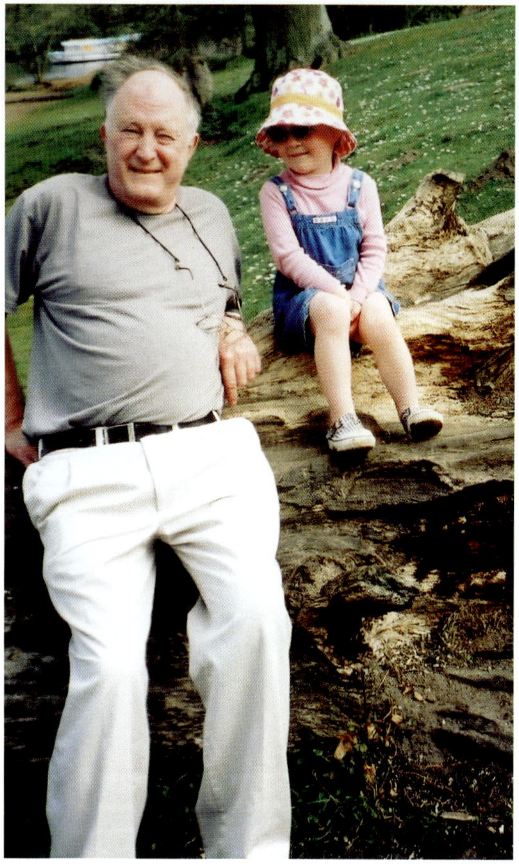

Finally when I felt that I had at last achieved some degree of balance in my life, and that it was favourably tilting towards leisure and fishing, I was persuaded by Adrian to have a final end-of-career exhibition at his gallery. Judy and the children felt that it would be a fitting climax to round off my artistic life and so, slightly reluctantly, I agreed.

Over the years I have never enjoyed the luxury of being able to amass canvases for exhibitions as we have obviously relied upon a regular steady income. Fortunately, my style has been popular with the buying public. It is a great source of pleasure to me that despite the foreboding of my parents, and all the pitfalls and vagaries present in the art world, and having worked and survived through two financial recessions, I have provided adequately for my family.

I was well aware of the commitment necessary to put together an exhibition. To create sufficient paintings in a variety of sizes working to an agreed deadline would be a real challenge. I knew that it was going to be tough.

Relaxing with Florence at Salhouse Broad, Norfolk.

Exhibition 2004

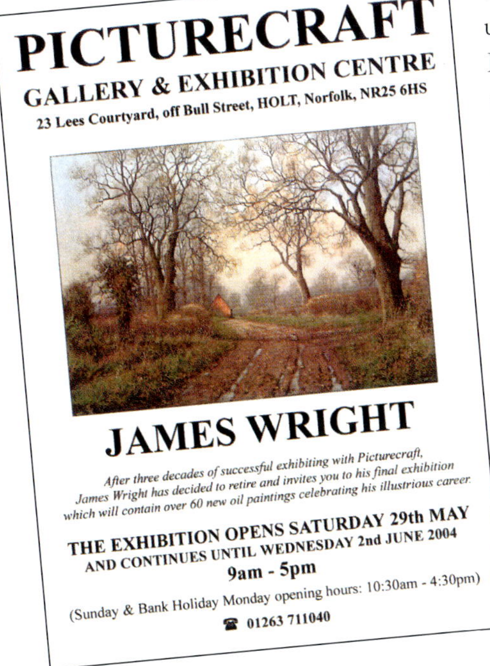

This turned out to be the understatement of the year. By the time I had completed the task I was emotionally and mentally drained. I had found no problem in selecting the variety of landscapes that I thought would make for a worthy display as I had naturally collected an enormous body of suitable subjects that I still wanted to paint. The challenge was more of a physical nature – the large canvases measured 24 inches by 36 inches and proved a daunting task in respect of area to be covered. Dutifully I disappeared hermit-like into my studio and eventually emerged, if not exactly triumphant, satisfied to have reached the end. After the laborious and mechanical task of framing 60-plus paintings was finally completed it only remained for us to transport them safely to Holt.

Thankfully leaving Adrian responsible for the final details of sorting and hanging, my thoughts turned towards the preview night.

Right: *Waiting nervously for guests to arrive, dutifully supported by Nicola who was determined that I would enjoy myself! Granddaughter Florence, six years of age, getting ready to provide light relief.*

Preview Night

I have never ever been comfortable with the social demands expected when attending one's own opening preview. Being self-employed for such a long time had succeeded in making me even more unsure and nervous about conversing with strangers, even if they were attending because they presumably admired my work. I liken the experience to putting one's head above the parapet and then waiting to be shot at. Surfice to say that I would have preferred to remain at home – an unthinkable choice not to be contemplated as my family were suited and booted and ready for the off. So all spruced up I reluctantly went along.

Well supported by my family and friends, and a glass of wine, I gradually relaxed and began to enjoy it. It was gratifying to see my work hung and displayed with all the advantages of superb lighting and the people I met said some very flattering things. We returned home on a high and looked forward to relaxing.

Shatteringly the next few days were the worst we had ever experienced with the sudden and tragic death of our granddaughter Maude. At just seven months of age she succumbed to bacterial meningitis. The following years were very difficult for us all but gradually we began to pick up the pieces once again, although I understandably became even more resolved to consider retirement. Little did I guess what was waiting round the corner.

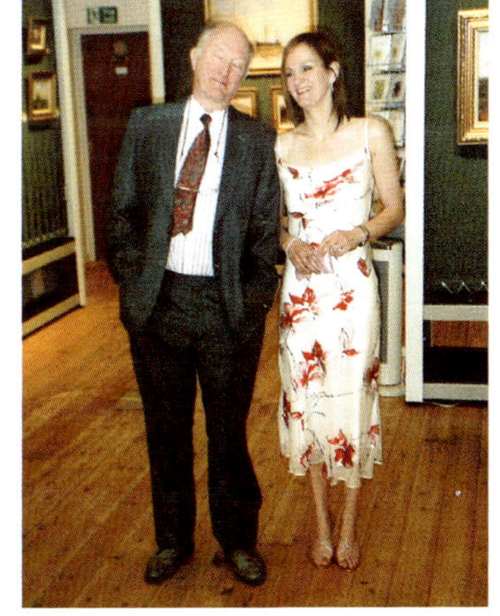

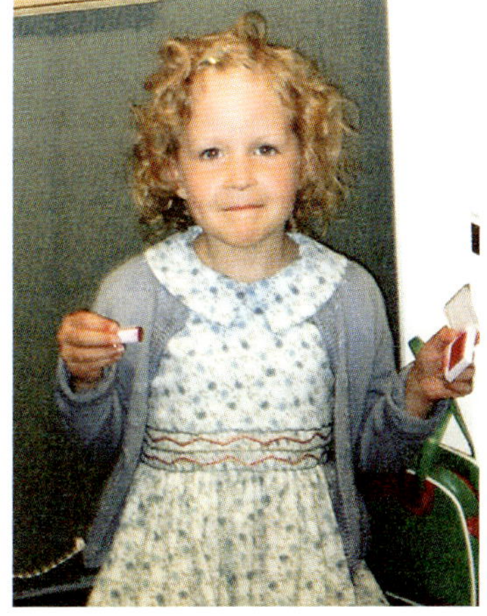

New Territory

With the very real thought of retirement in mind I decided that the first step was to spring clean my studio. Over the years it had also become increasingly cluttered with my many carpentry jobs as Nicola had previously claimed the woodwork room for her ceramics workshop. I knew that if I was ever realistically to enjoy making model boats I had to first create enough space to spread out. After much grumbling and moaning (tidying up is not my favourite activity) I reached the stage where I was ready. I had cleaned my palette and packed away my paints, replaced tools and disposed of lots of rubbish. Thankfully, the task of clearing the floor of sawdust, pieces of wood and all the other mess accumulated along the way fell to Judy. Then the day that I had longed for finally arrived – I lovingly unpacked a purpose built kit and settled down to read the plans.

On cue the telephone rang. It was a call from Steven Pugsley representing the book publishing company Halsgrove. He said that he was familiar with my style having seen the most recent in the Barle Gallery and was exploring the possibility of recording my life in landscape. Any resulting book would also give an insight into the highs and lows of the self-taught artist, ranging from the business practicalities to the influences that had guided my career.

I didn't know whether to laugh or cry, the timing once again seemed so ironic – was I ever to retire? After further pleasant and amicable discussions I warmed to the idea of being able to tidy up loose ends before drifting into obscurity. So about turn once again, away with the boat and out with the paints.

Reflection

Methodical as ever I retreated to my now spotless studio and set about the task of providing the extra canvases needed to satisfy the publishers. Once I had mastered working to slightly different proportions I happily progressed with new vigour and enthusiasm. I enjoyed revisiting my hoard of sketch books (many much the worse for accompanying tea stains) and selecting both new and familiar scenes to explore in paint. True to form the mornings have been spent focussed in the studio but the afternoons have consisted of much discussion and many laughs.

Judy and I have enjoyed reminiscing about the eventful journey we have made together. Many hours have been spent remembering long-forgotten anecdotes and the rediscovery of places we visited and the people we met. Scrambling around to find all the material required to make a stab at producing a record of my varied and satisfying life has made us appreciate how lucky we have been.

Judy of course has been my scribe, and as ever a calming influence when panic has set in. On looking back my life seems to have followed a path consisting of hard work and dedication to an idea that I have never wavered from. I have been blessed with the total support of Judy and the love of our family. I can still hardly believe that I have travelled so far, from policeman to labourer and from teacher to artist. I only know that I have been incredibly lucky to have been able to spend the majority of my working life doing something that I have continued to enjoy.

Being able to work from home has enabled me to see closely my family grow and develop. Interestingly, my eldest son Simon followed the traditional path and gained a Fine Art degree from Newcastle University. Stephen has followed in my early footsteps and is now a Police Officer in Devon. Nicola is a ceramicist and is at present teaching in Guildford and Deborah, who says she possesses no artistic talent whatever, is a Speech and Language Therapy Specialist in Autism in Peterborough.

The Future

During this last year I have enjoyed renewing acquaintances with people who know me as an artist. It was heartening to discover that Tony Crook particularly has been an avid collector of my work for many years and I am happy to say that this relationship still exists today.

I am looking forward to the trout fishing season once again. One of the only drawbacks to working from home is that it has been a solitary occupation and whilst I am usually happy with my own company, I do enjoy discussing with fellow fishermen the intricacies of rod and line. It has been a great source of amusement to my family (who have all been involved in dangerous sports) that I am the one who has frequently ended up in the casualty department to have a fly hook removed from my head and recently the cornea of my eye. This last visit caused instant fame as photographic proof was required to act as a teaching aid for all would-be ophthalmologists!

Long ago as a teenager I became interested in classical music and can remember collecting the old 78 records to play on the must-have radiogram. Where this interest came from I have no idea – my parents were definitely not smitten. However, when painting my background music is always Classic F.M. and I am keen to pursue this passion and to see opera performed live instead of on the television.

I am also hoping to experiment once again with watercolour. Long ago I stocked my studio with ample supplies of paint, brushes and a variety of quality paper. Since then I have tried a few times to master this very difficult medium, but have never managed to persevere long enough to achieve any kind of success or satisfaction. I find it extremely daunting to overcome my natural style. Having spent the majority of my career using oils to produce detailed images I am well aware that adapting to the fluidity and suggestion of the medium will not be easy, but I am looking forward to having a go. Likewise the opportunity to work in pen and wash also has its appeal.

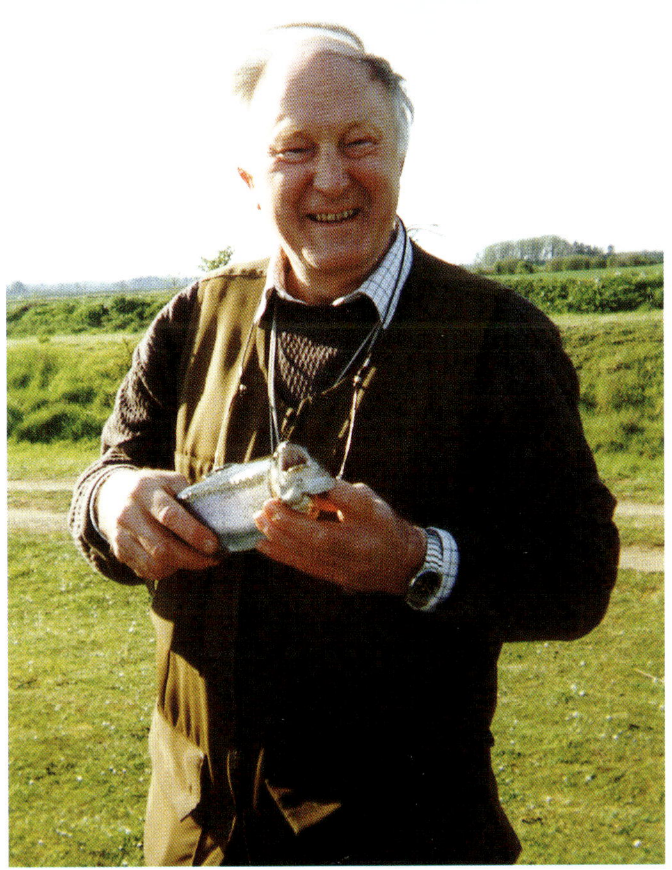

The fisherman. A successful catch, trout fishing at the Kingfisher Fly Fishing Club at West Deeping. Hopefully many more of these days to come.

Postscript

Finally to us. I now have the freedom to paint when I so desire. I am enjoying pottering in the studio and know that it will always be part of my life. Now the only pressure that I have concerns Judy as I have promised to fulfil a long overdue promise to paint specific canvases of our favourite places for us to enjoy in our own home. We are still happy here in Lincolnshire and continue to visit all the places that have been such an influence on my career.

We have recently revisited Southwold in Suffolk where the rambling boatyards extend along the meandering river. Reassuringly, there are still boats being repaired and a fair number of fishermen are still going out to sea. The delight of purchasing a wide variety of fresh fish from the small sheds along the moorings is a real blessing. The original ramshackle fishermen's huts still remain and I have already earmarked a possible subject. Across the river is the atmospheric Walberswick where long ago I painted the fishing huts and small boats. So who knows what next year will bring: I keep an open mind.

If, as a result of reading of our eventful life, other budding artists are encouraged to take the plunge into following their dreams, we know that they will not be disappointed.

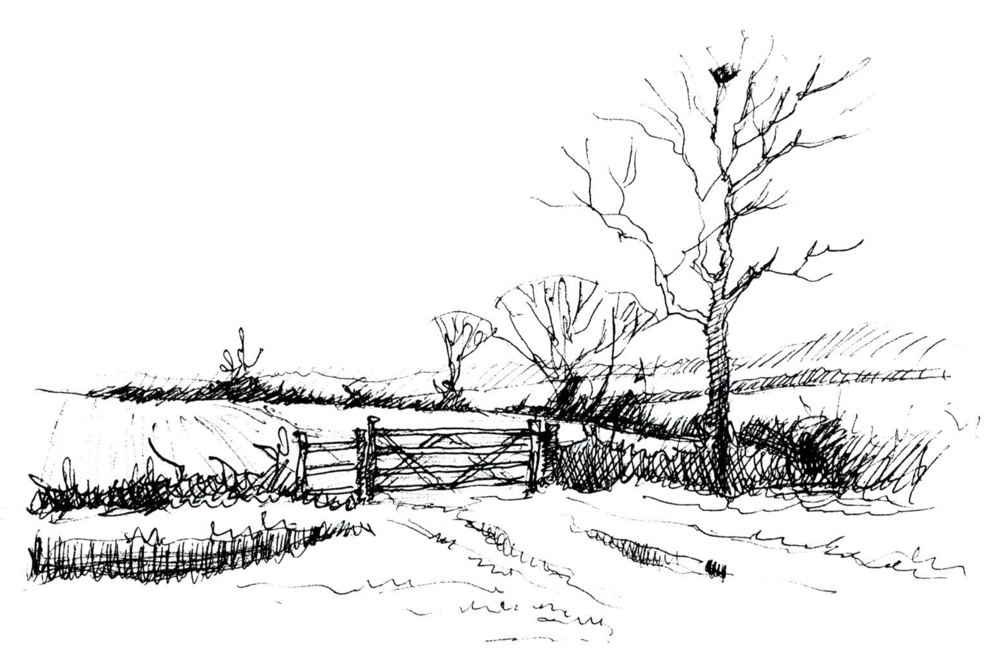

Opposite: *Cottage and Barns at Baston, Lincolnshire.*

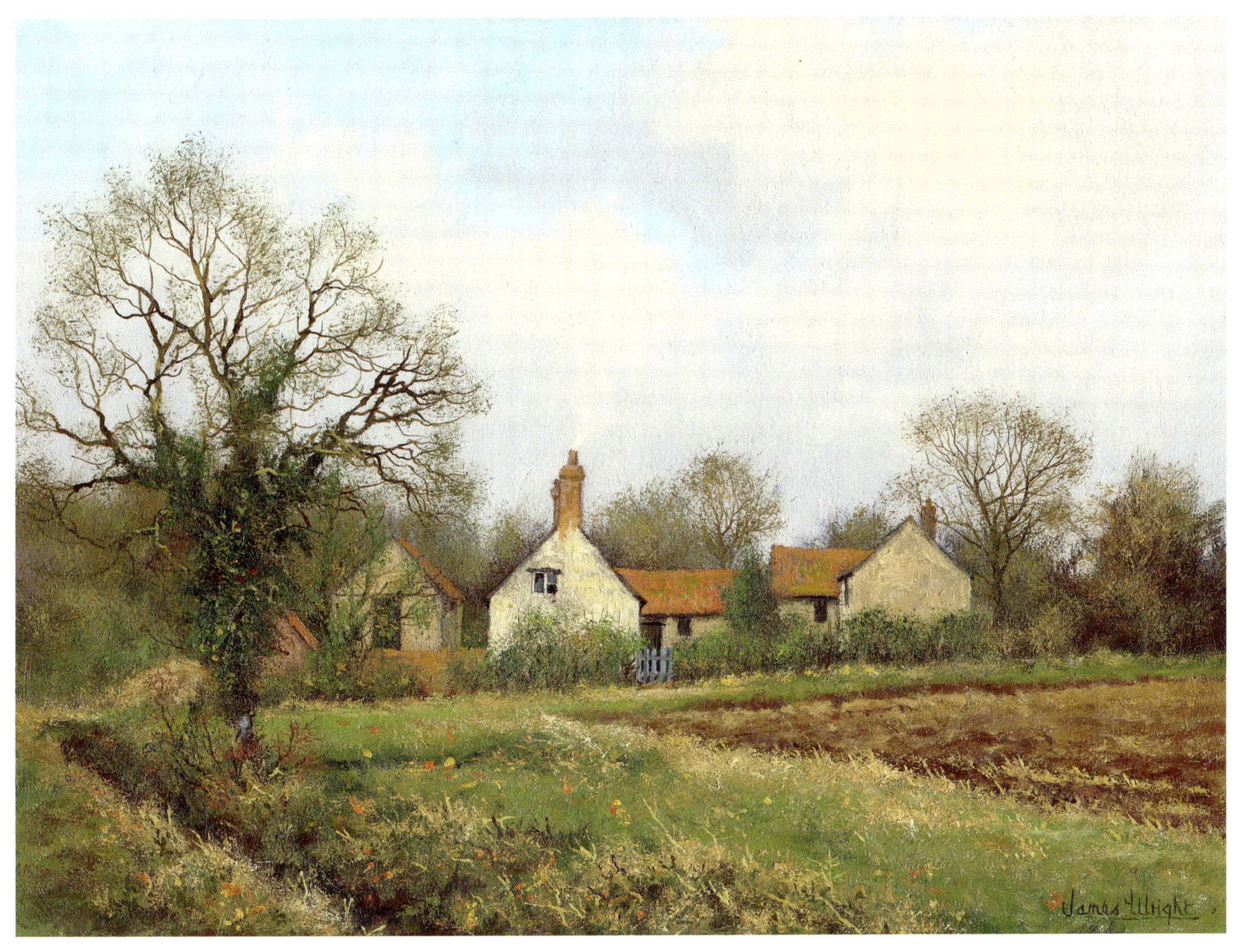

The Paintings

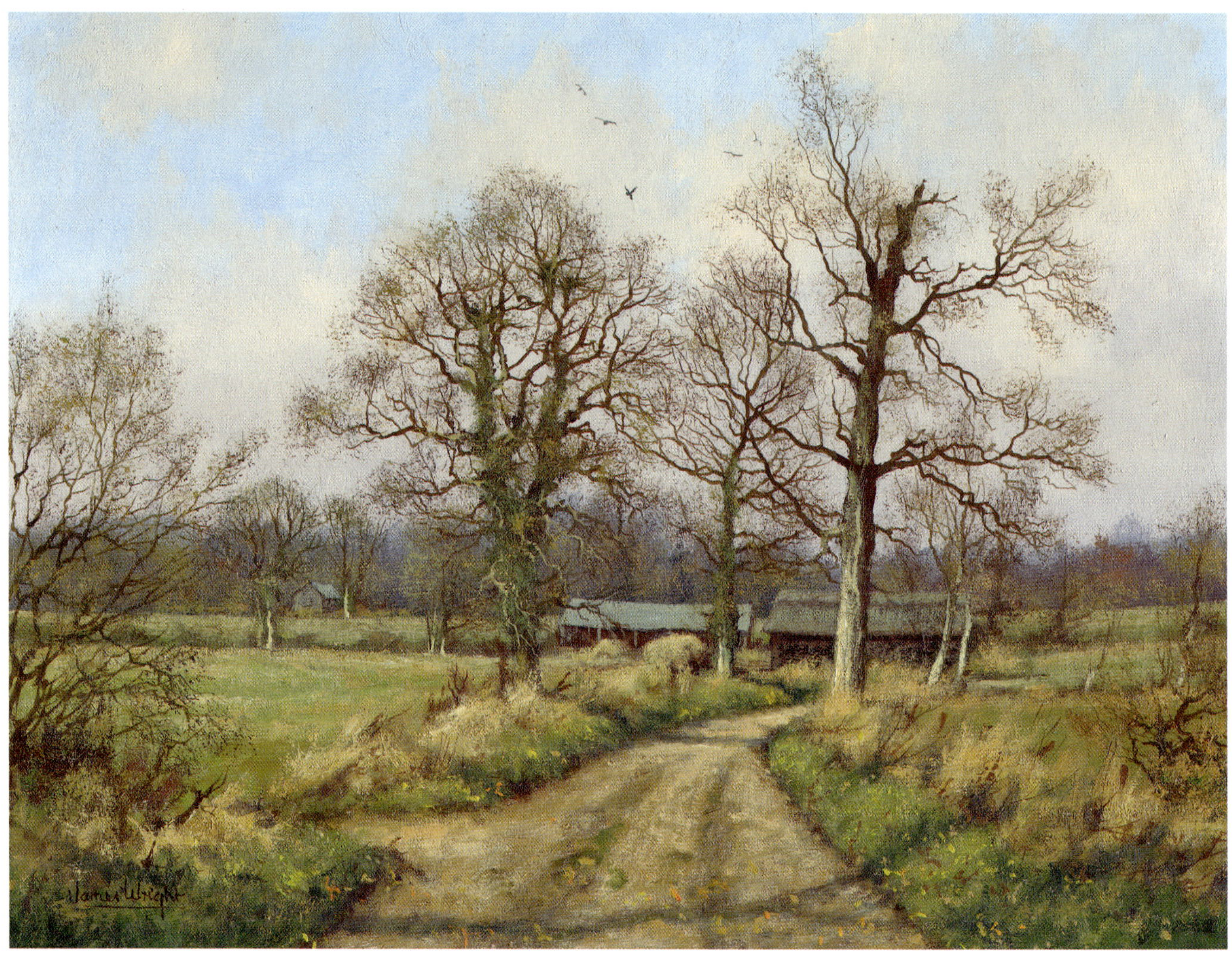

Country Lane near Woodbridge, Suffolk.

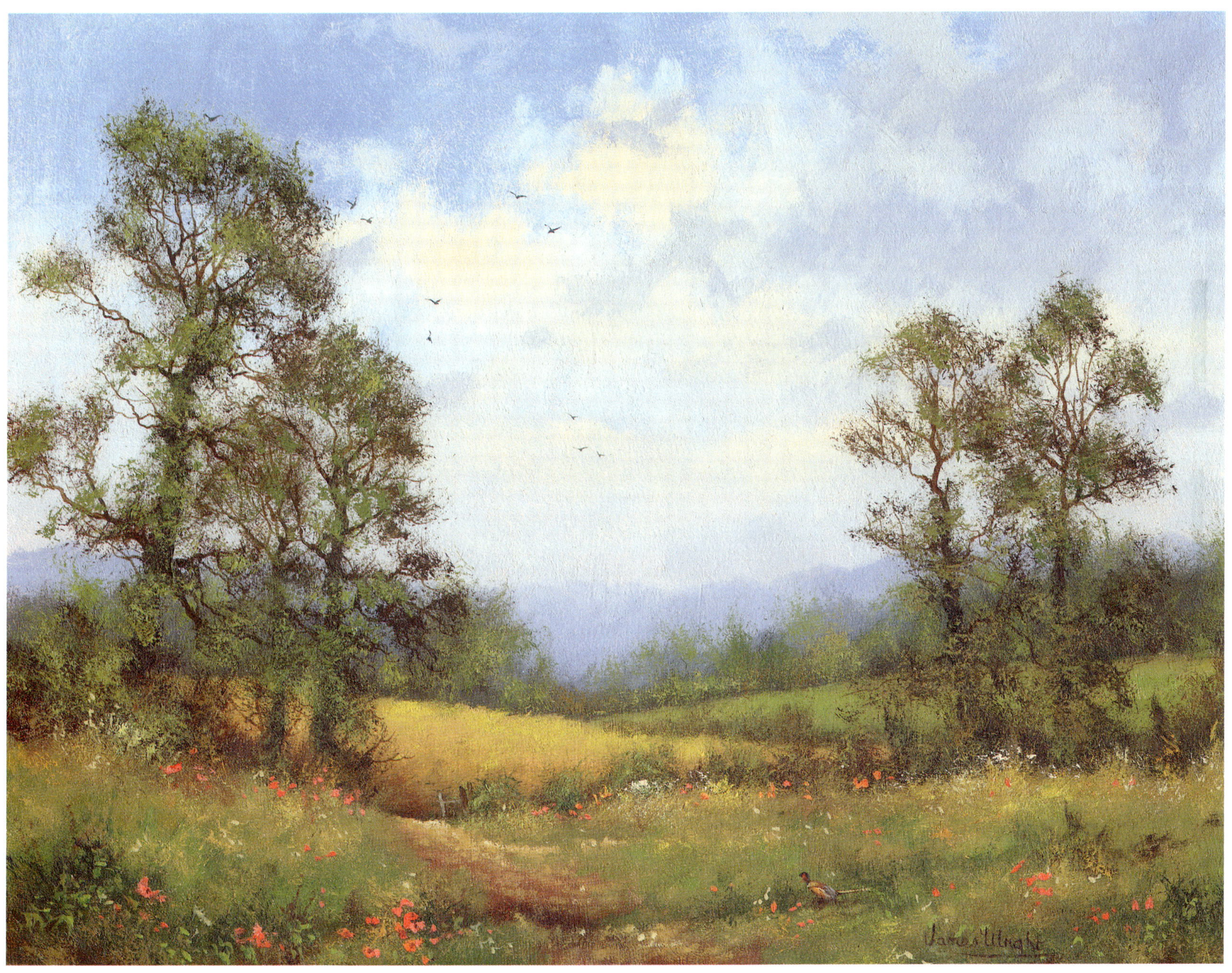

Summer Fields, Norfolk.

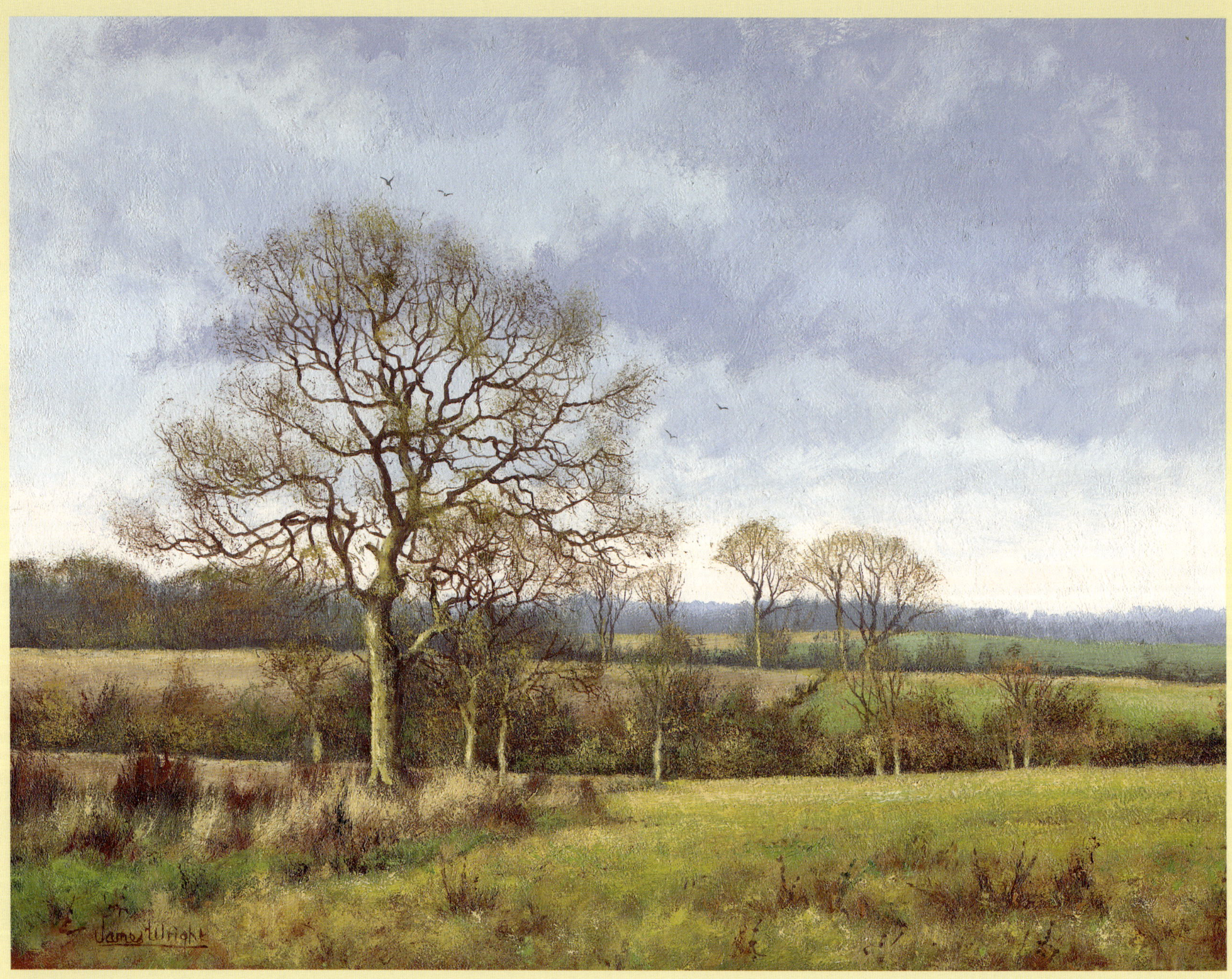

Norfolk Fields.

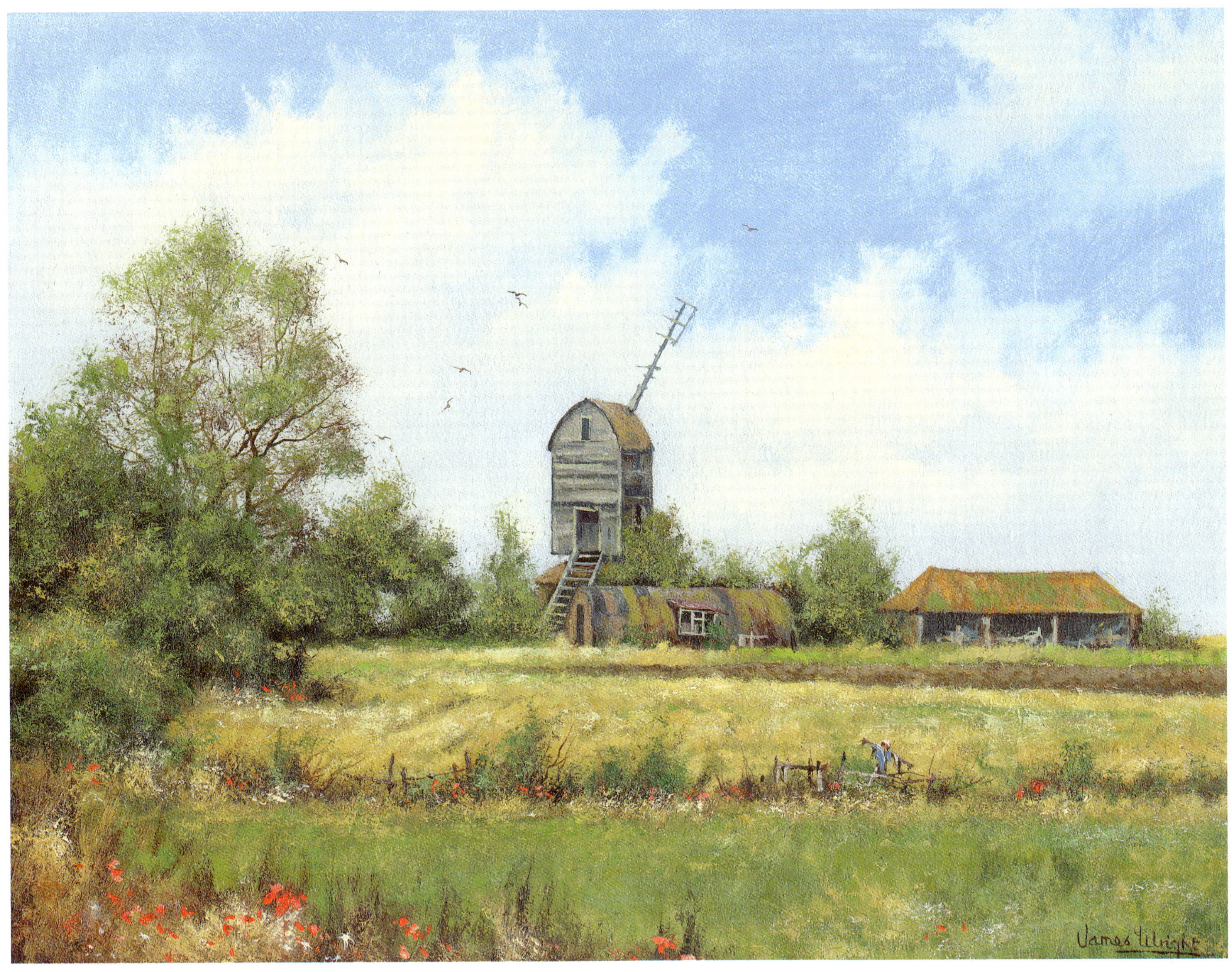

The Old Post Mill.

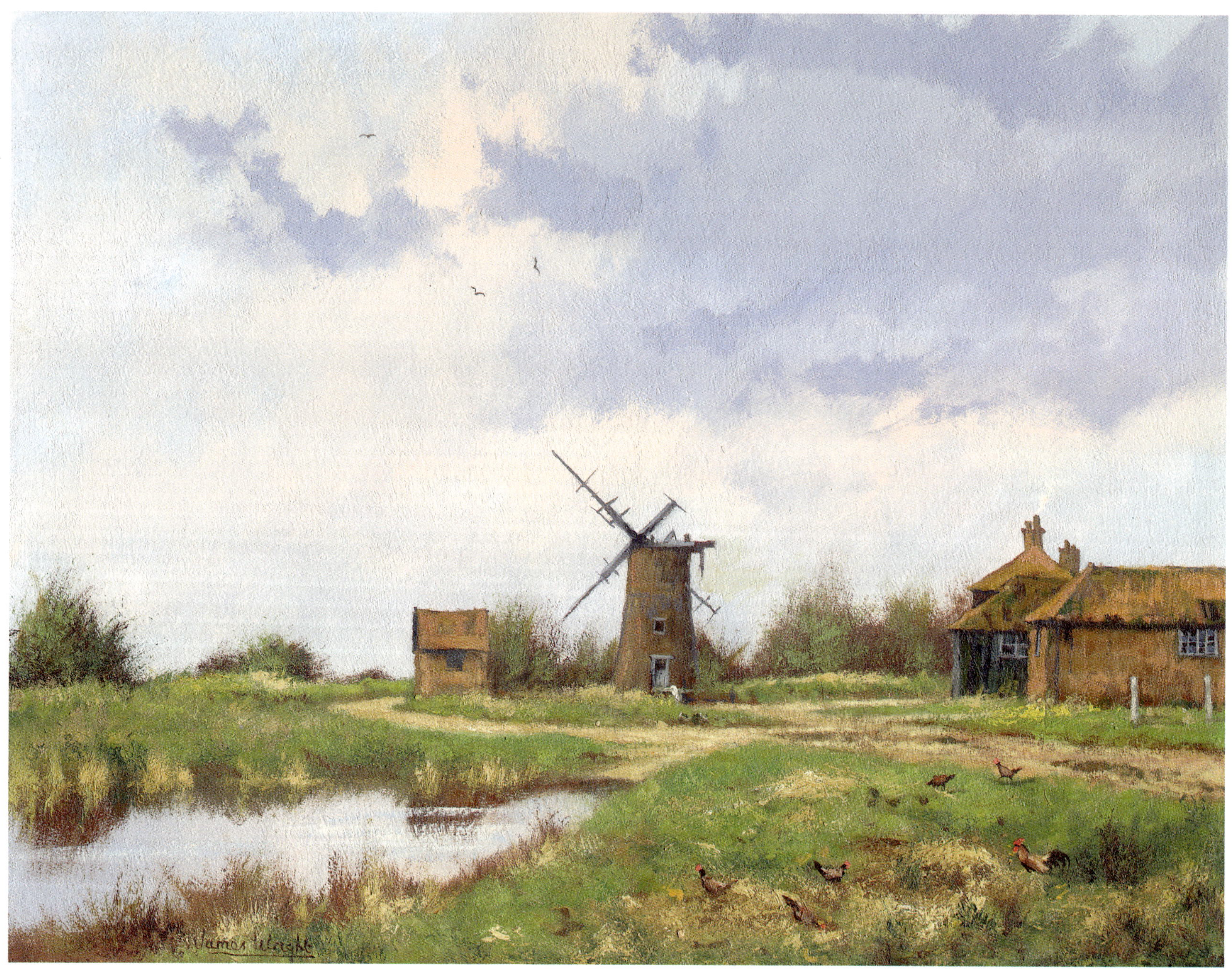

Mautby Marsh Farm, Norfolk.

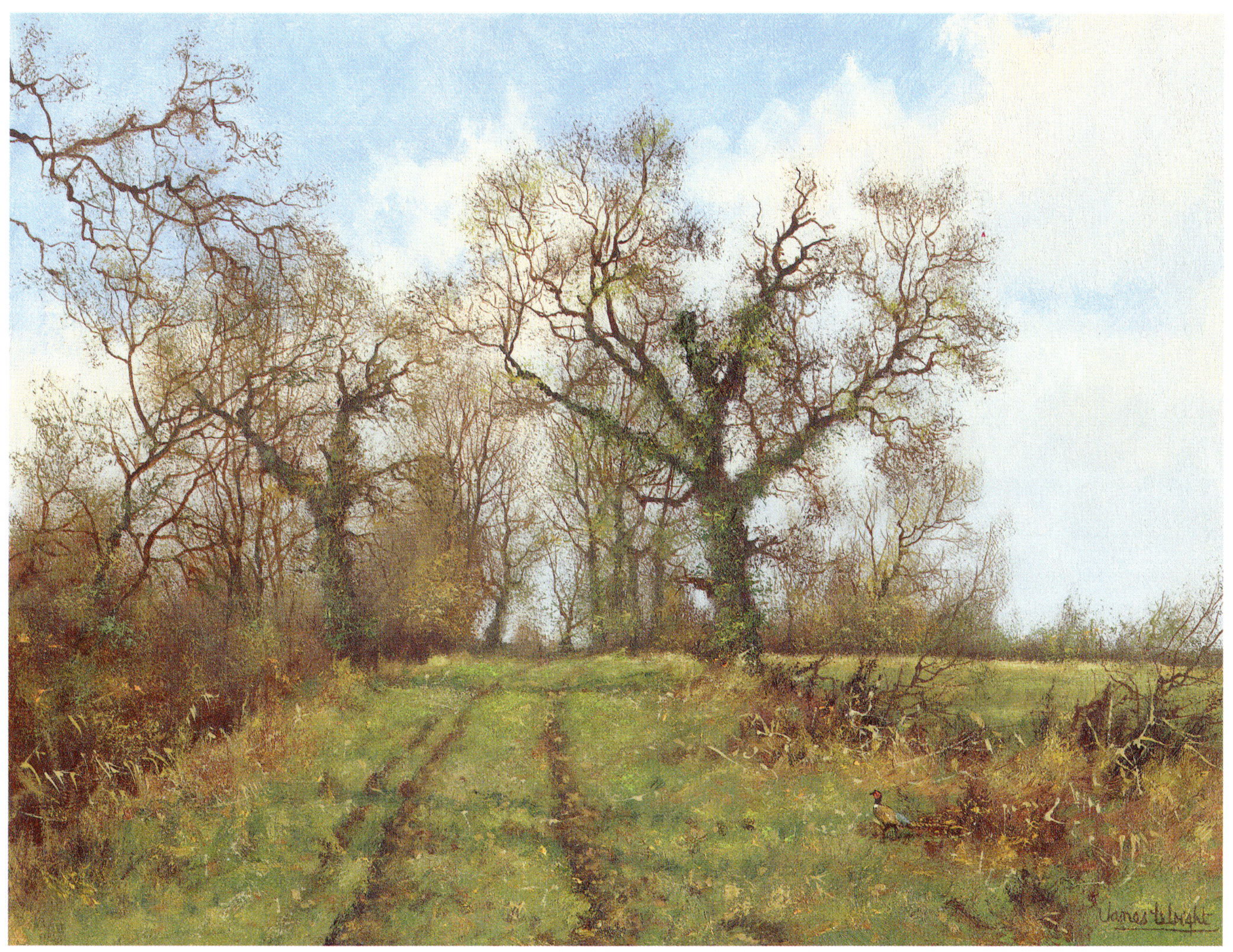

Cart Track, near Shipdham.

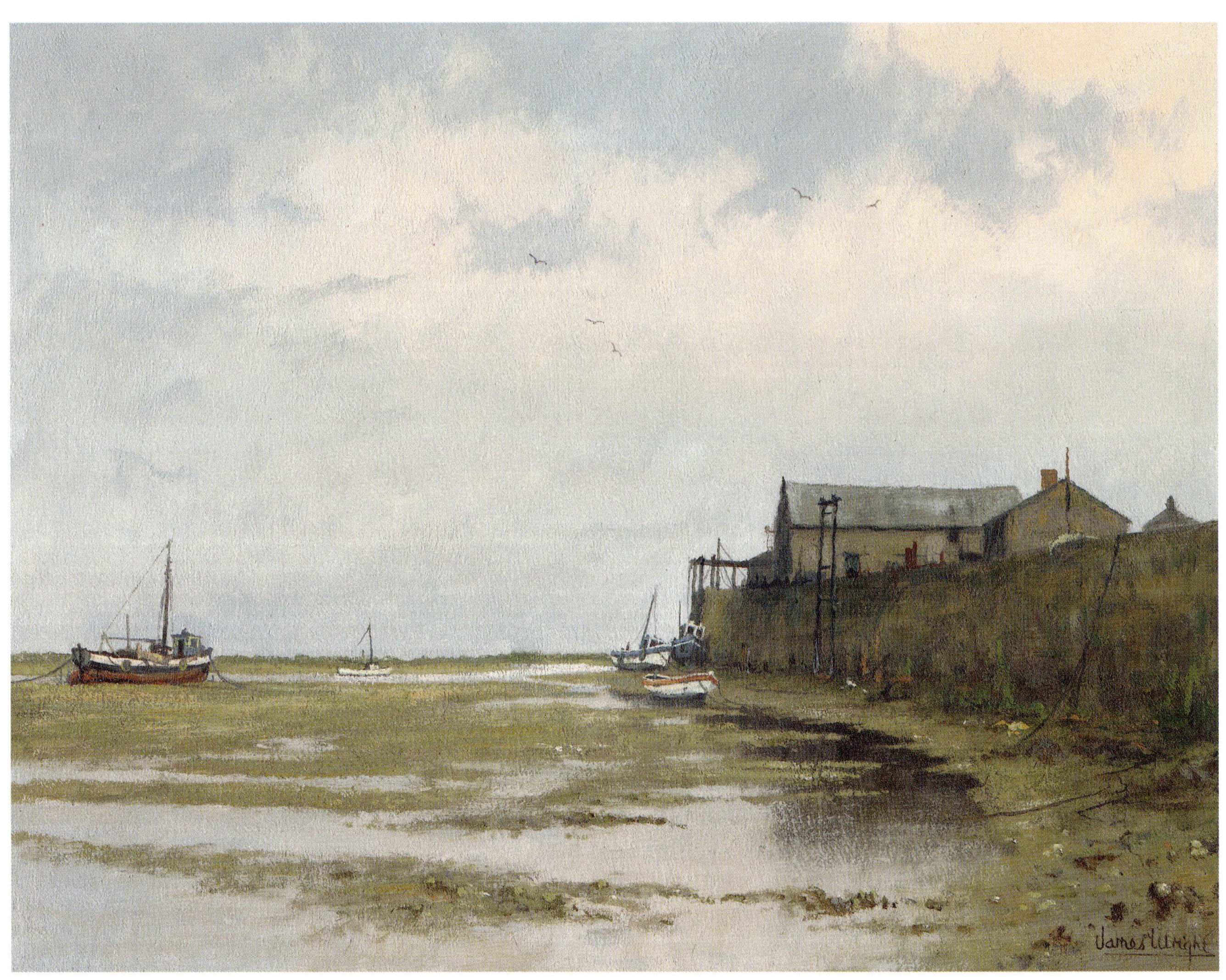

South Quay, Wells, Norfolk.

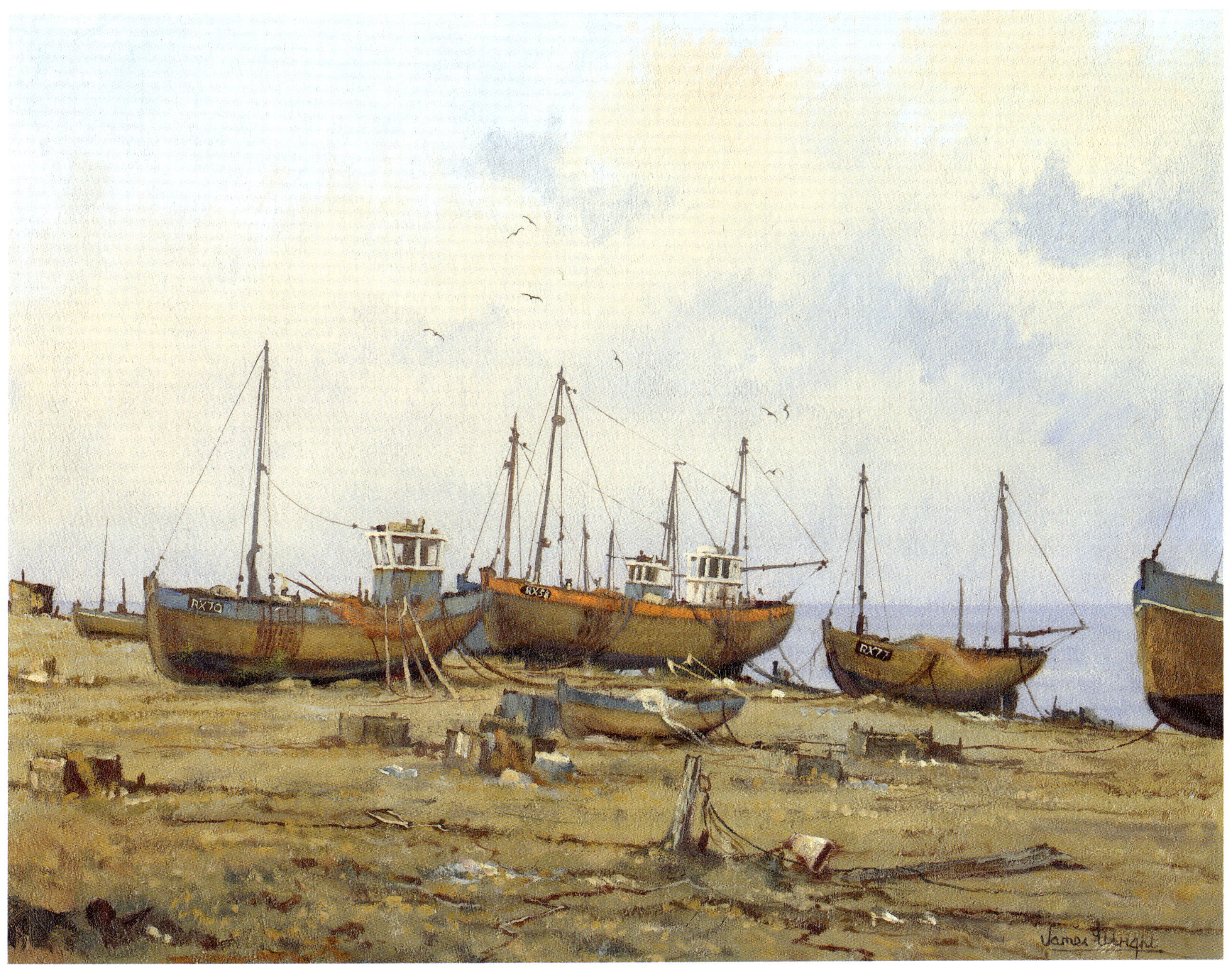

Hastings Beach.

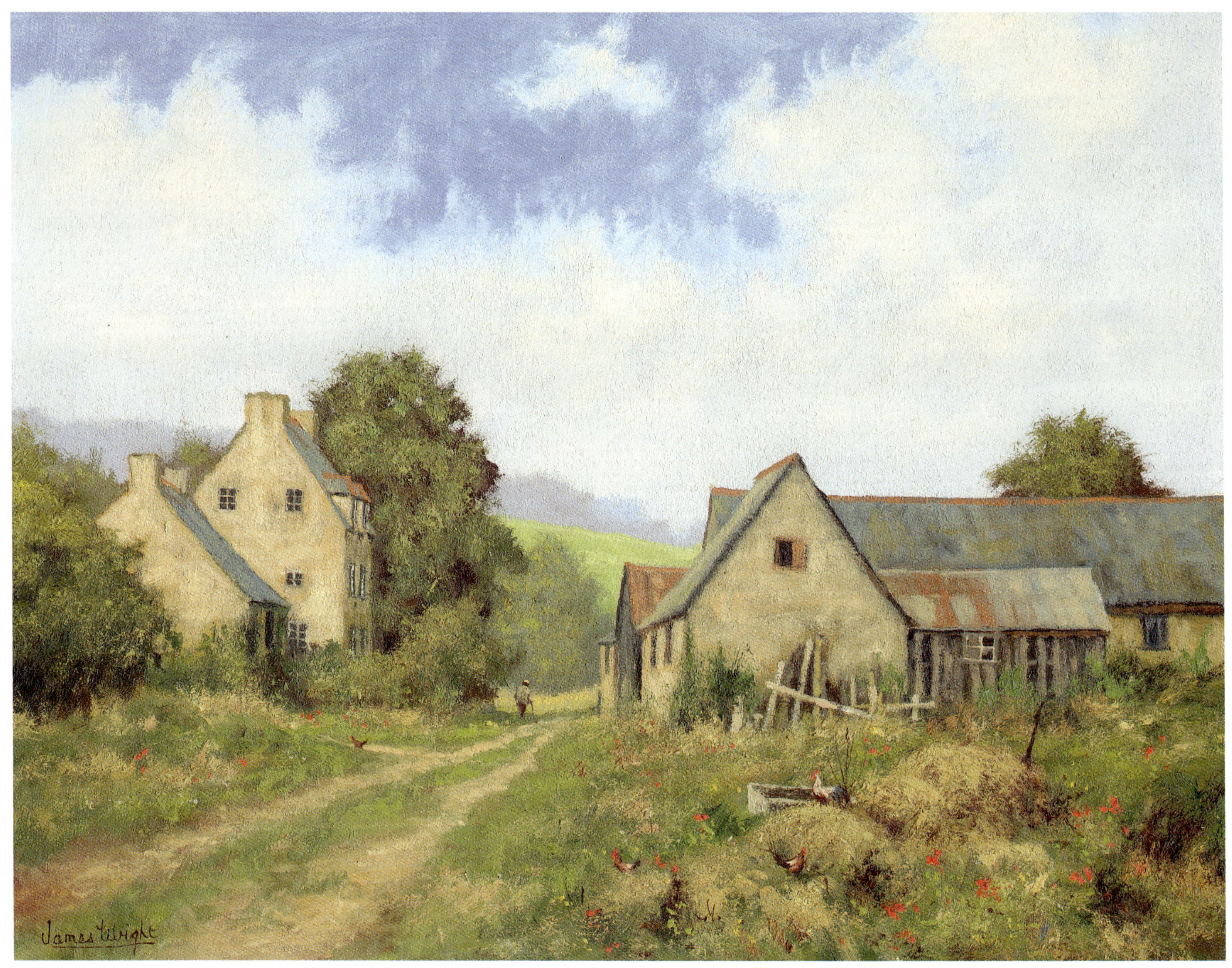

French Farm, St Goazec, Brittany.

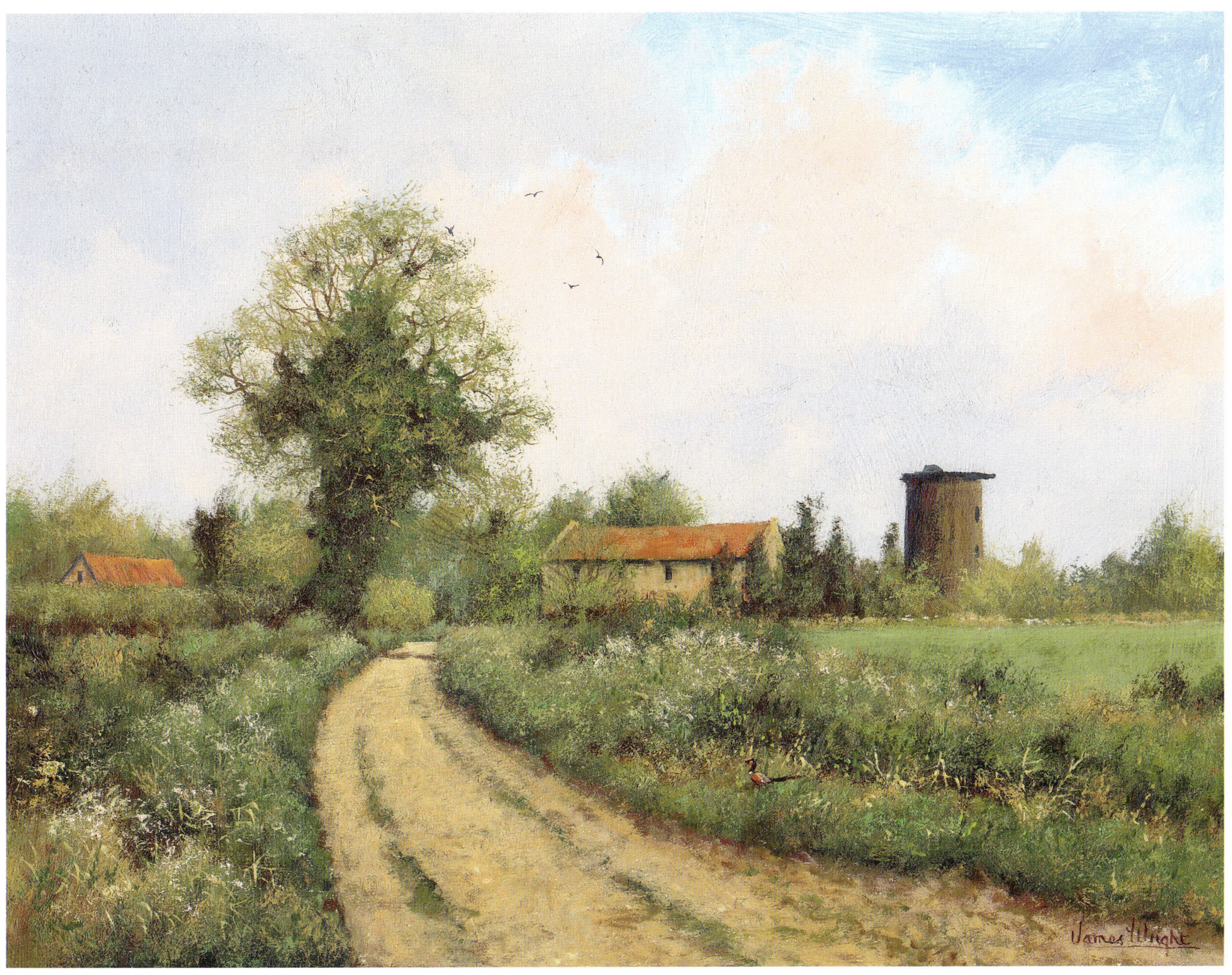

Old Buckenham.

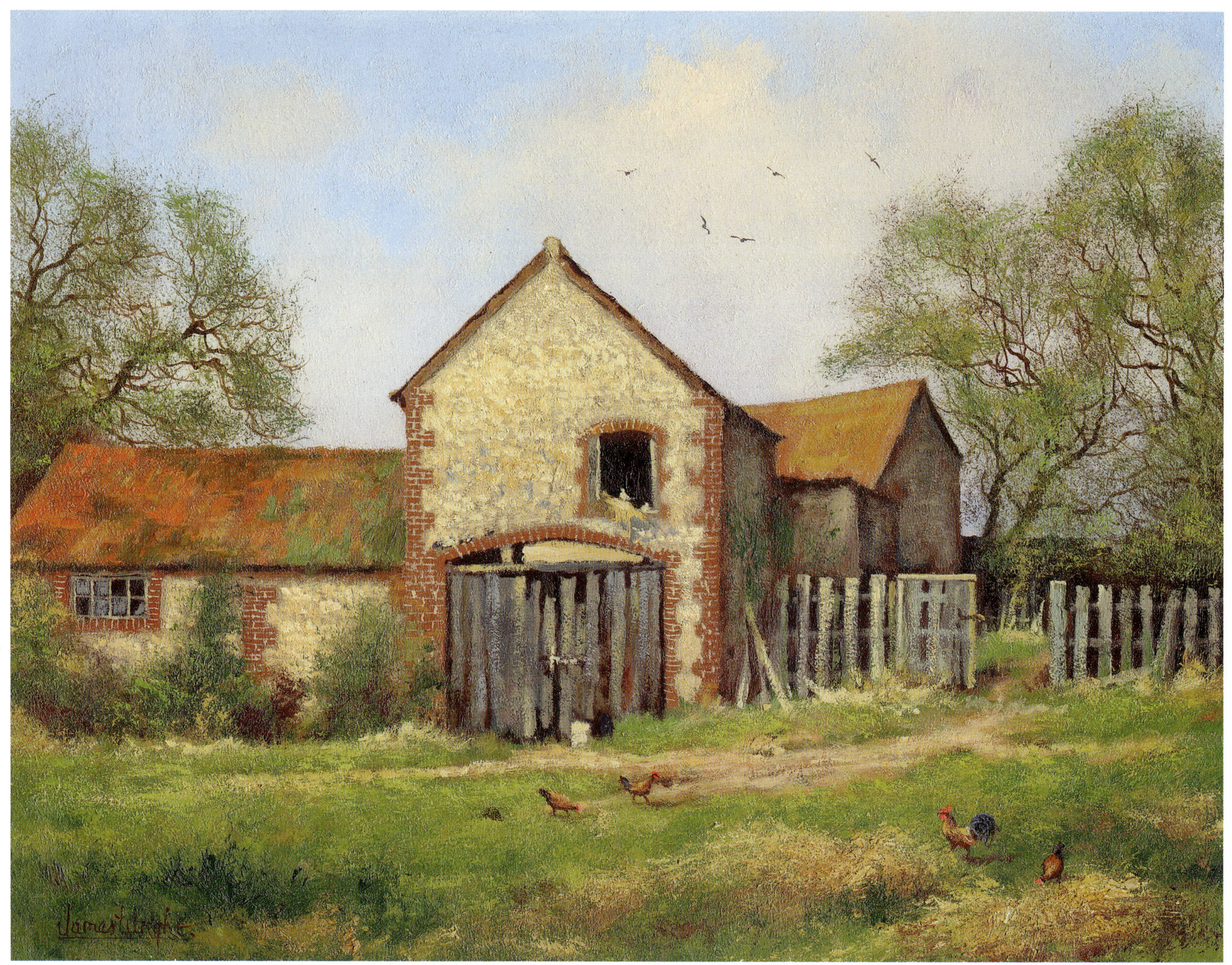

Farm Buildings near Holt, Norfolk.

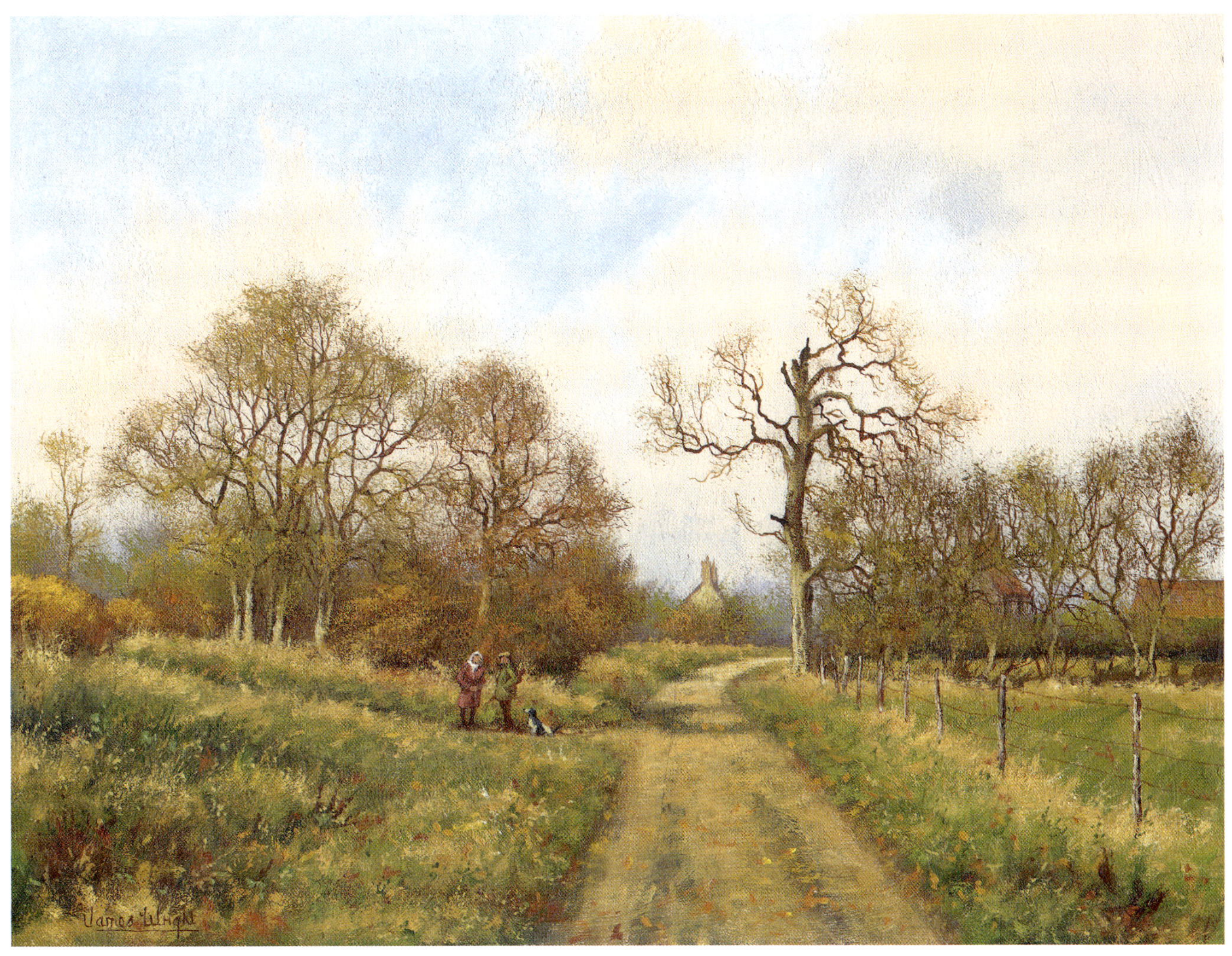

Norfolk Lane in Autumn.

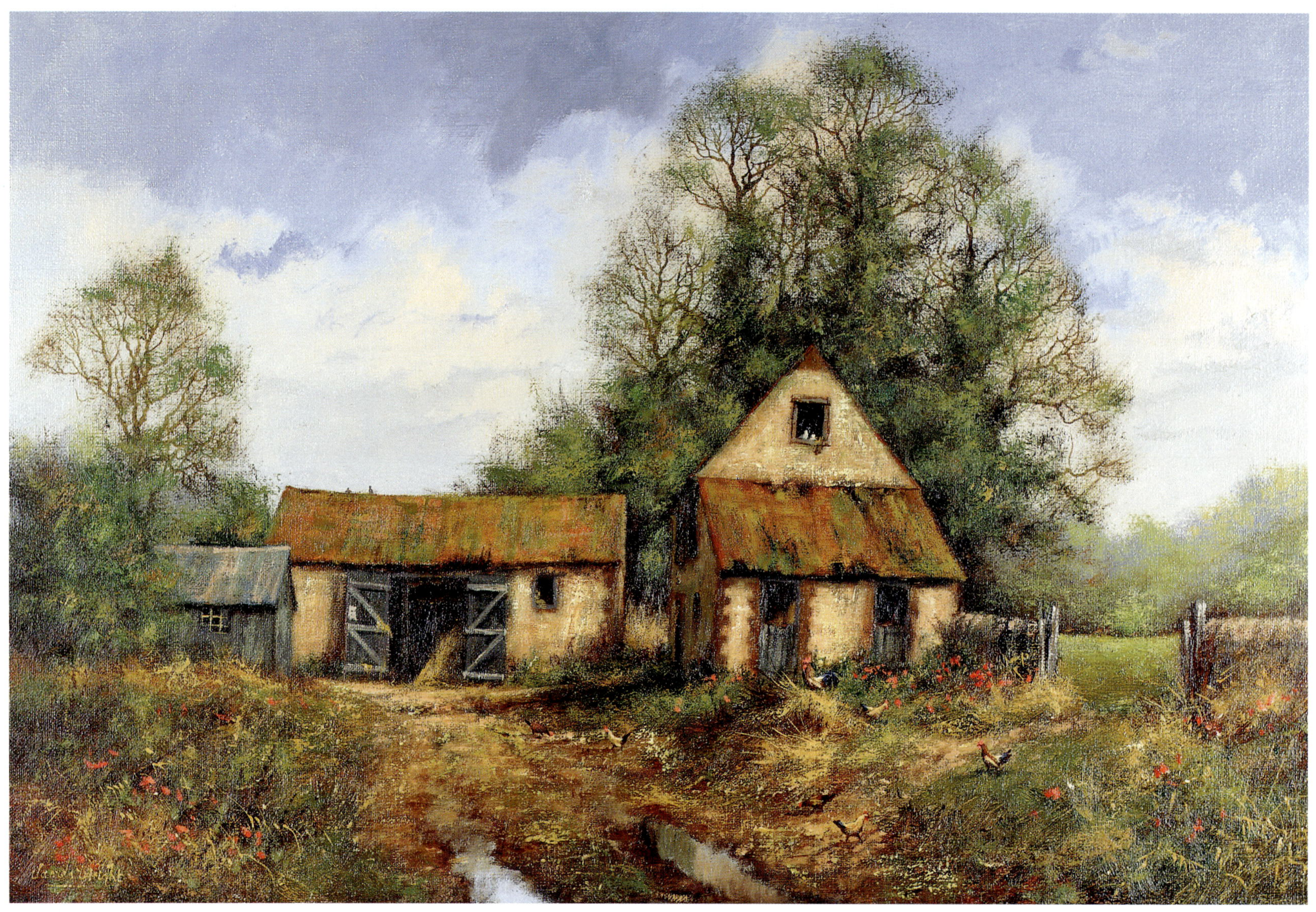

Norfolk Barn.

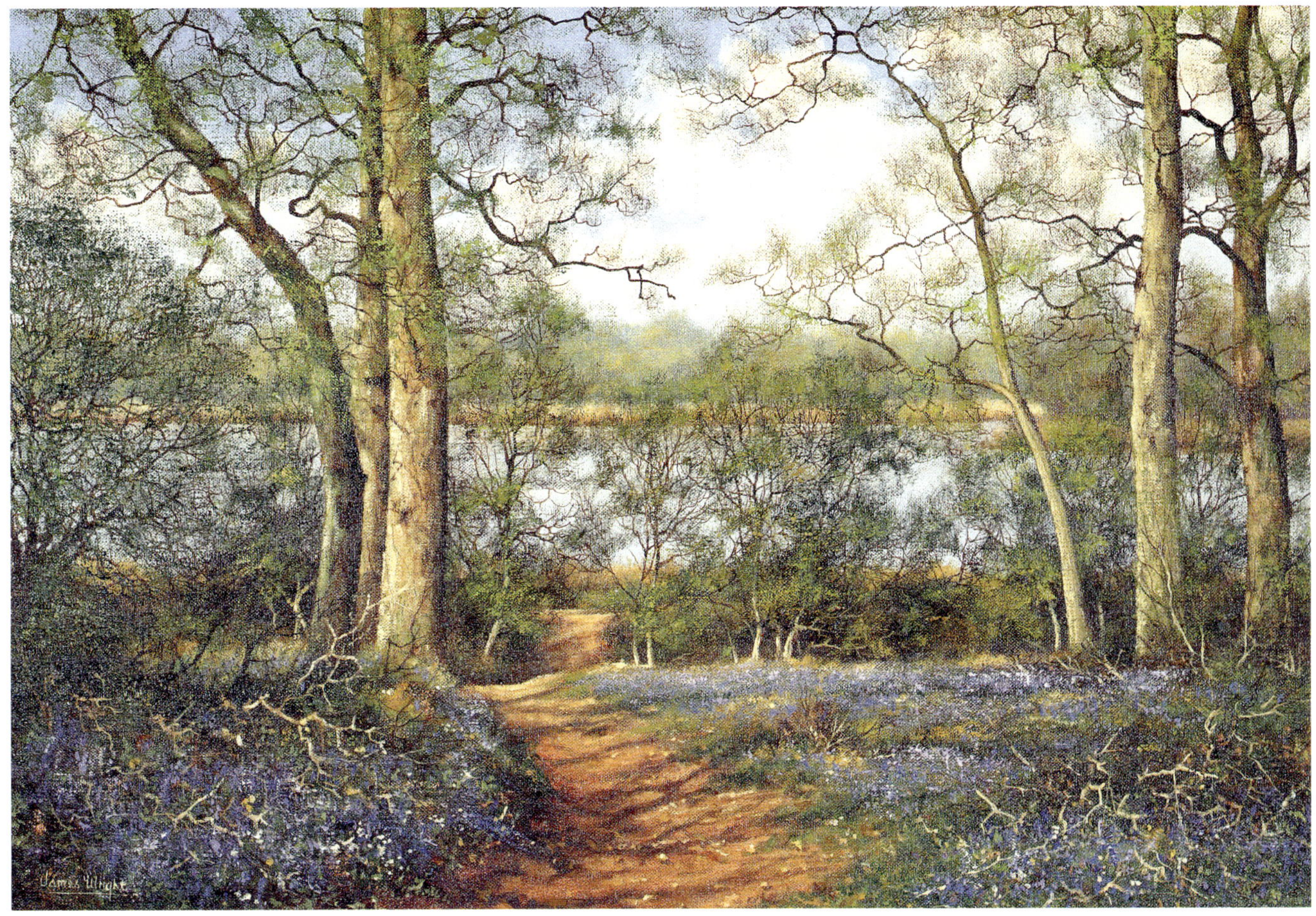

Bluebell Woods.

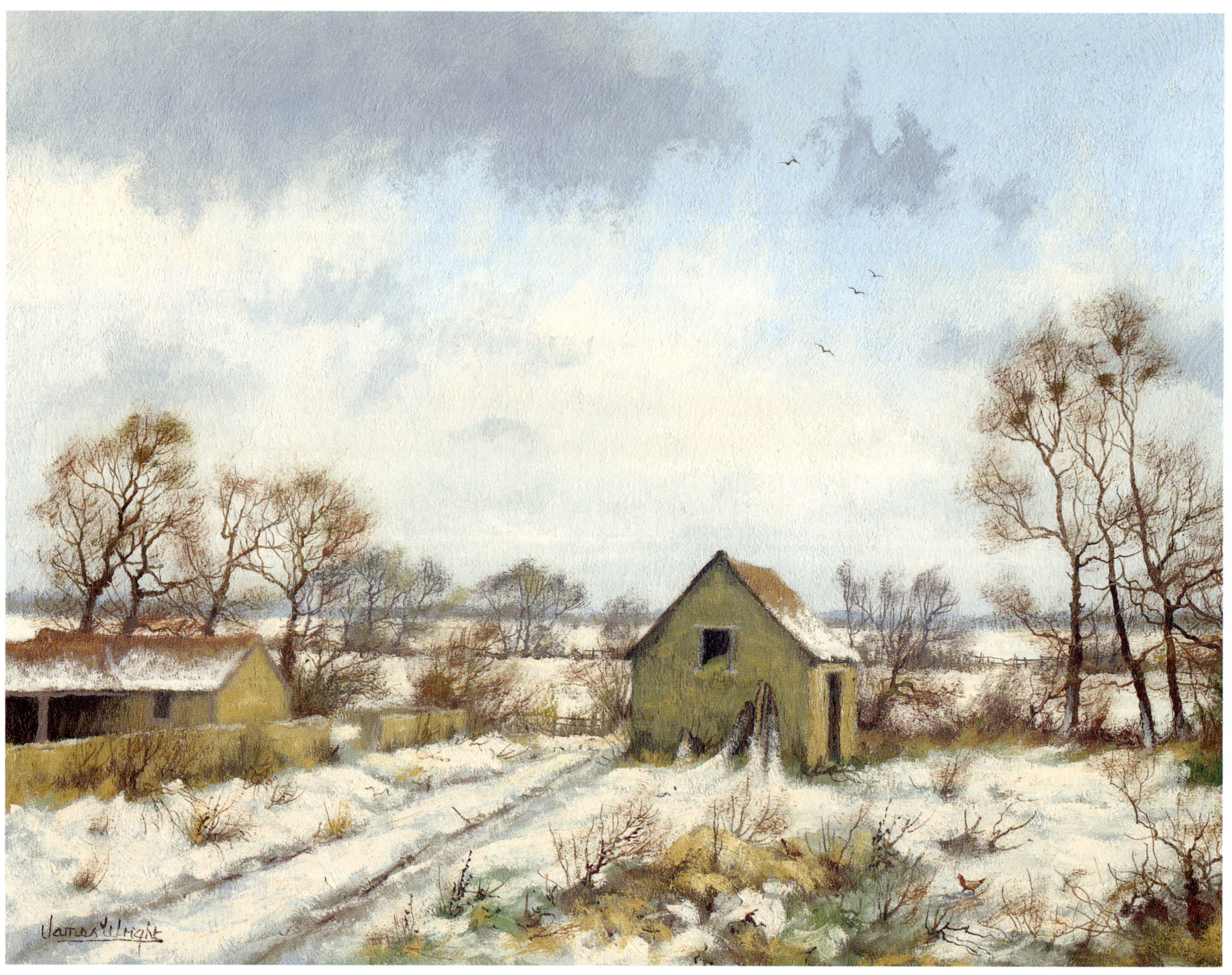

More Snow.

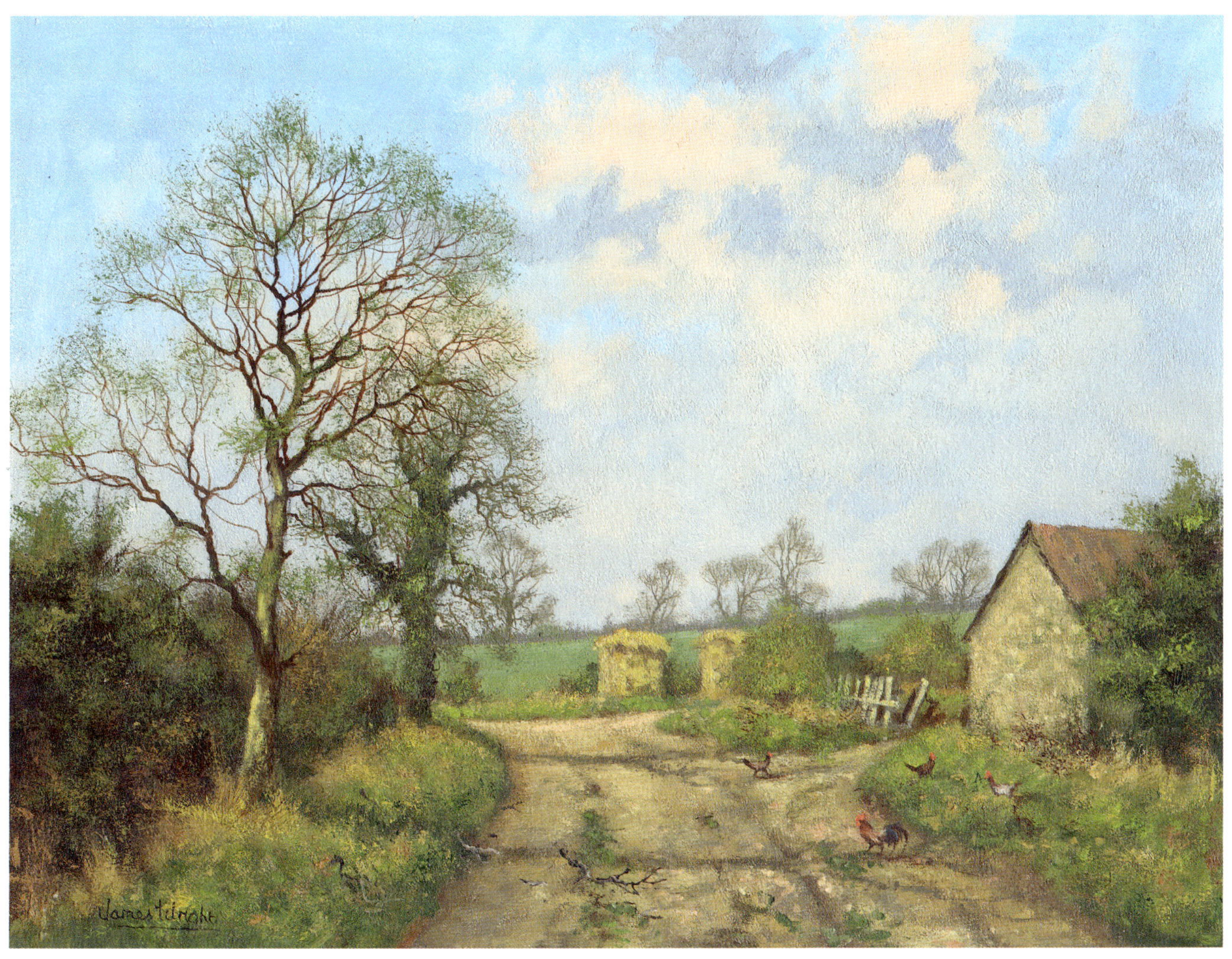

Country Lane, near Tattersett.

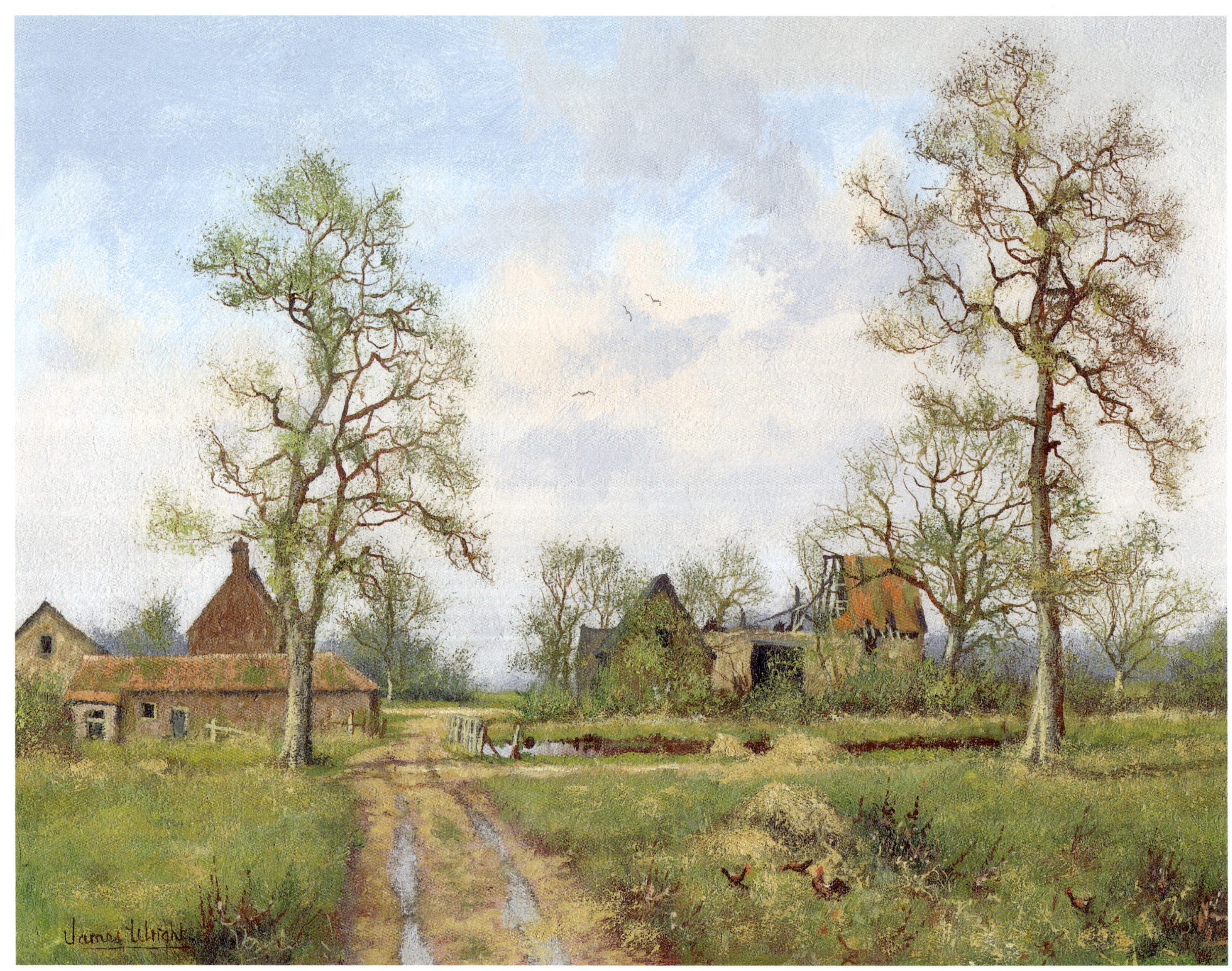

The Derelict Barn, Hanworth, Norfolk.

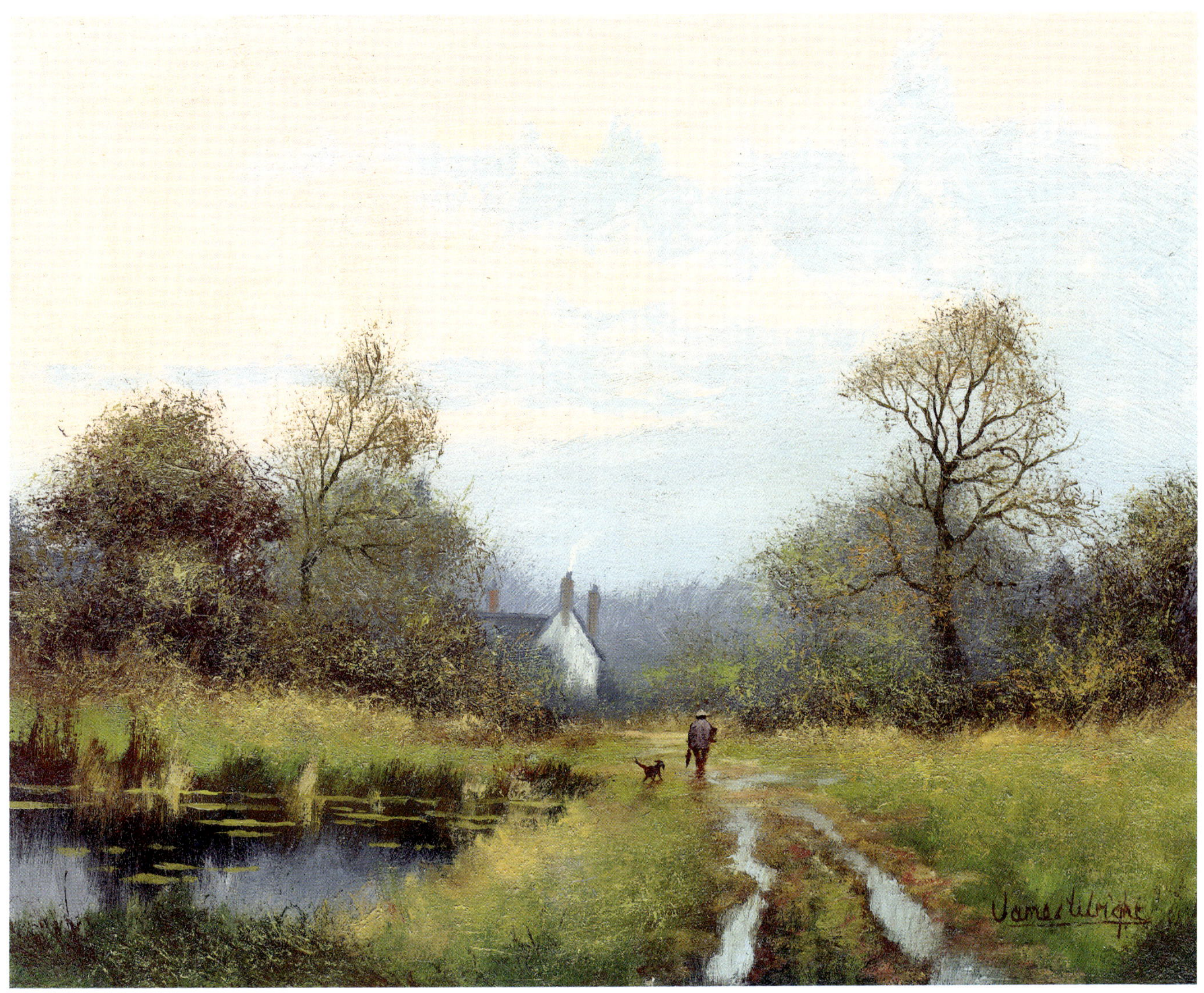

After the Rain.

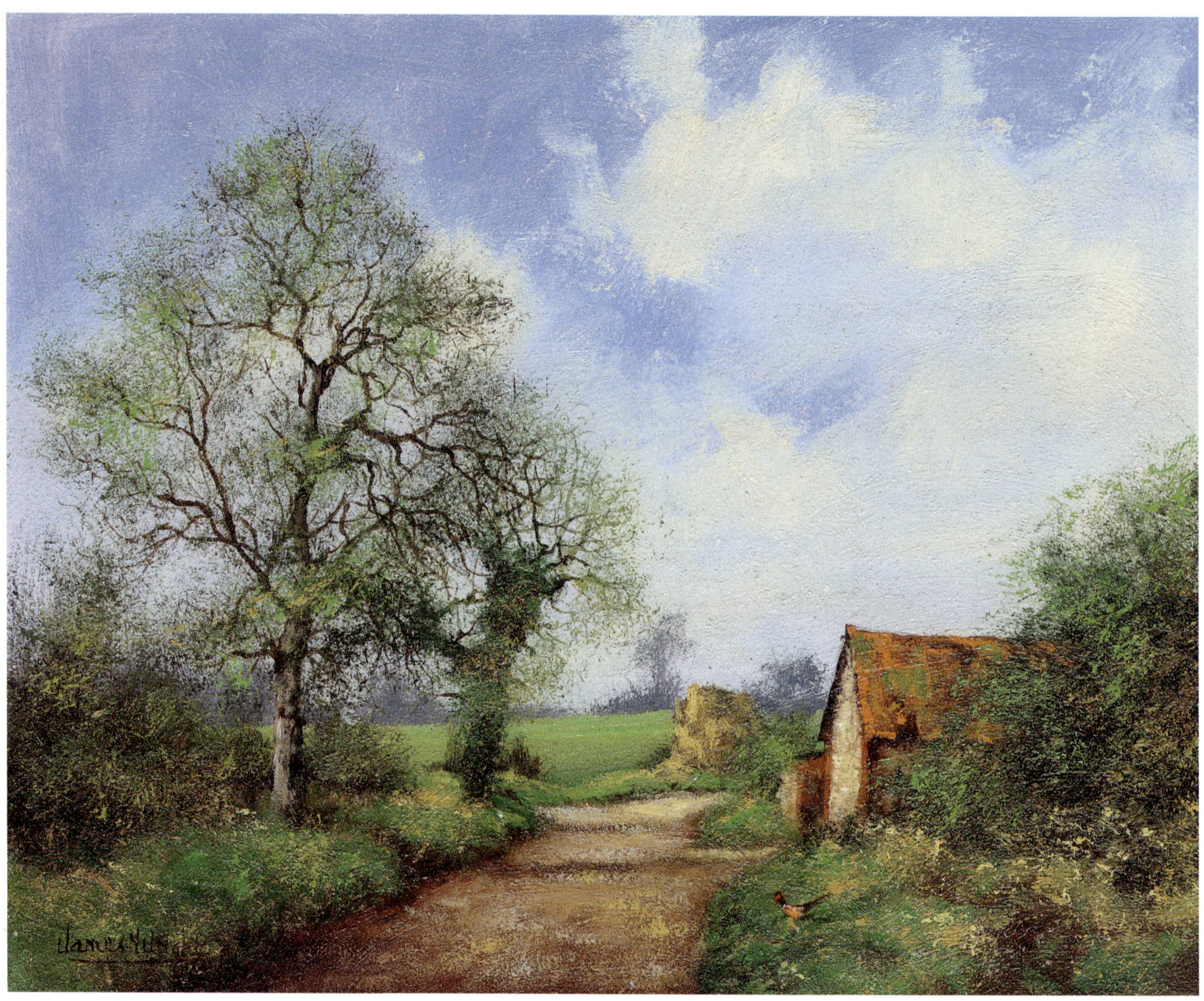

A Norfolk Lane.

Opposite: *Cottages near Narborough.*

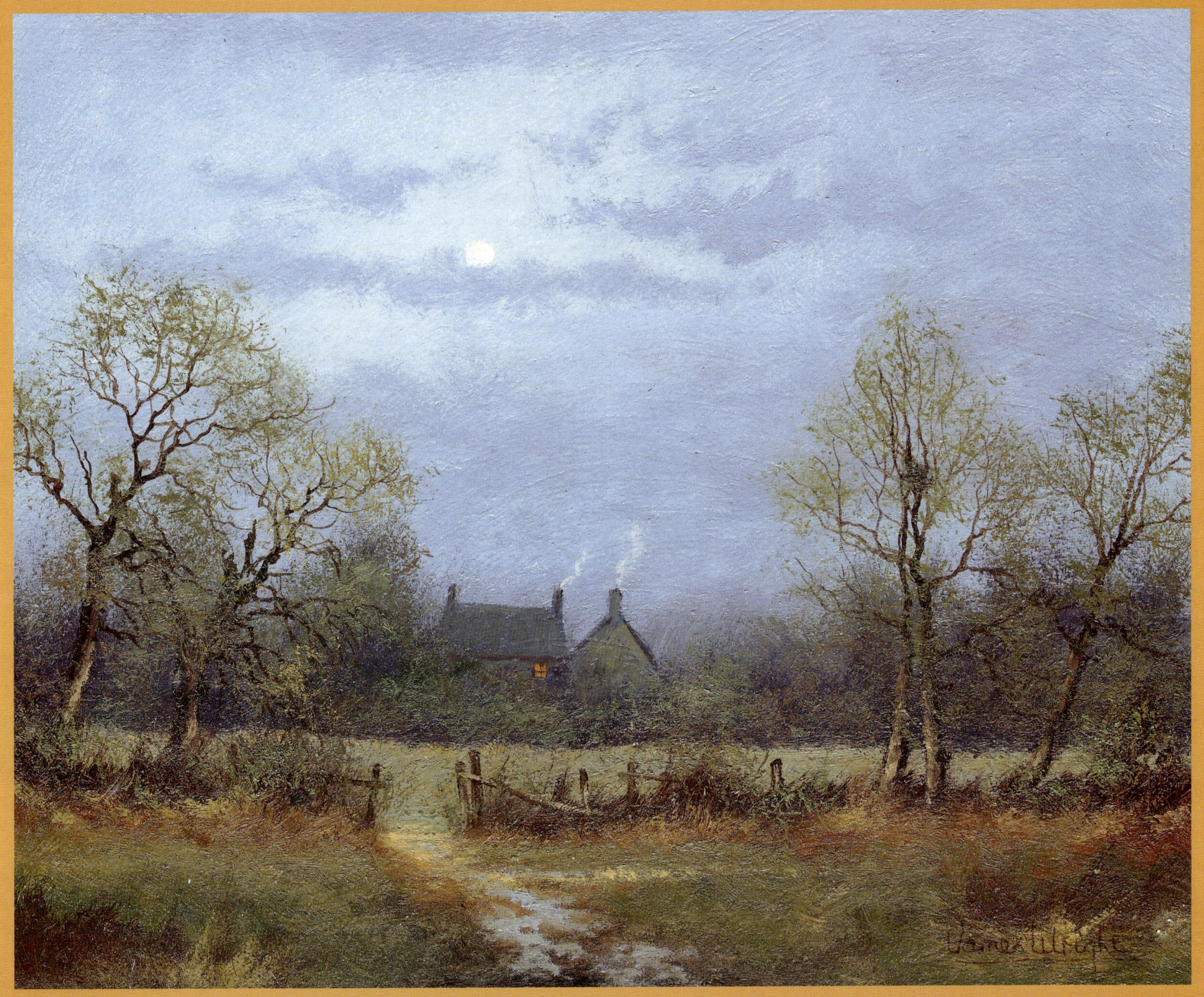

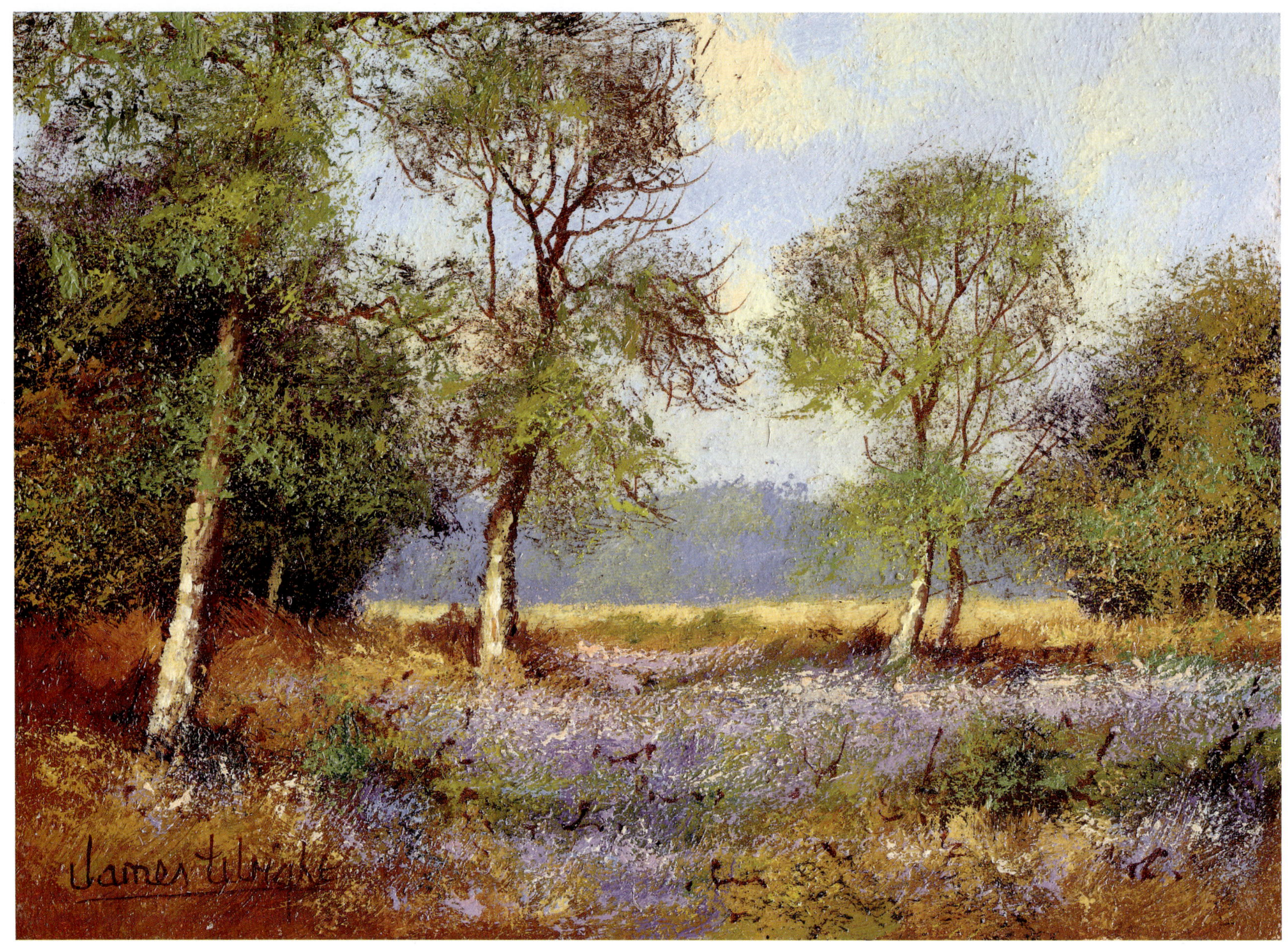

On the Edge of Bluebell Woods.

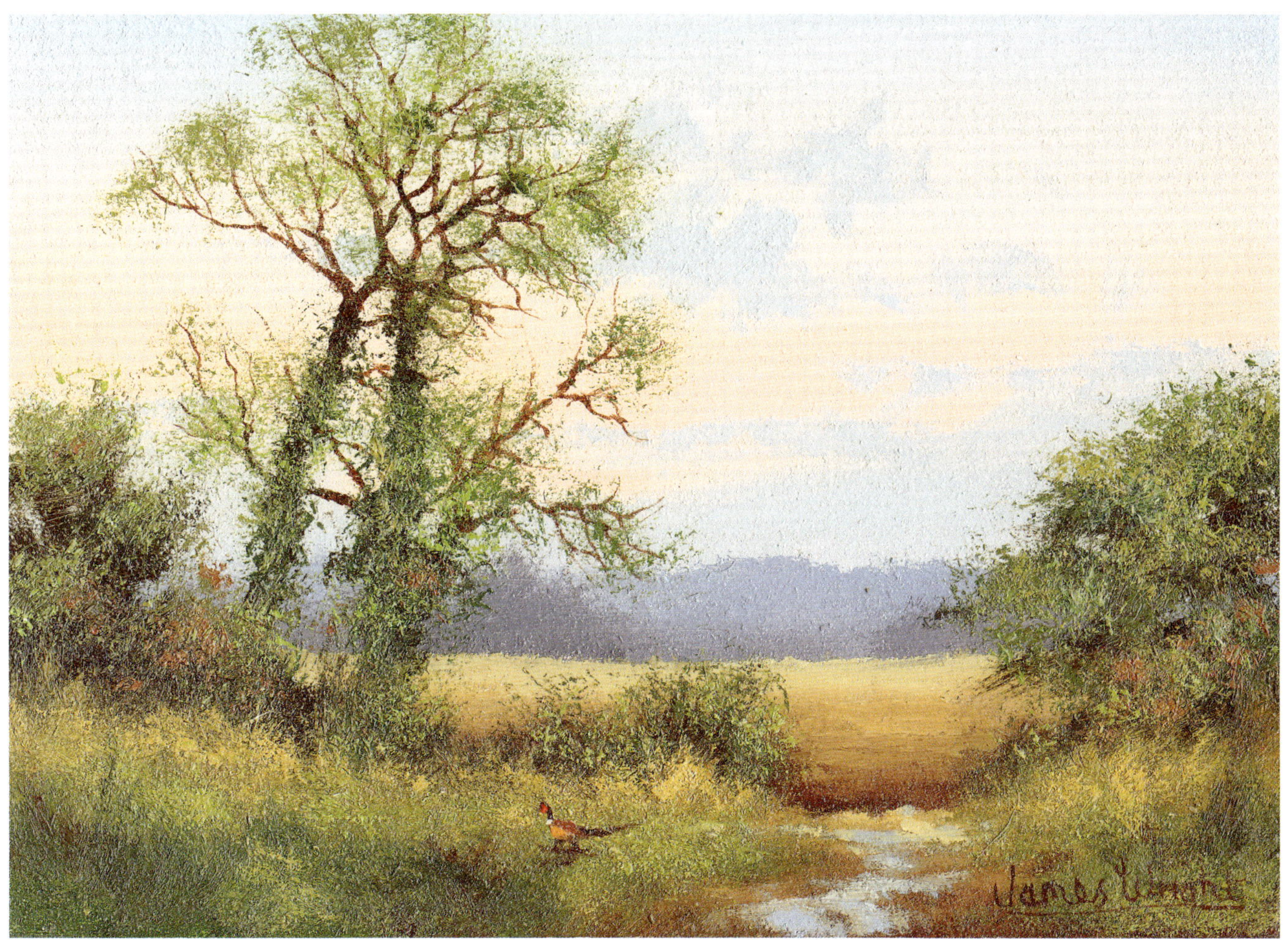

Evening Light.

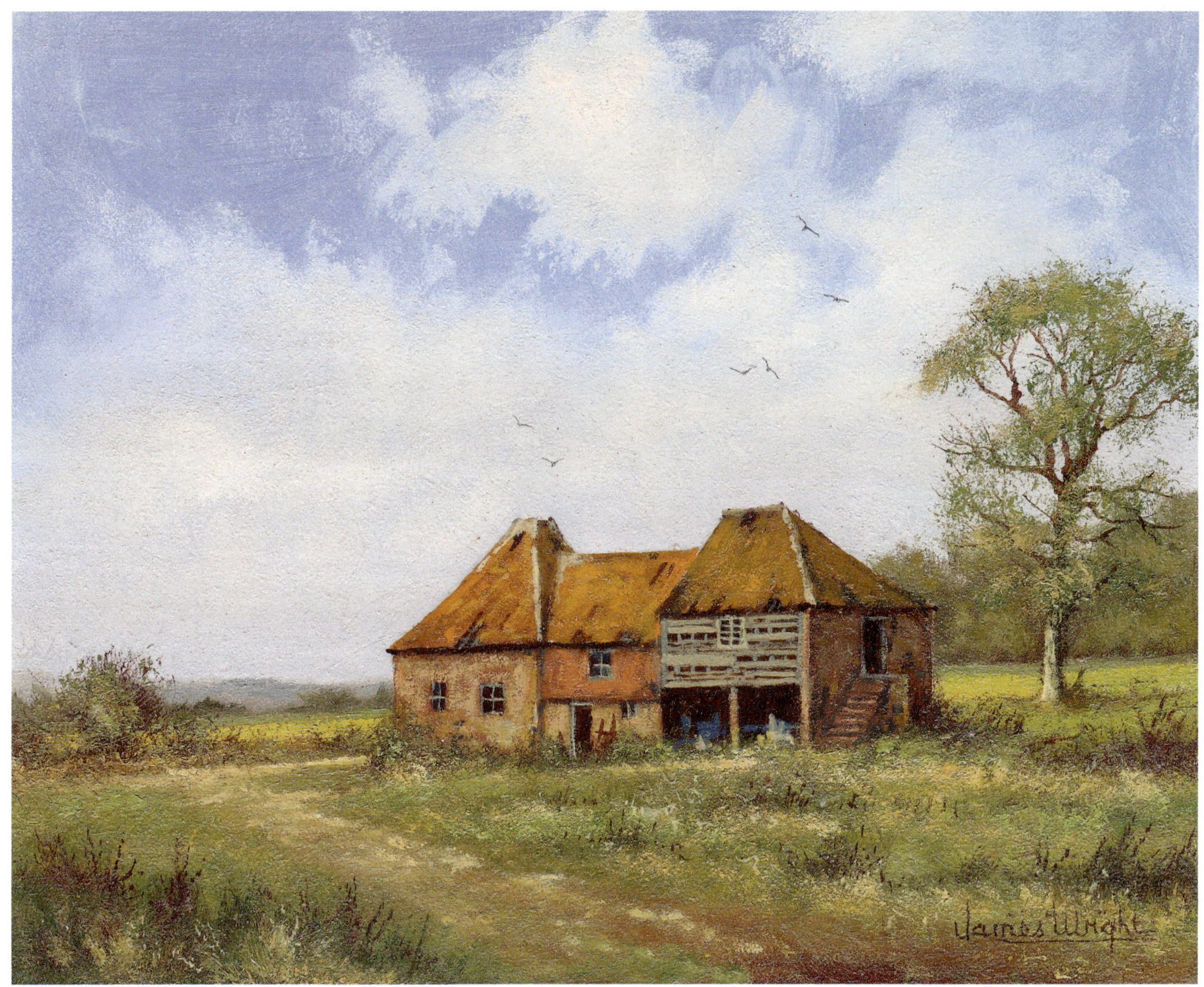

Derelict Oast House, near Hastings.

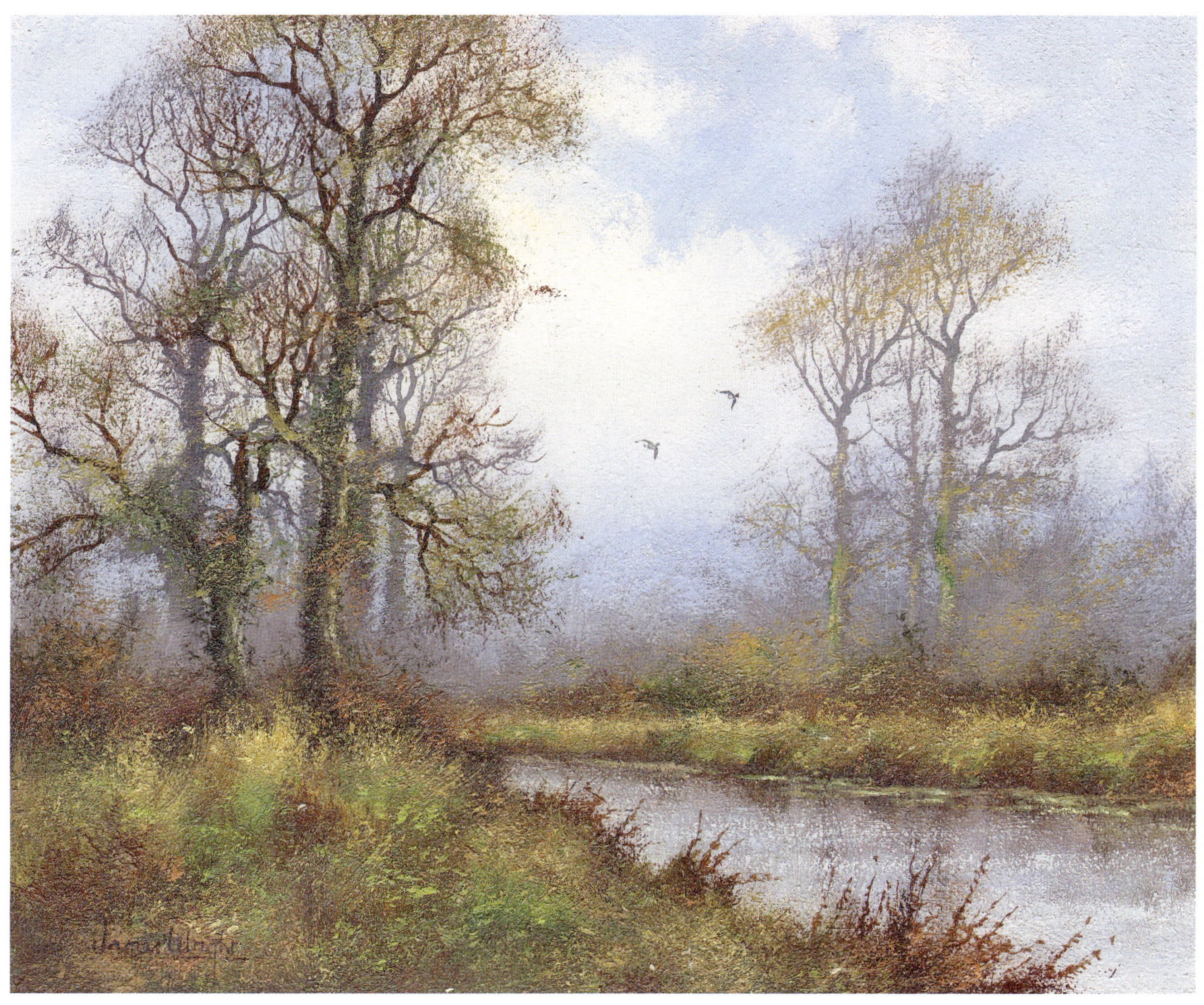

Stormy Weather.

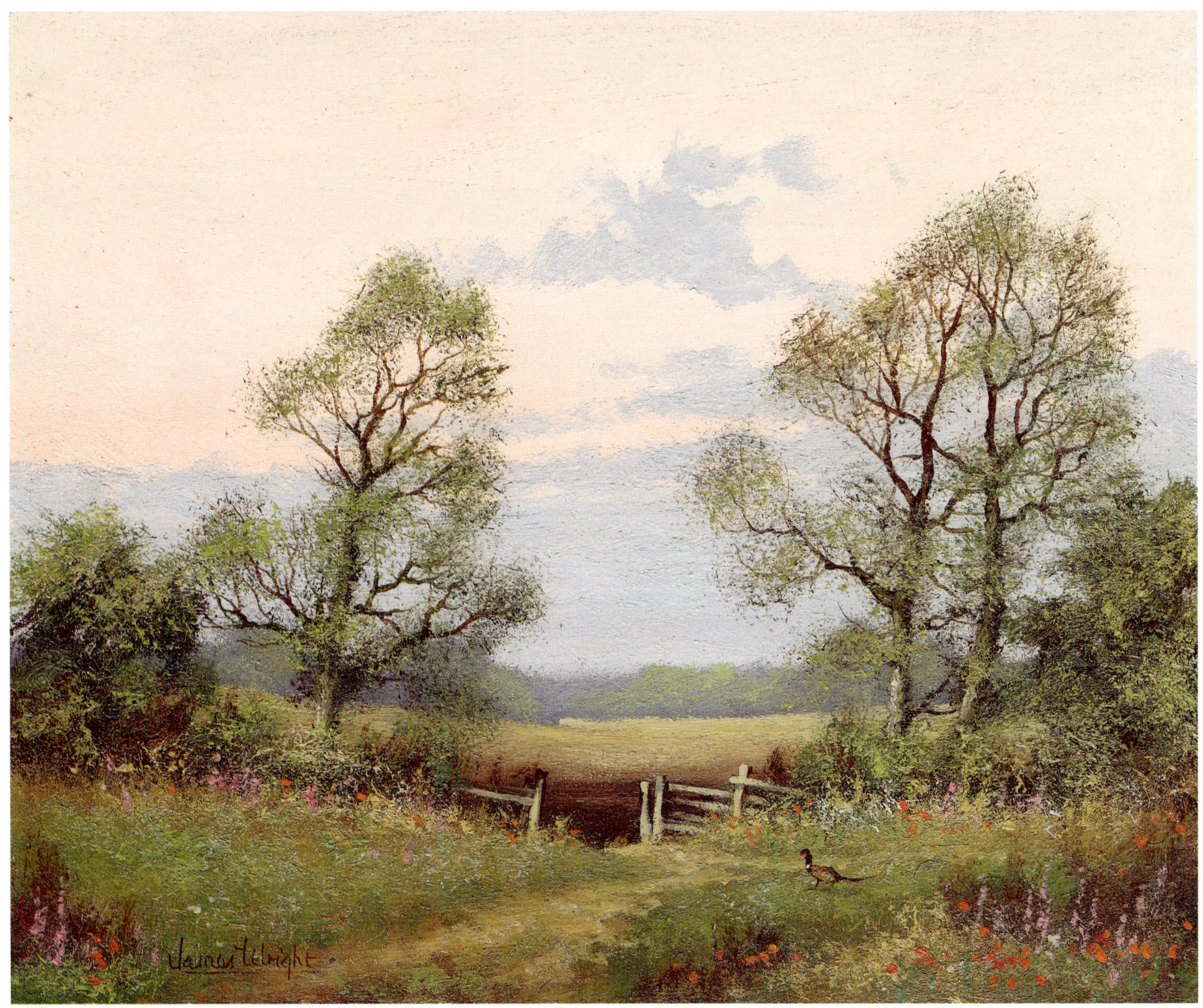

Pheasant on a Path.

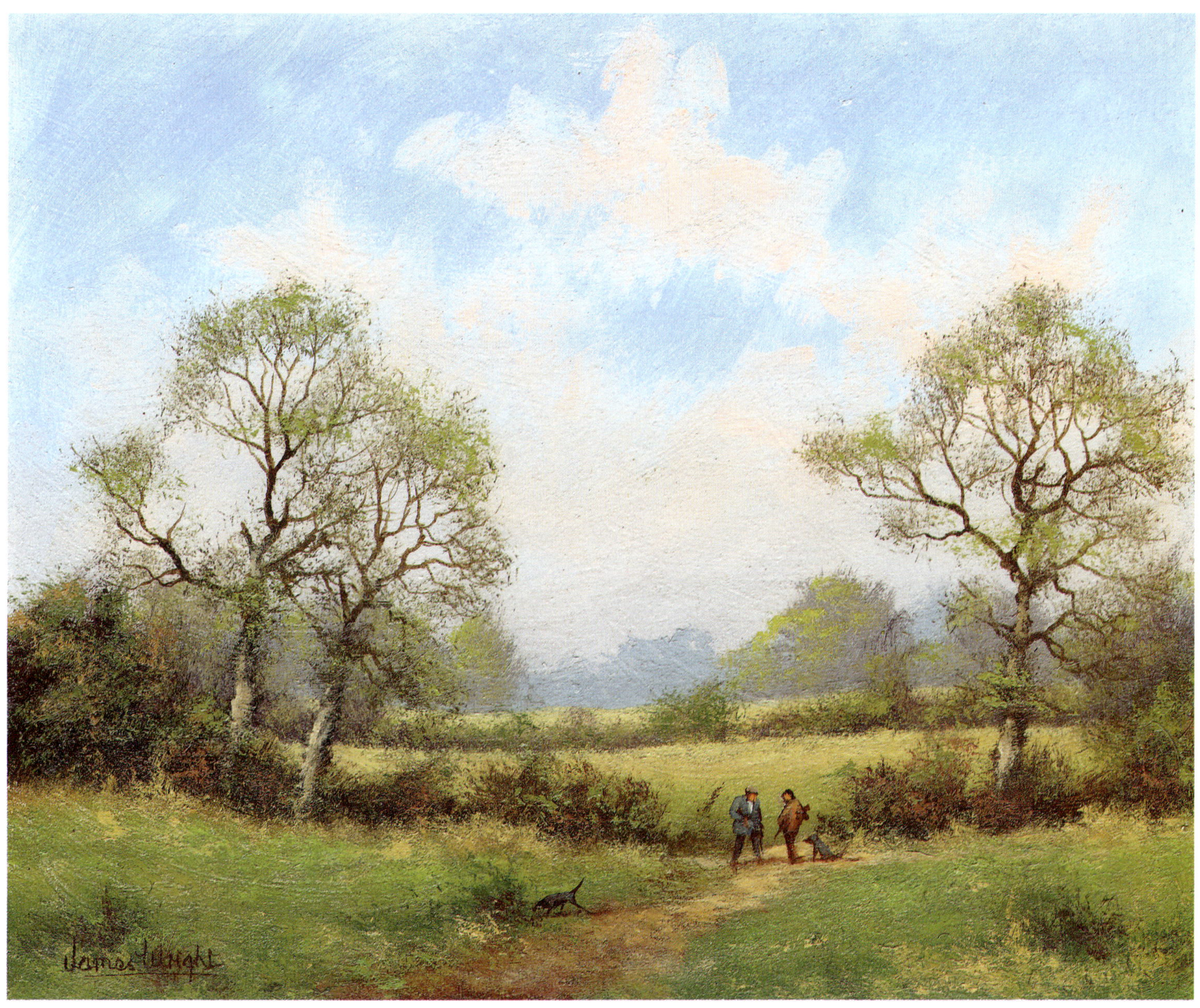

Discussing Country Matters.

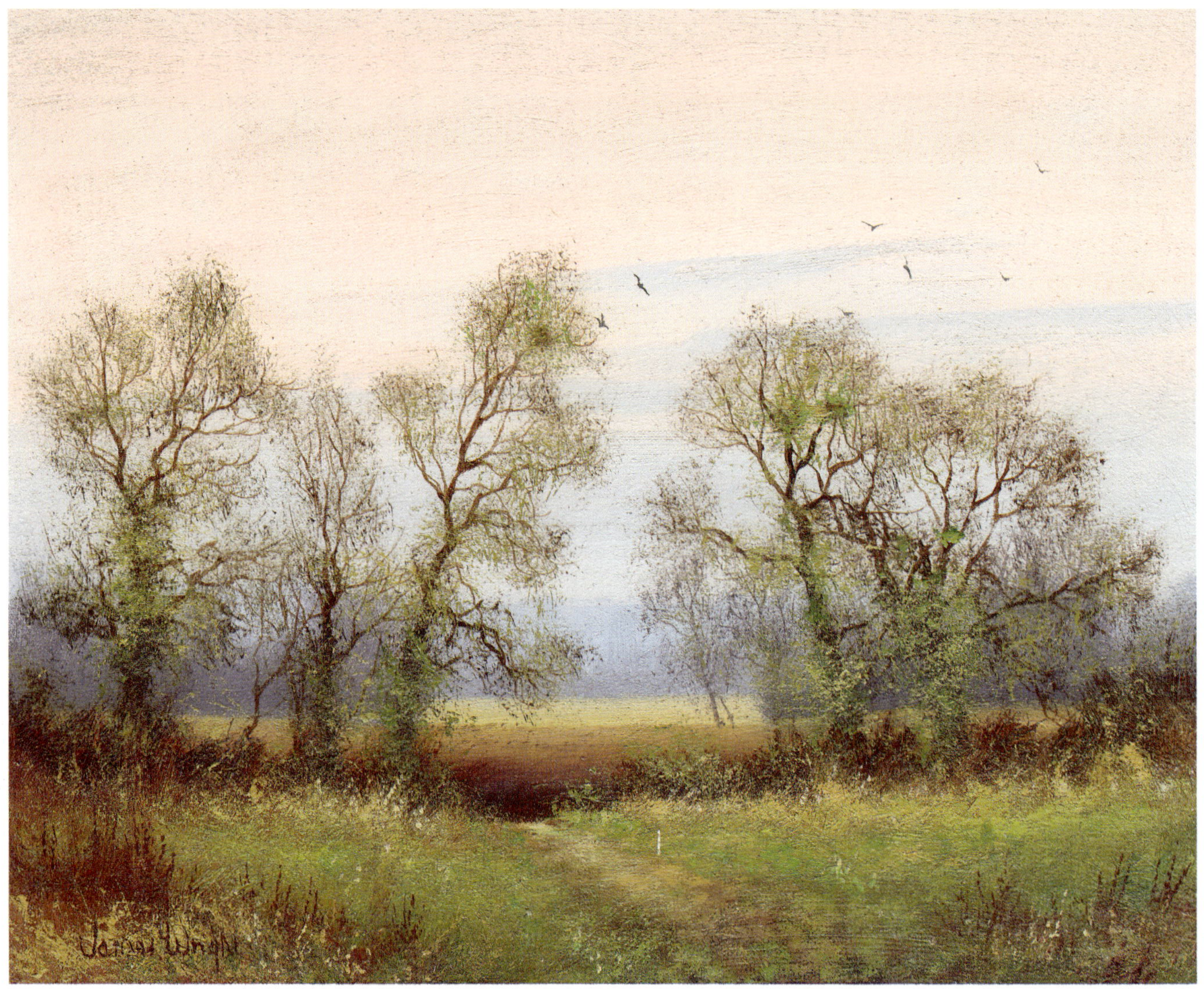

The First Signs of Spring.

Opposite: *Cart Track and Puddles.*

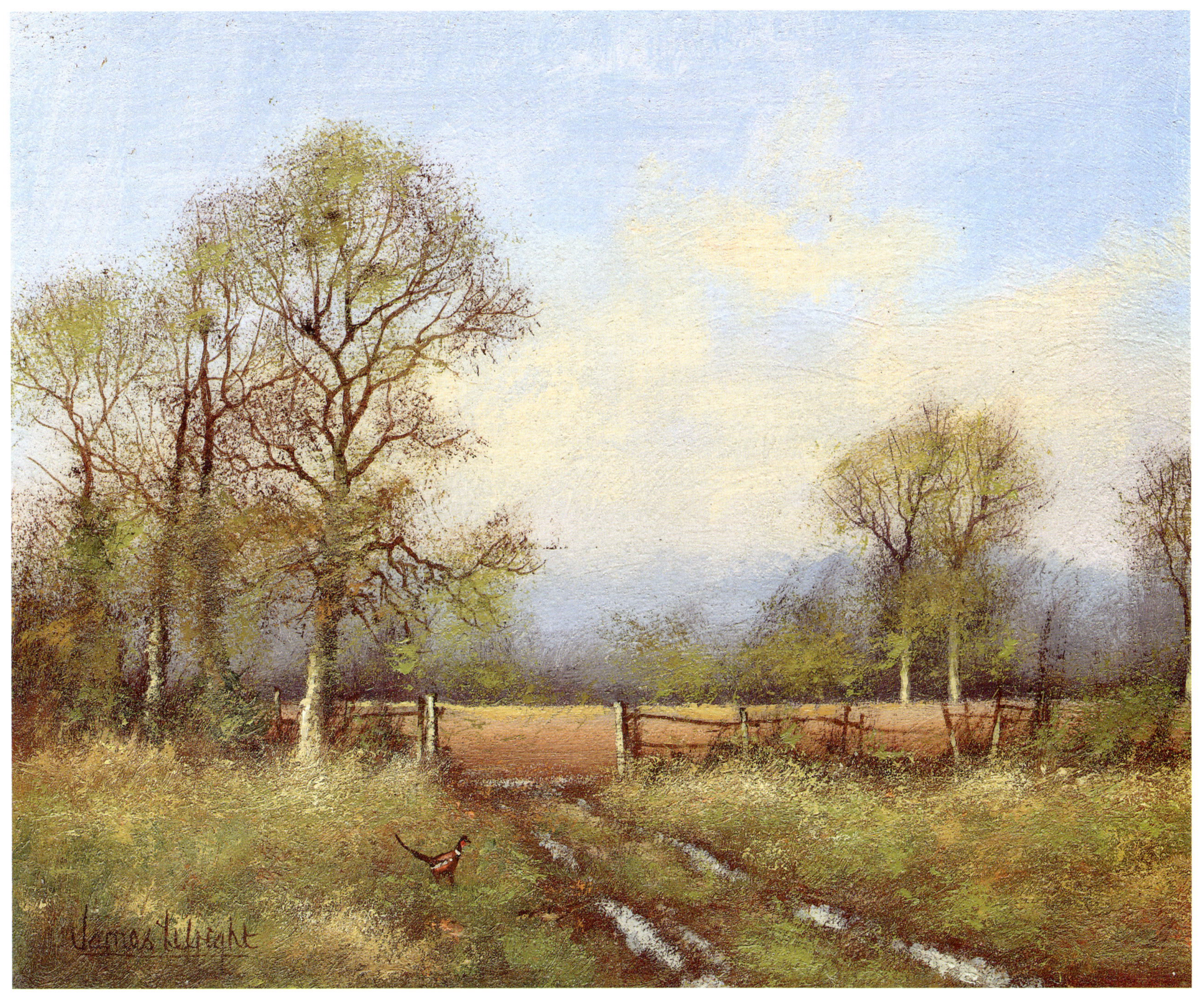

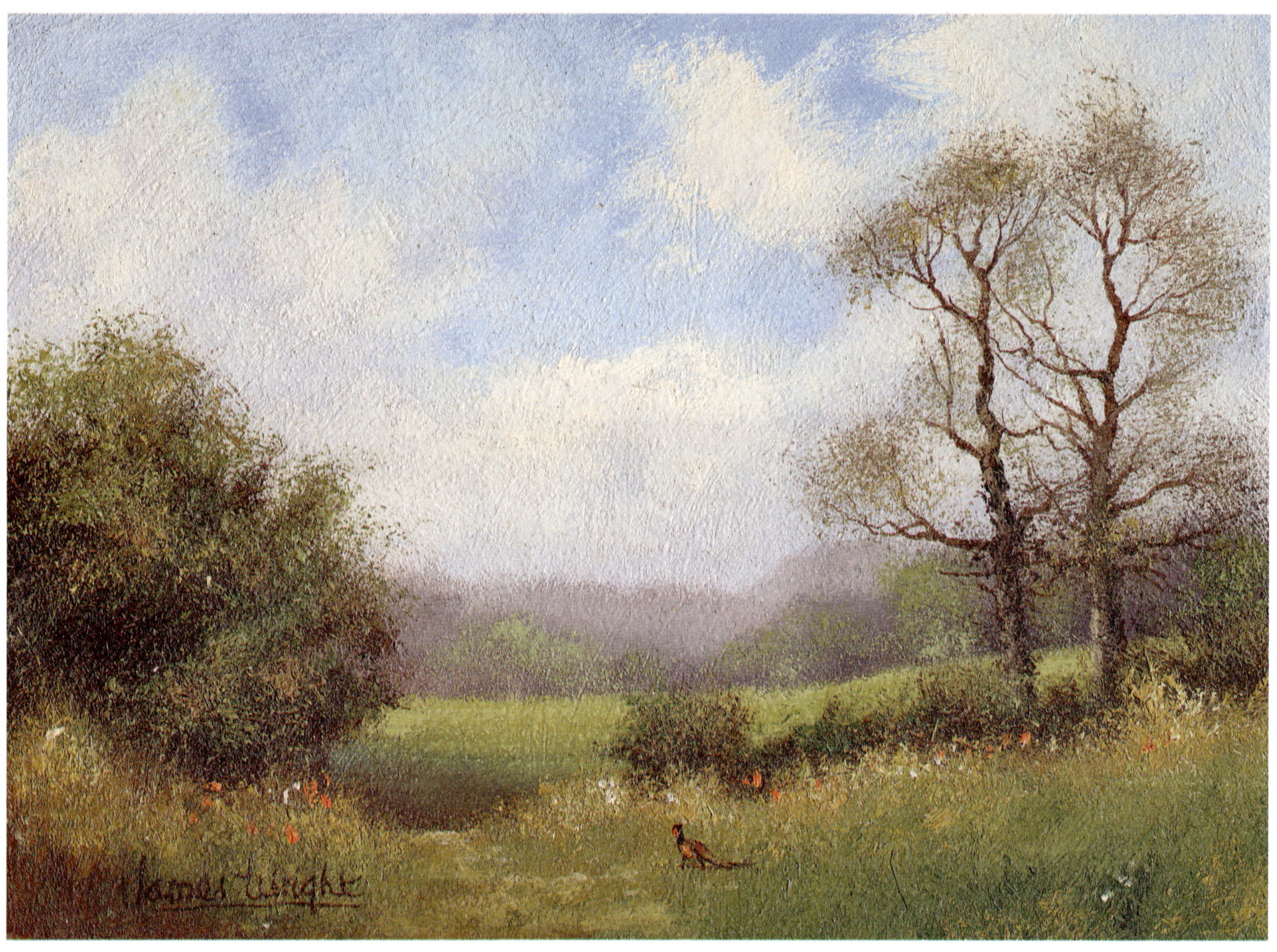

Suffolk Fields.

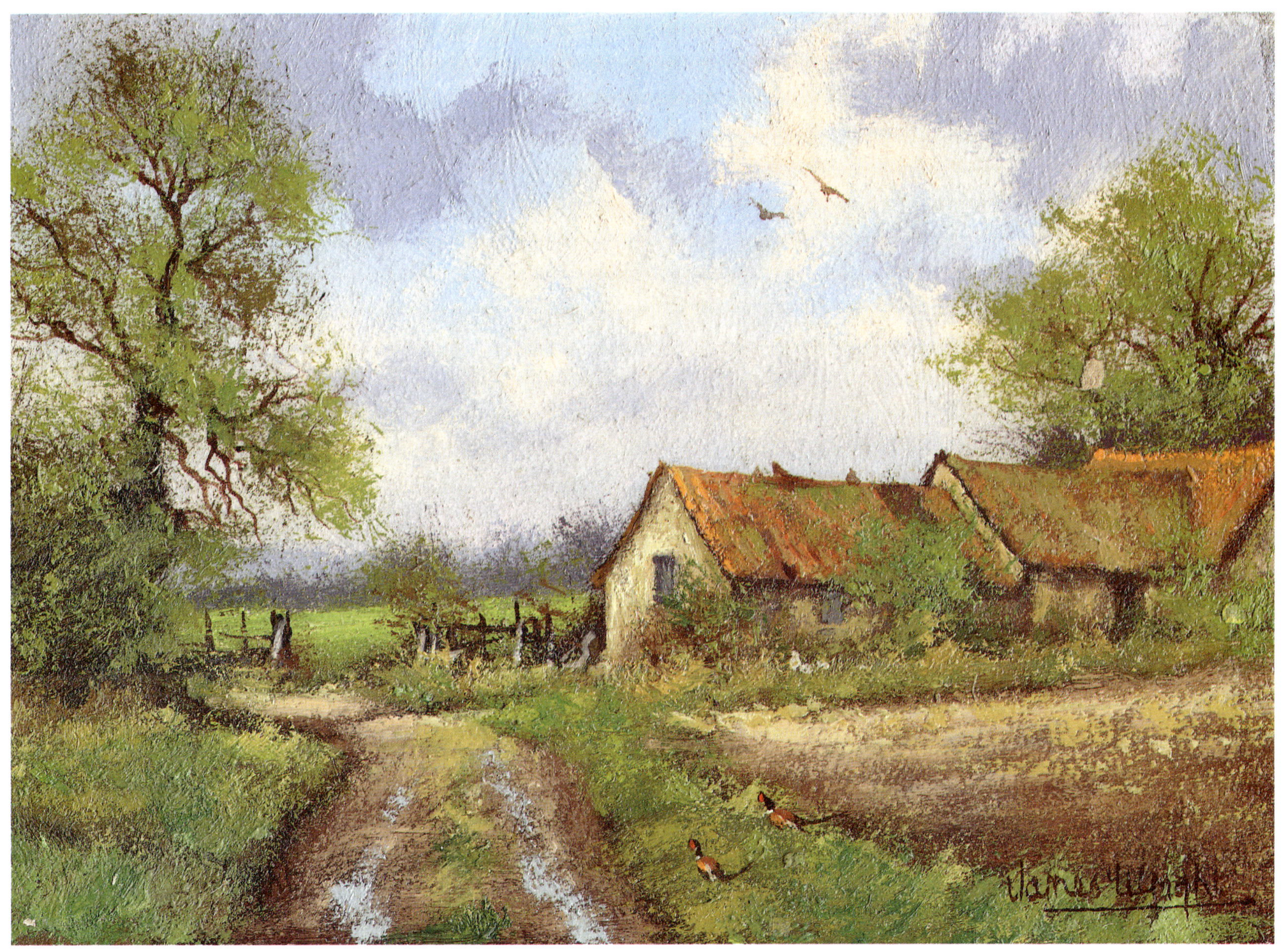

Farm Buildings at Elinor.

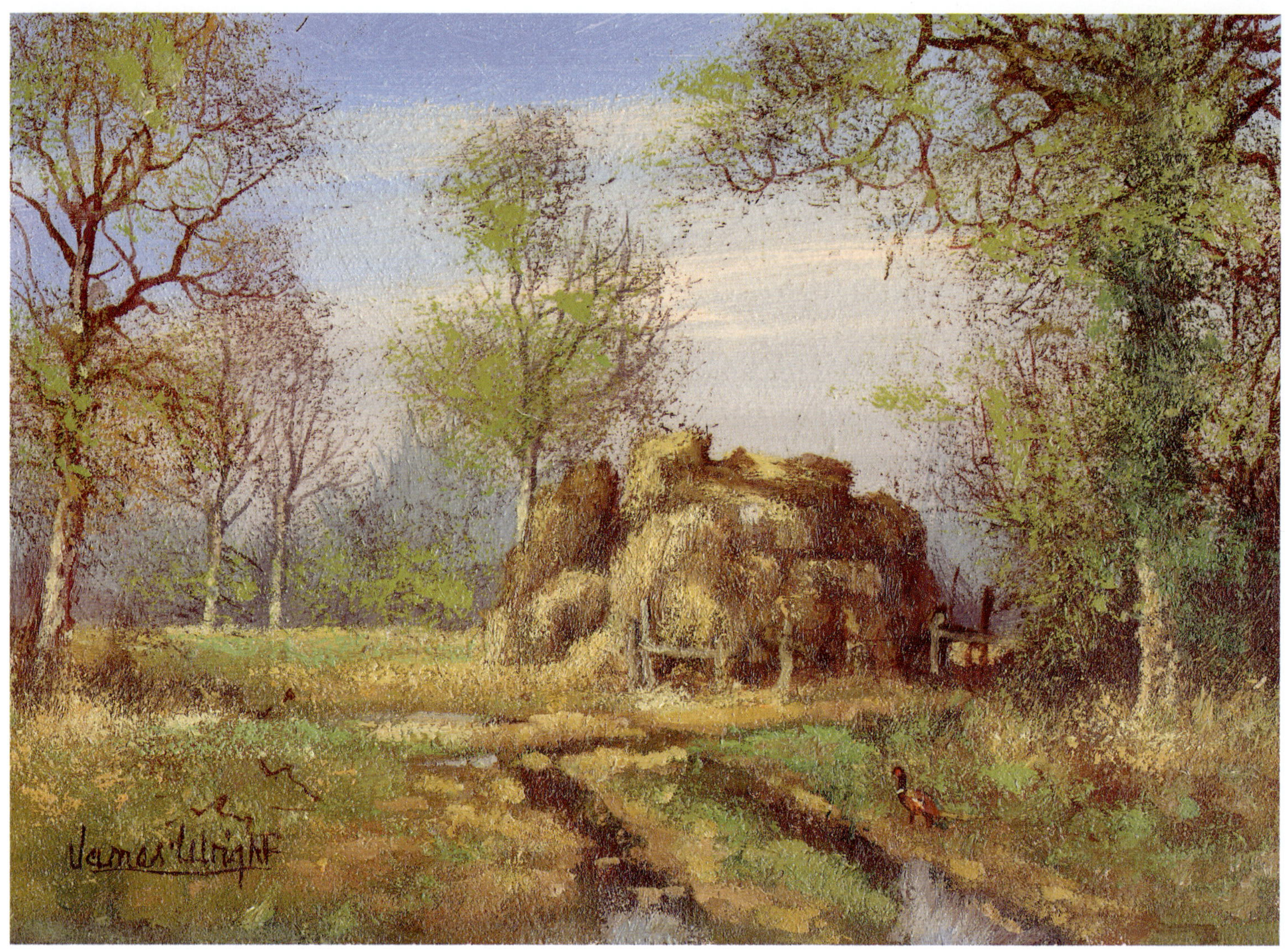

Haystacks and Pheasant.

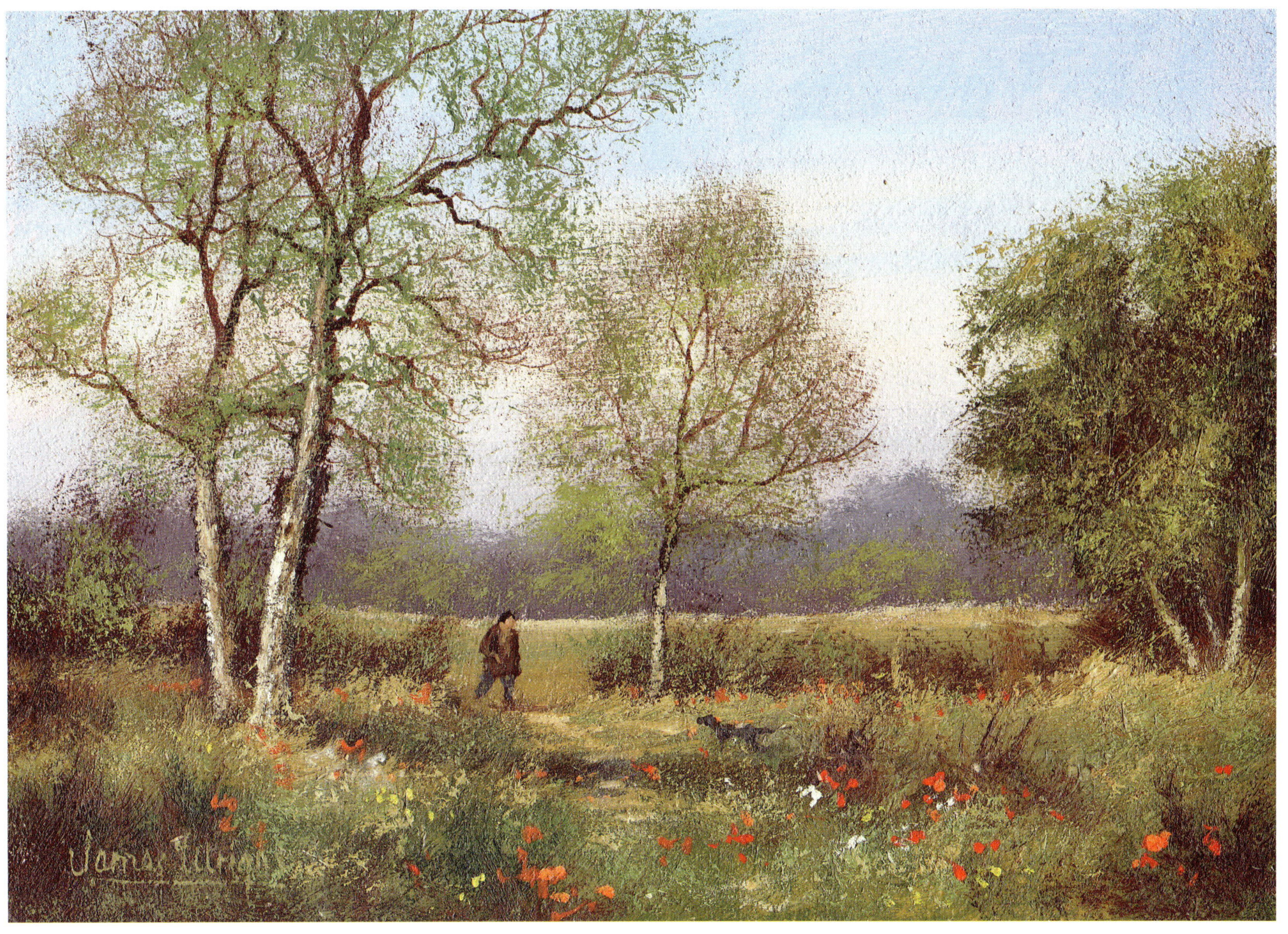

Out with the Dog.

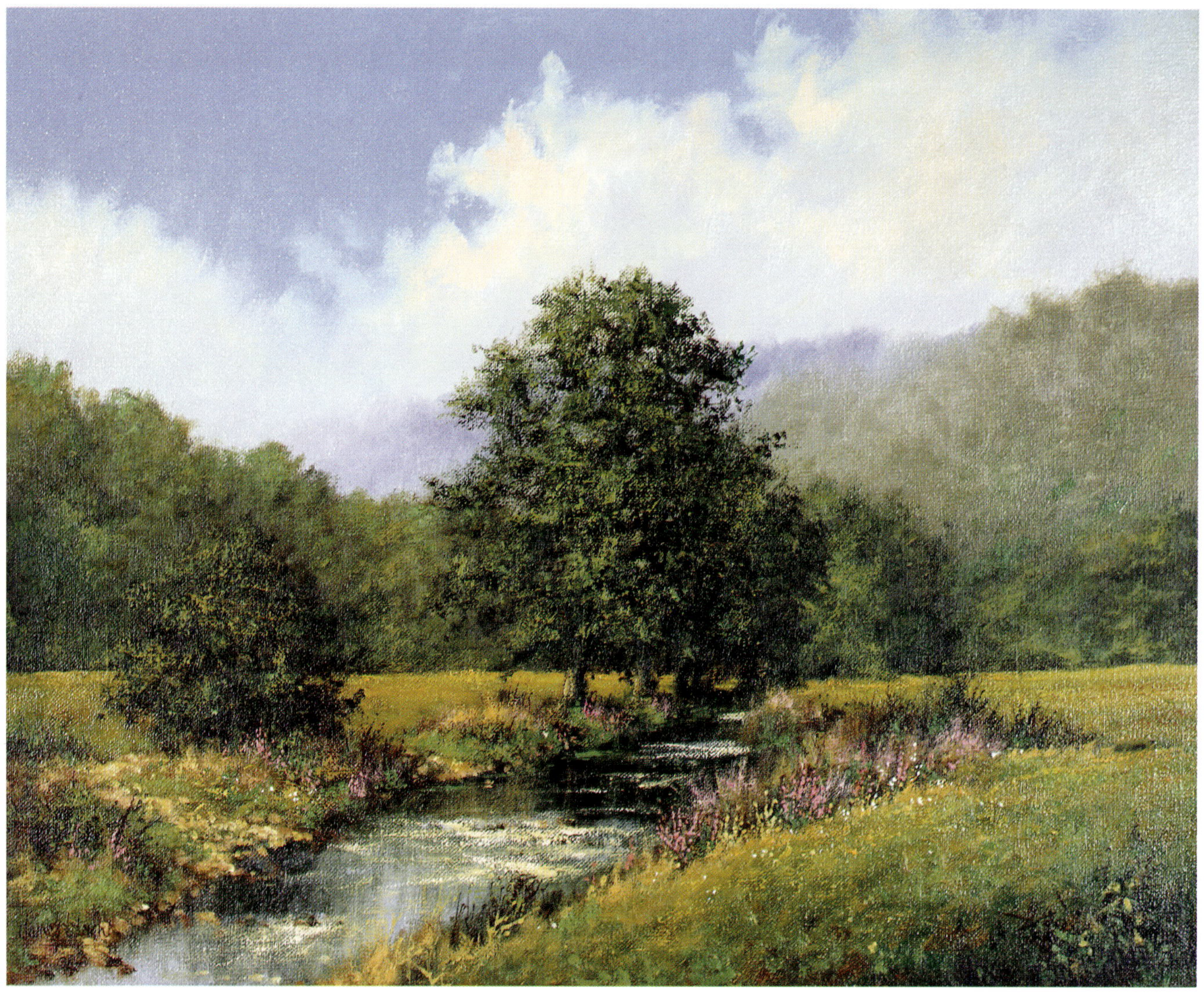

Exmoor.

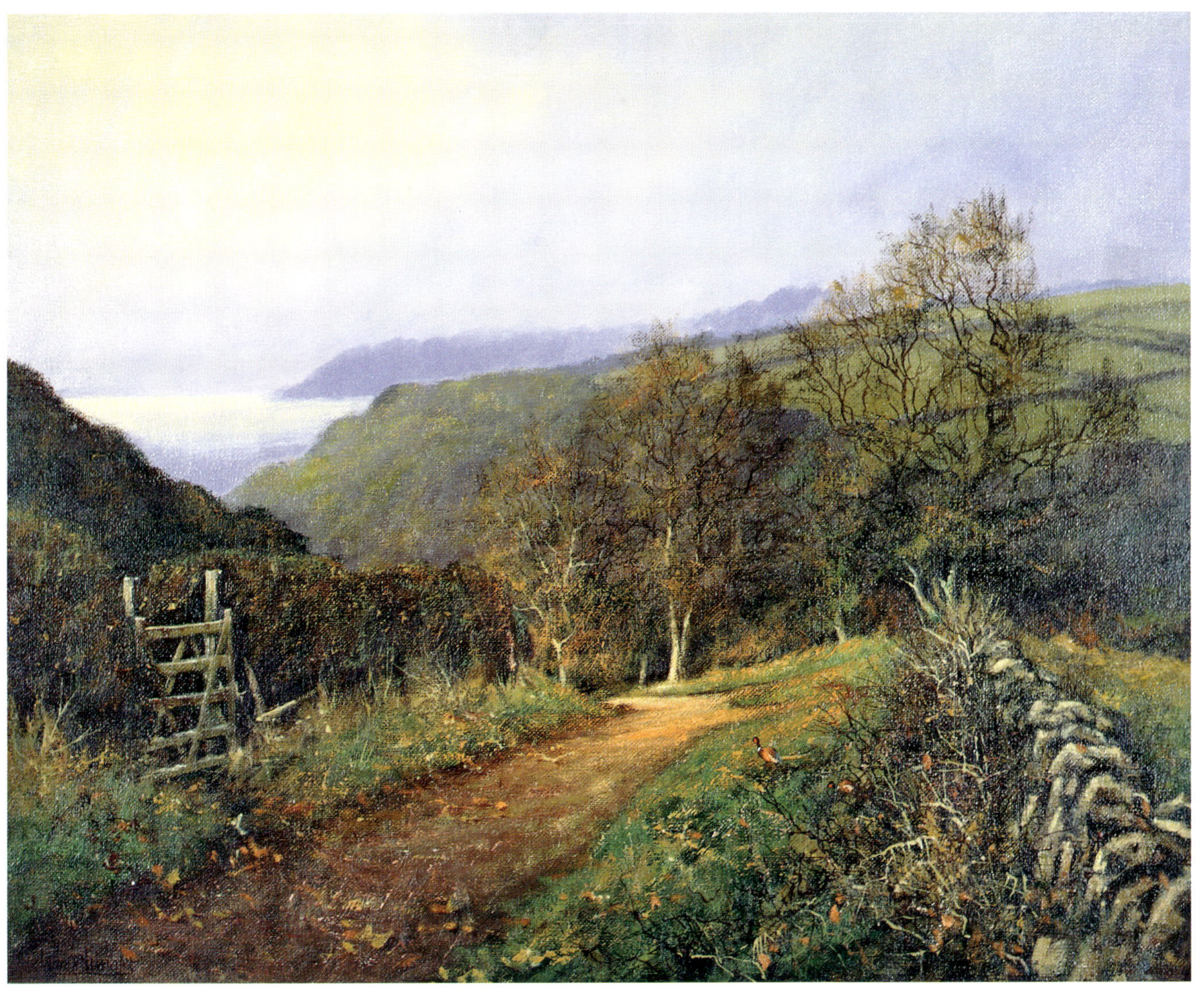

North Exmoor Coast.

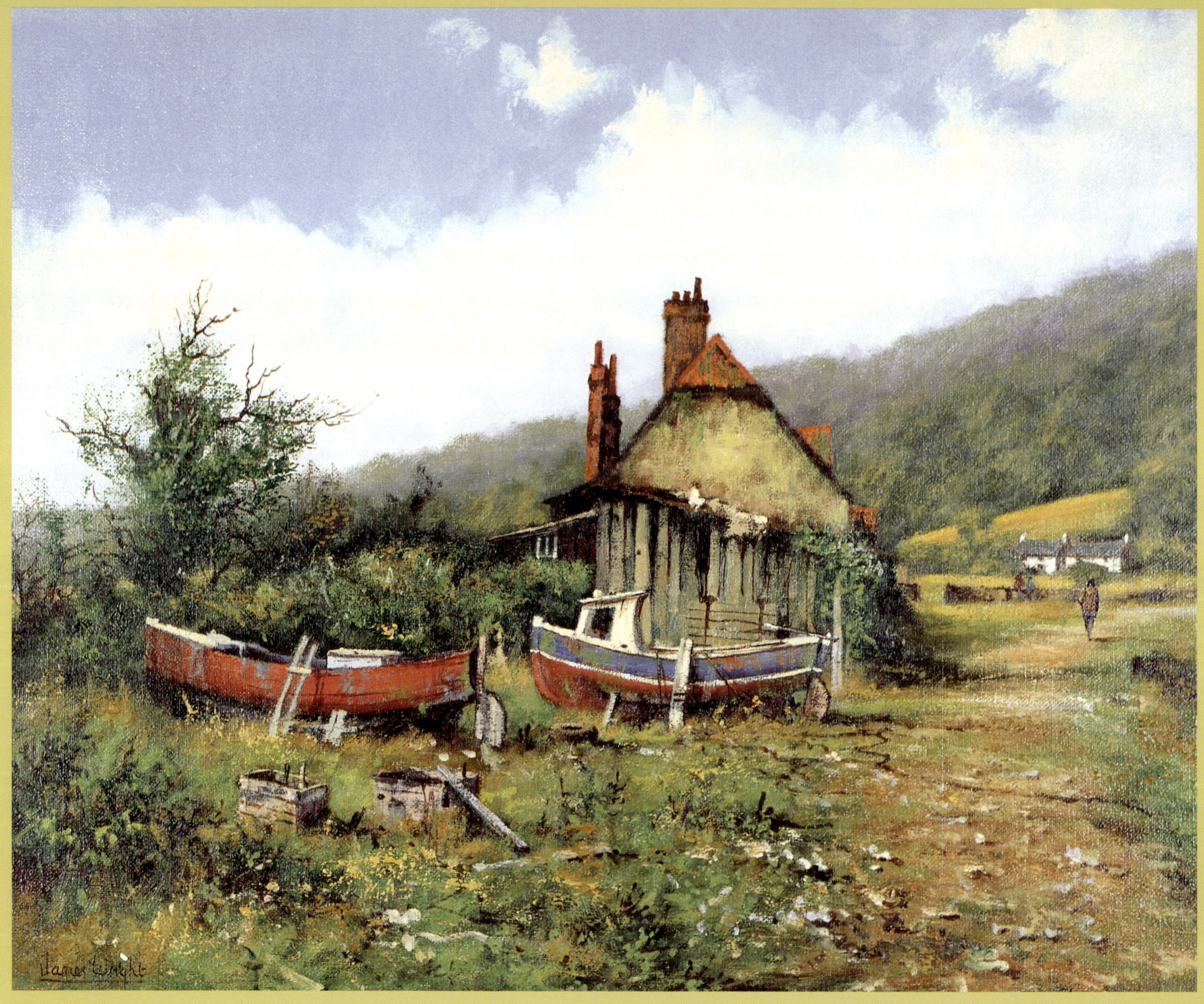

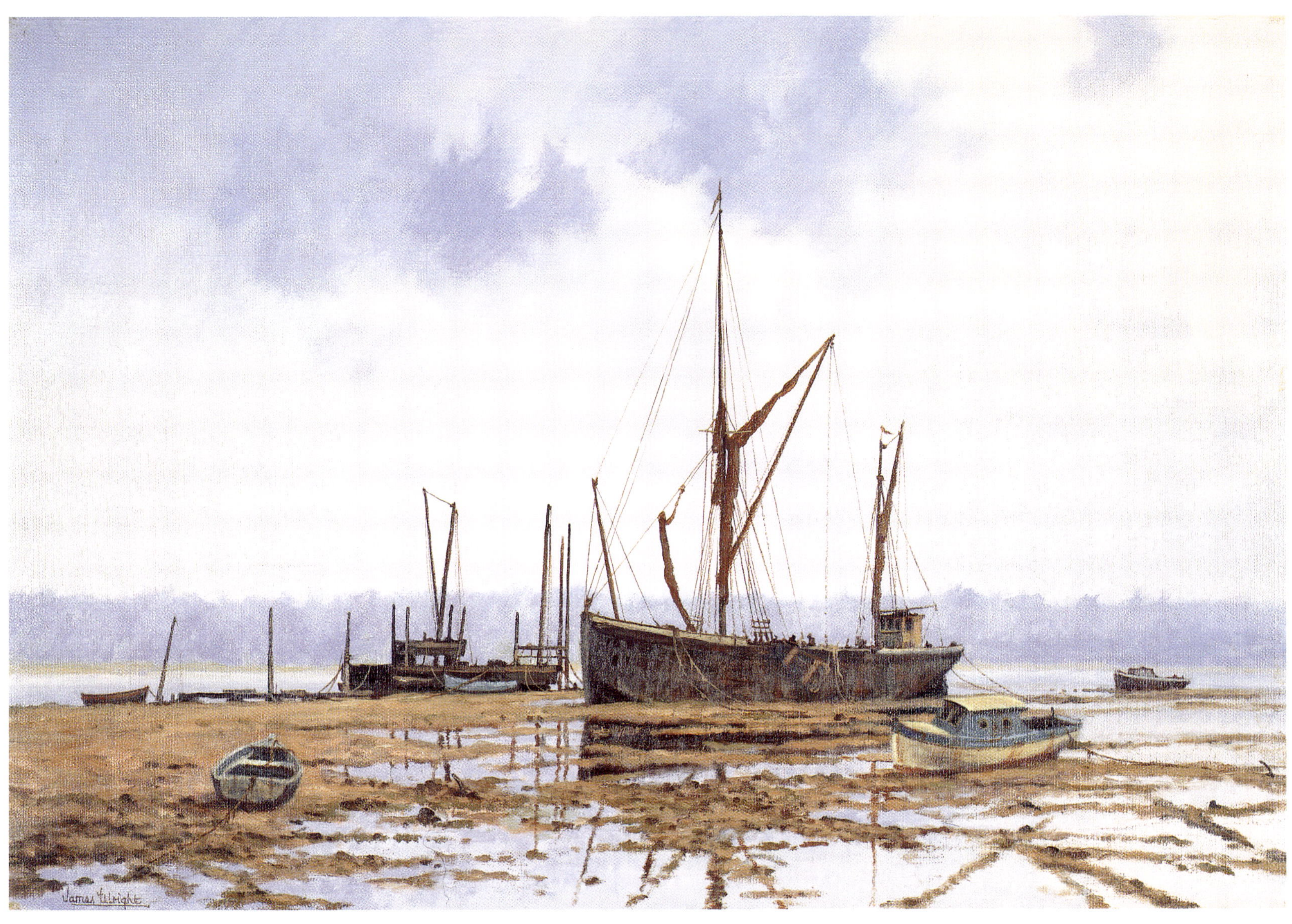

Pin Mill.

Opposite: *Porlock Weir.*

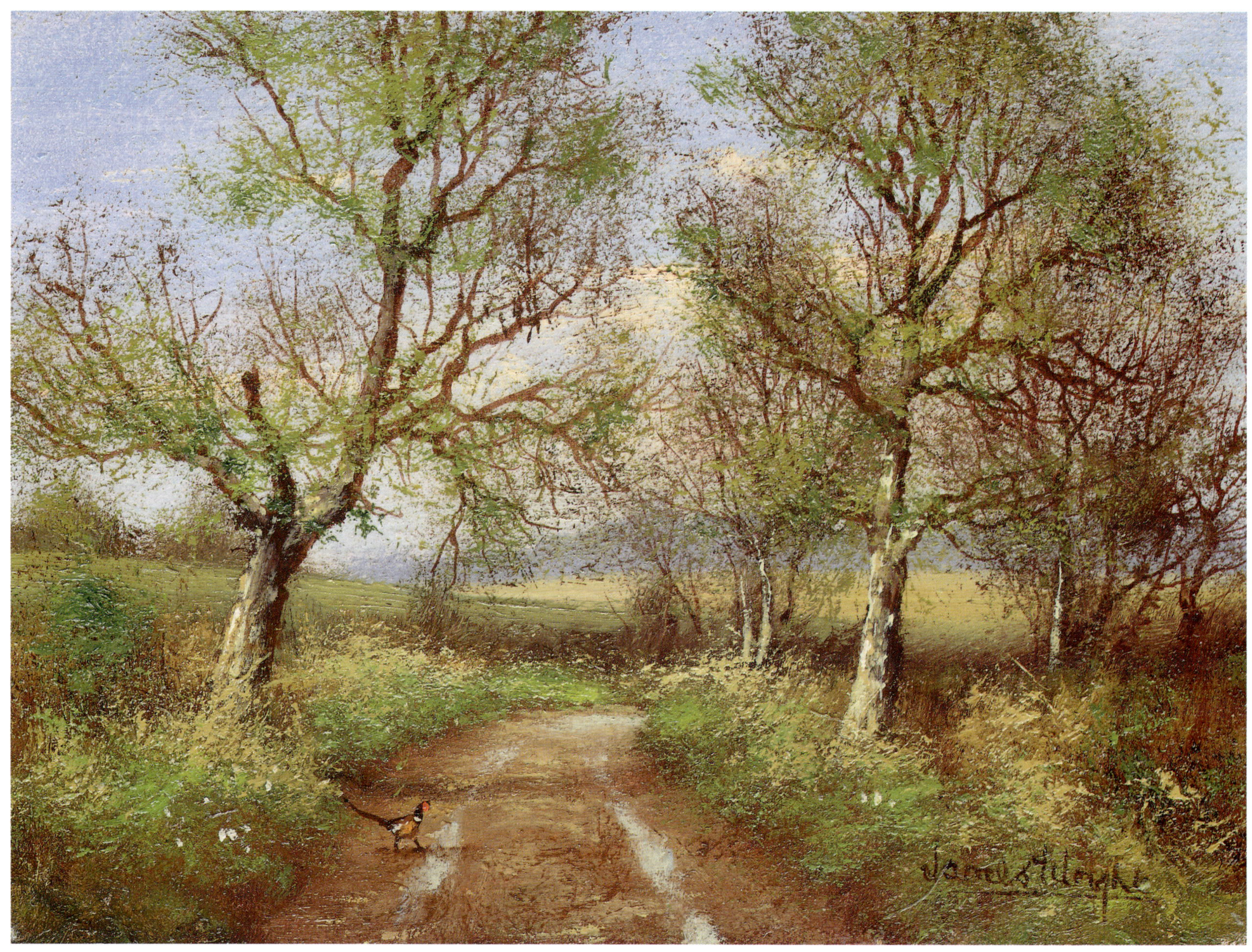

Country Lane in Spring.

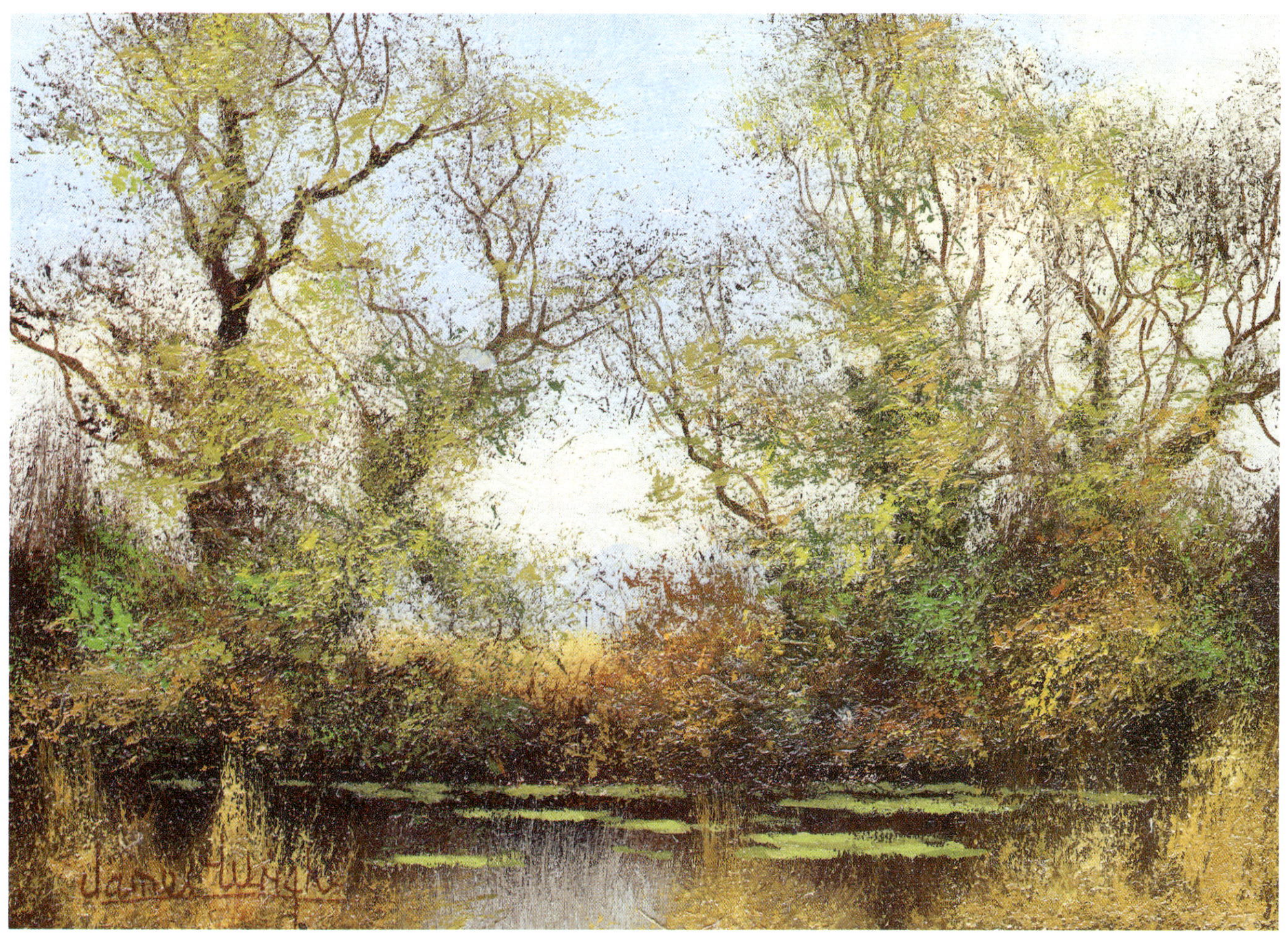

Still Waters.

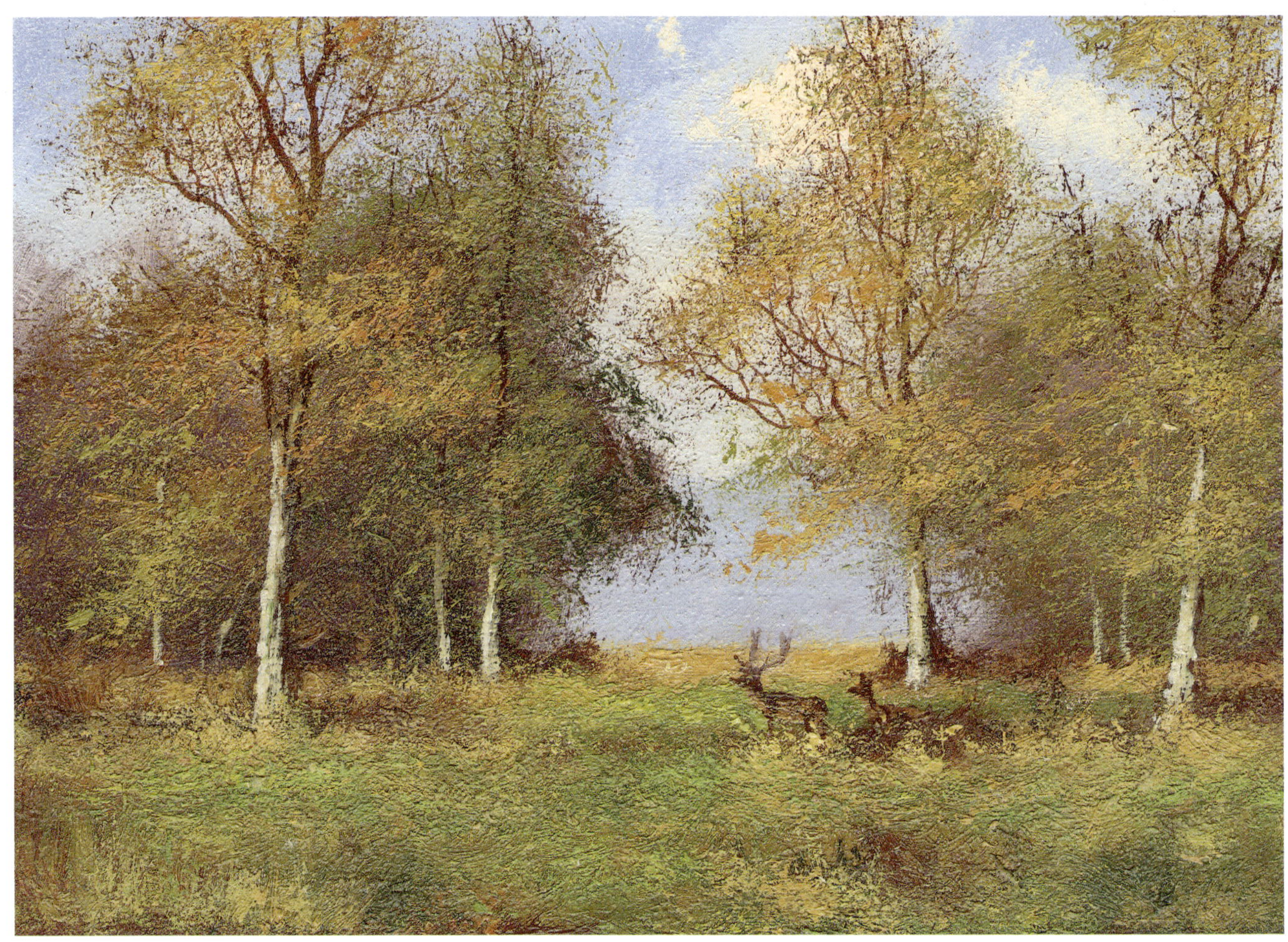

Autumn Woods.

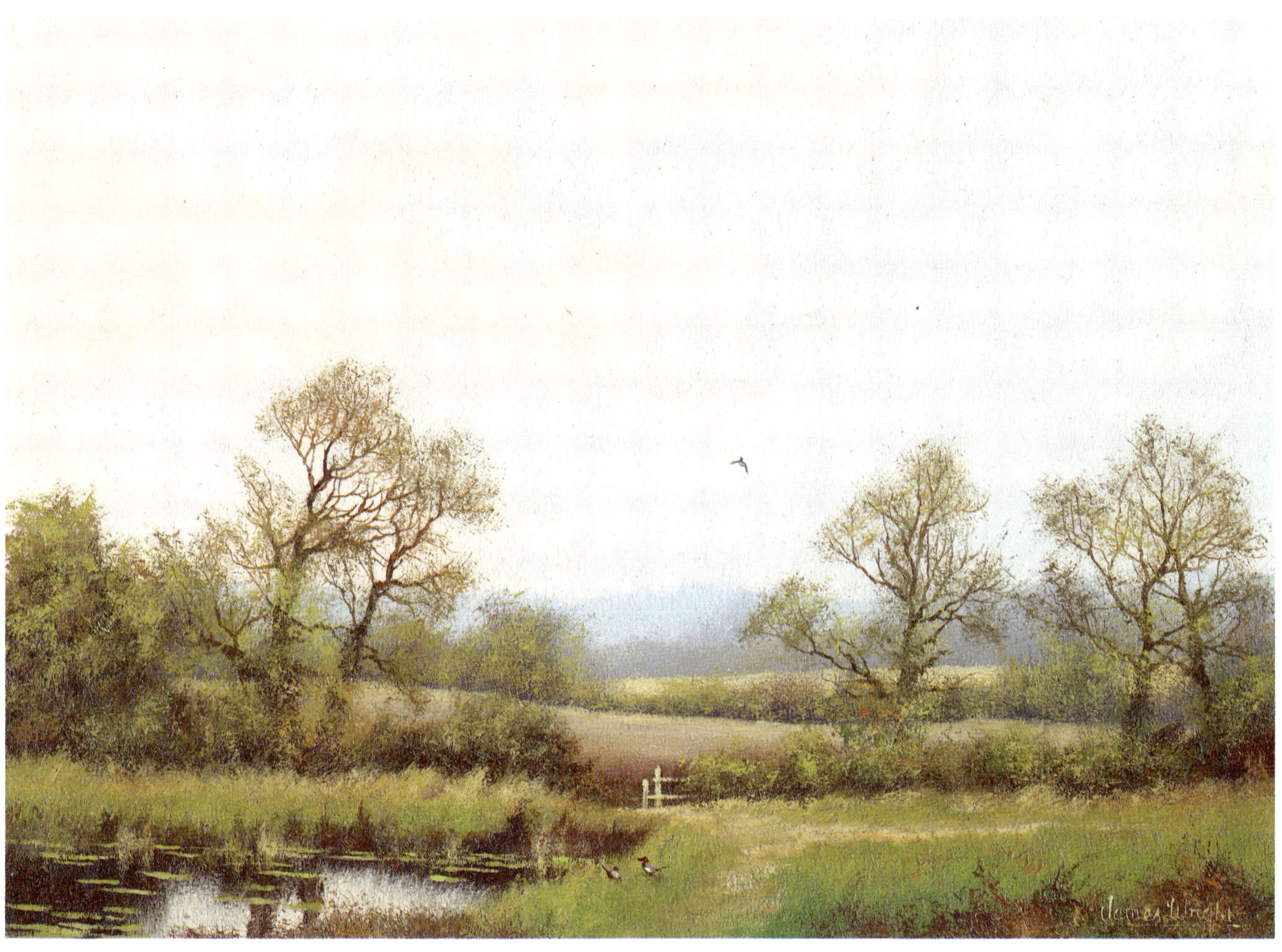

Norfolk Fields.

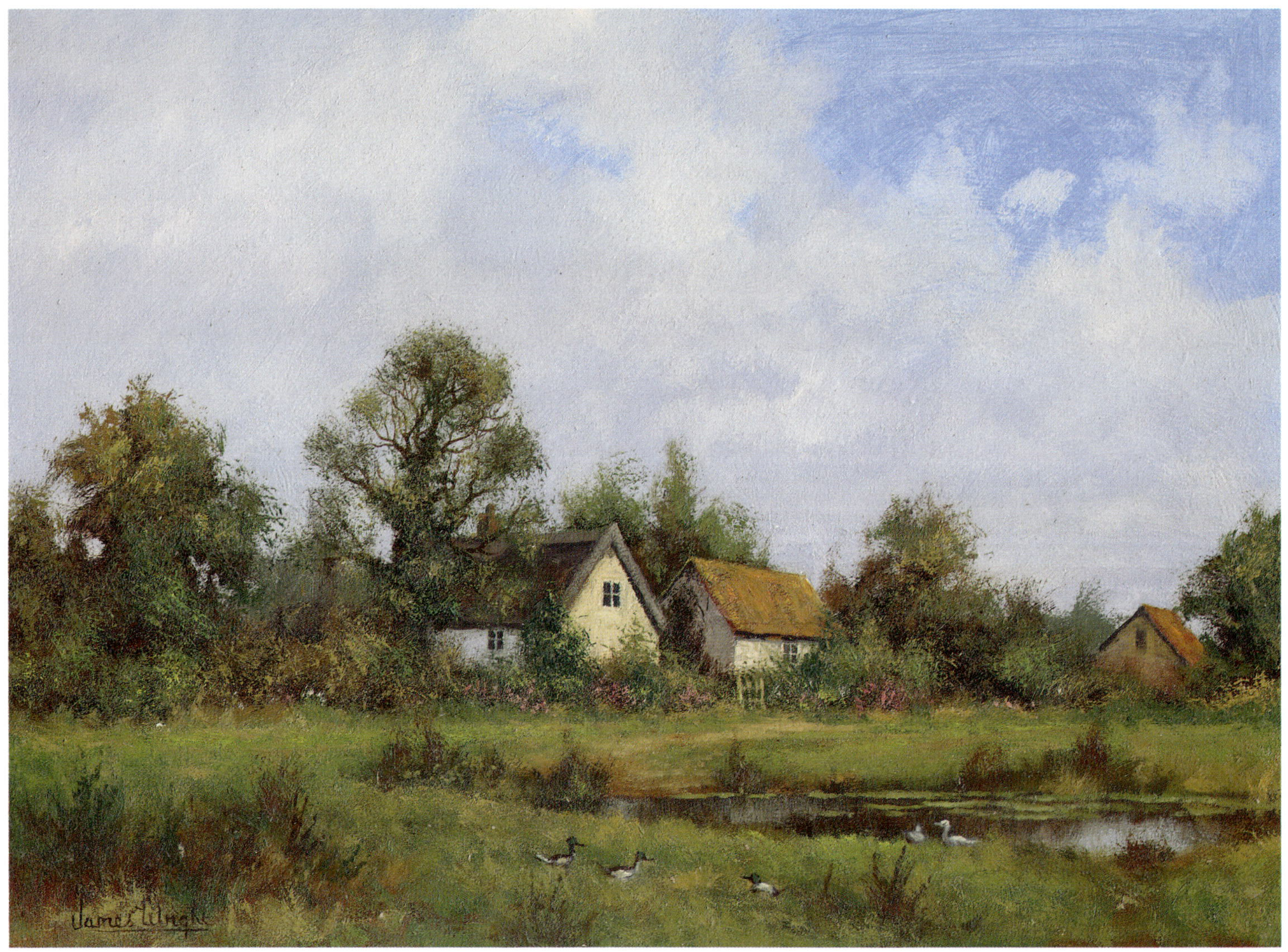

Cottages and Pond near Shipdham.

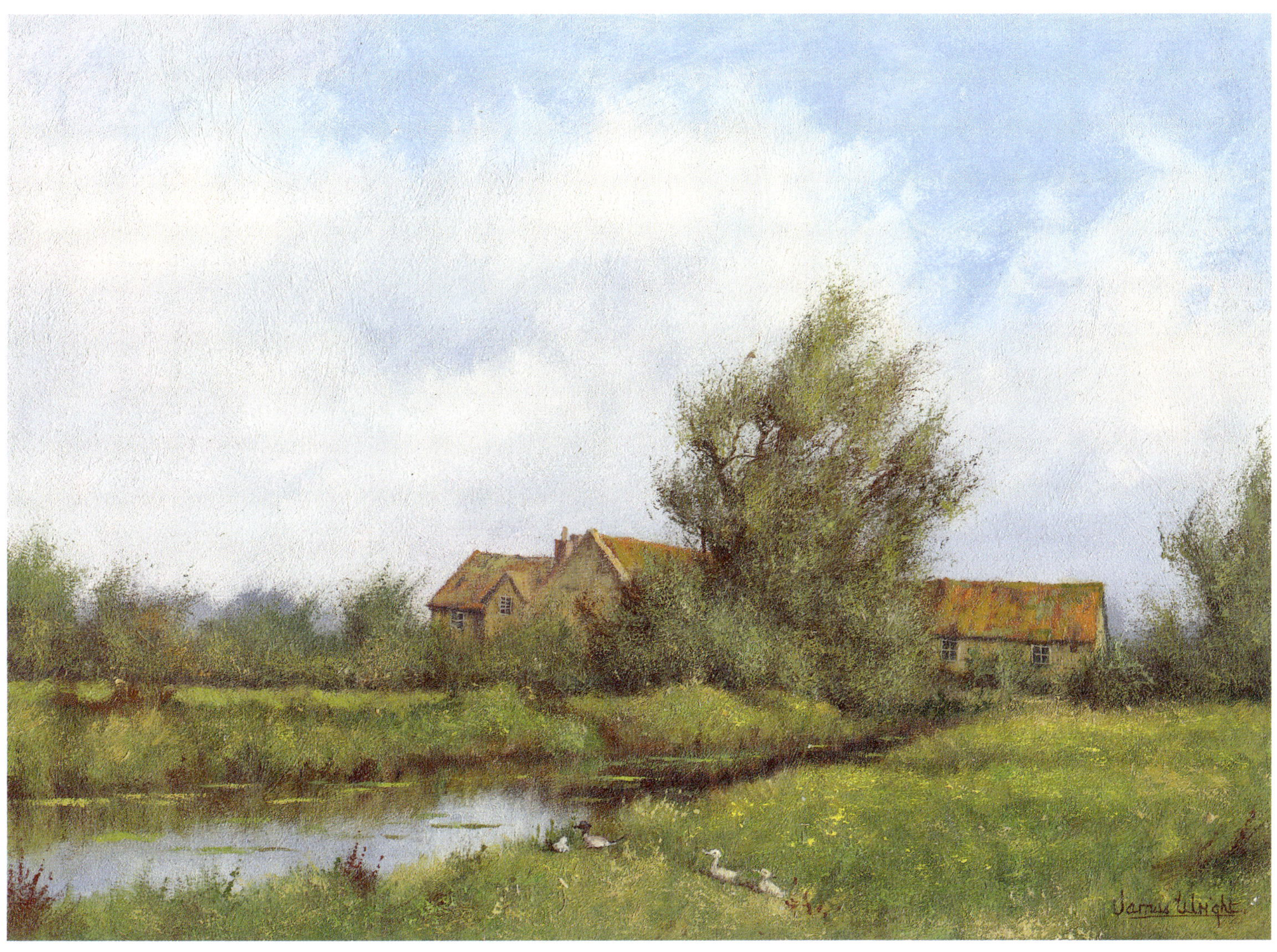

The Mill Stream.

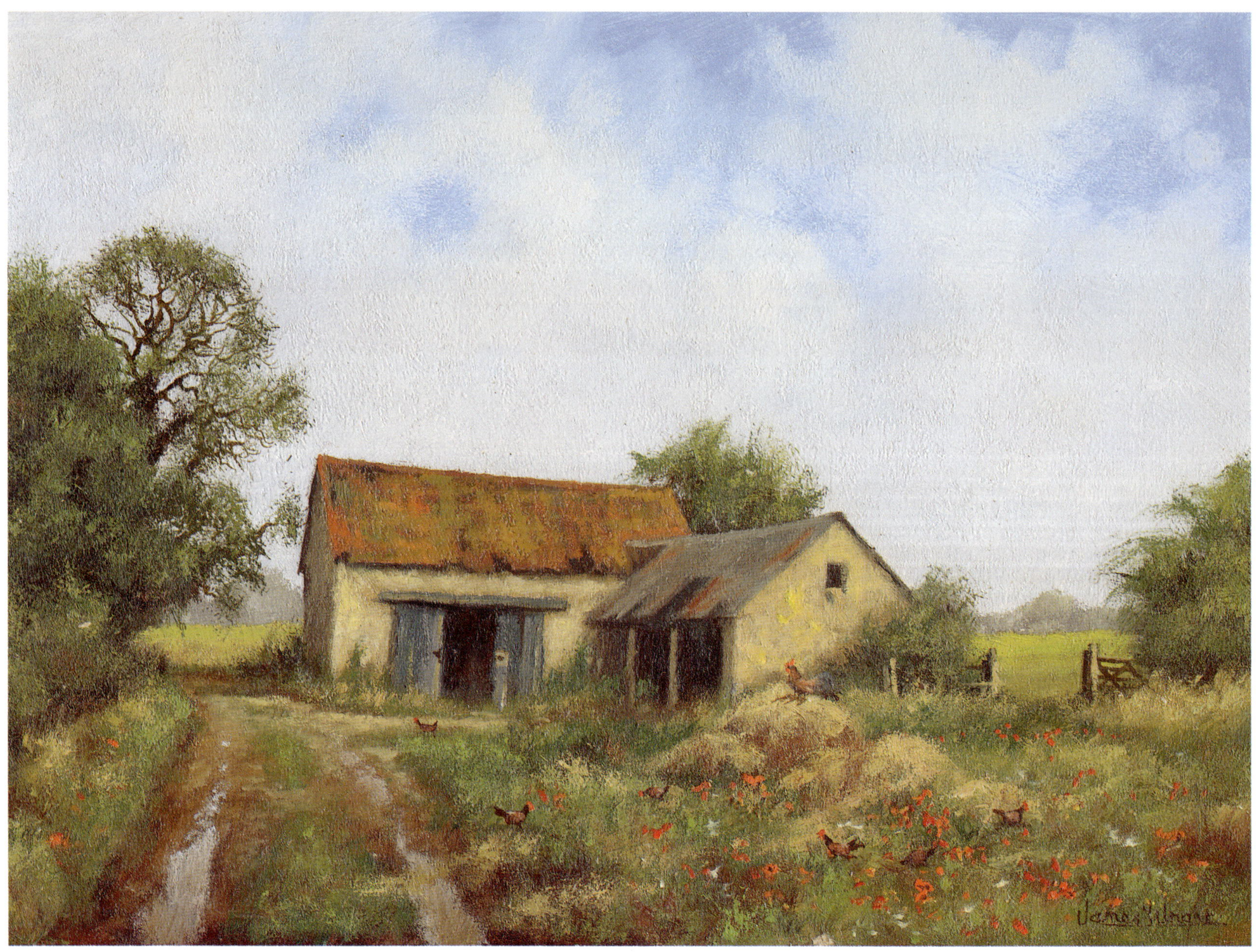

Barn and Poppies.

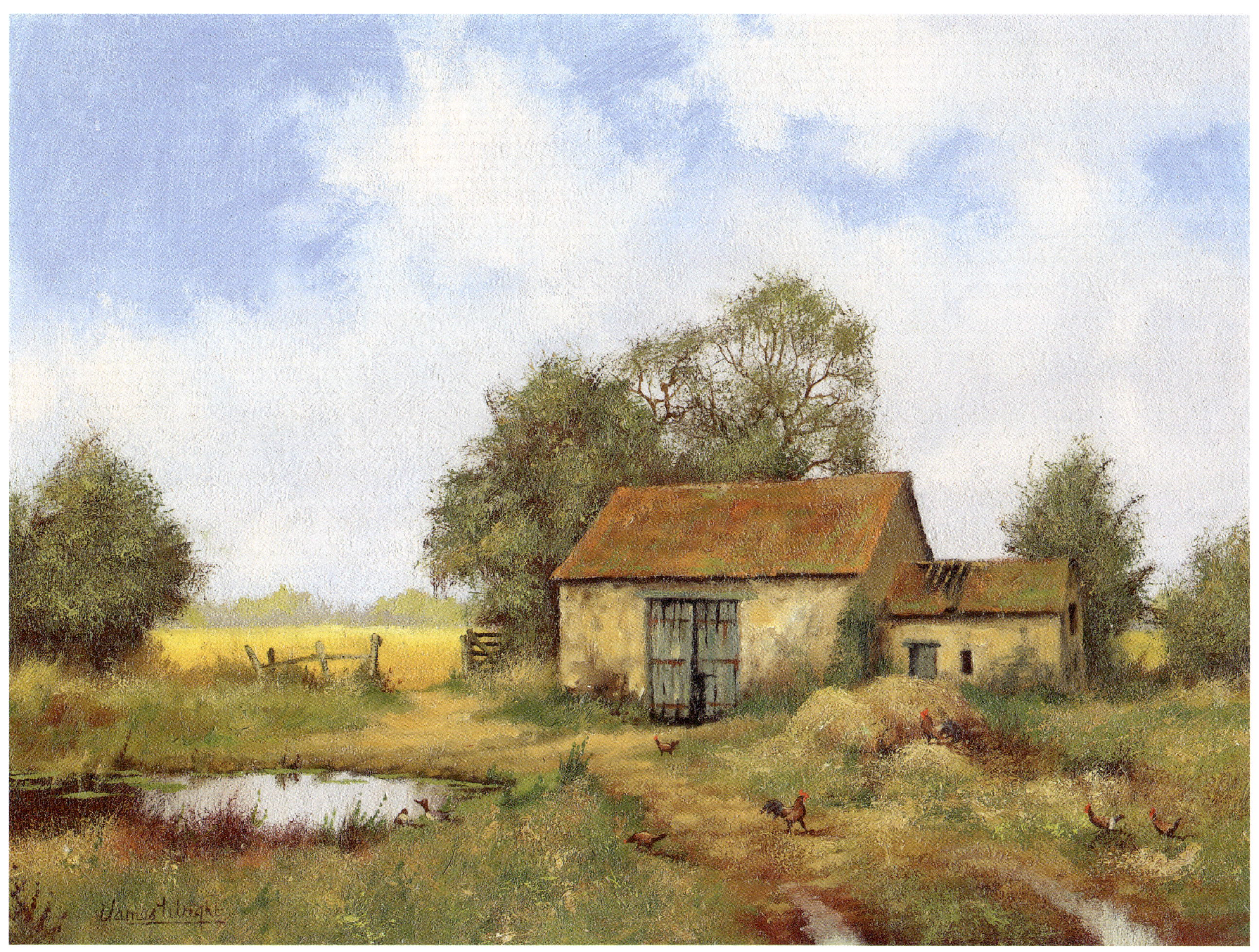

Farm Buildings and Pond near Woodbridge.

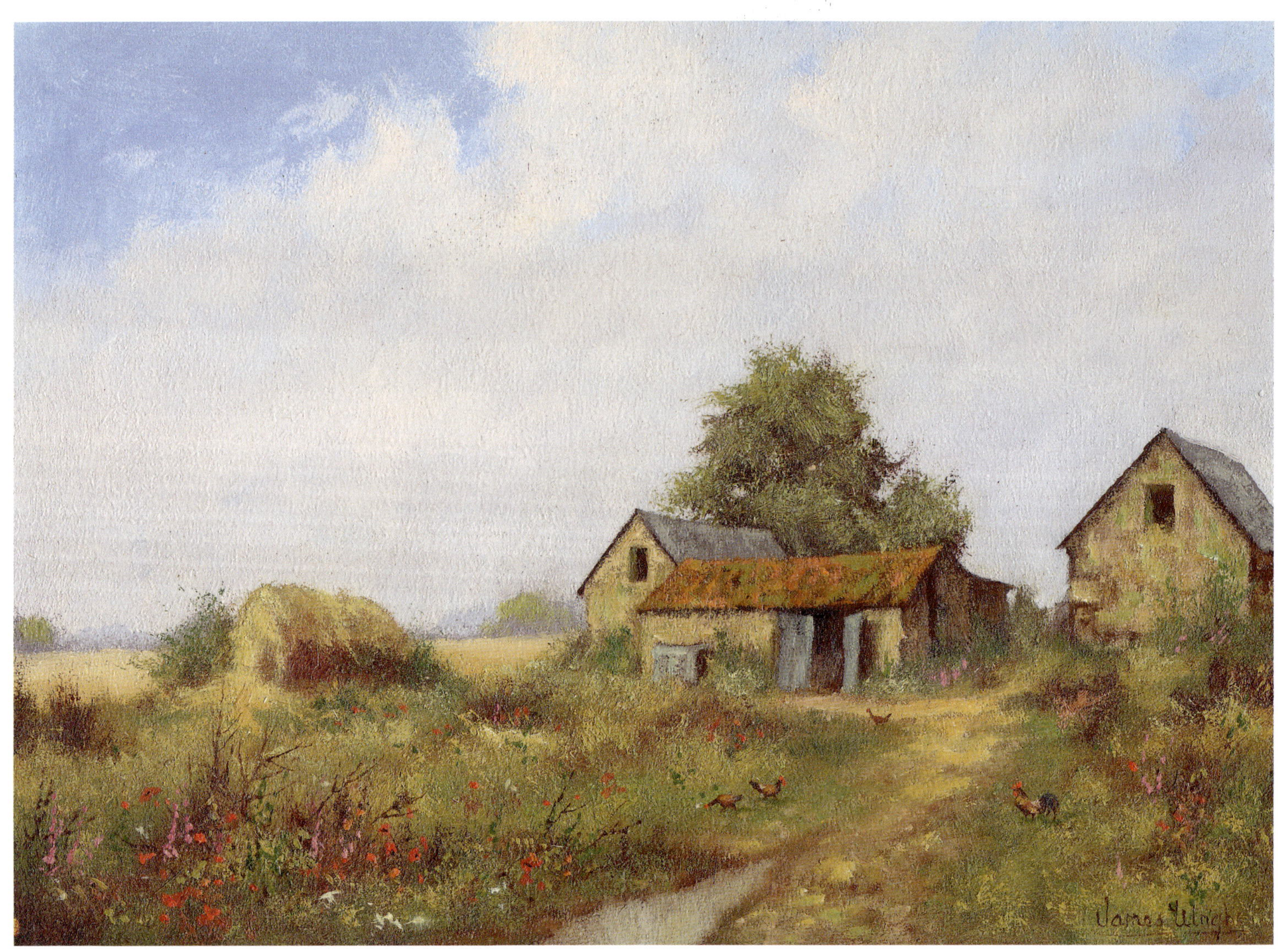

Farm Buildings, Salters Lode.

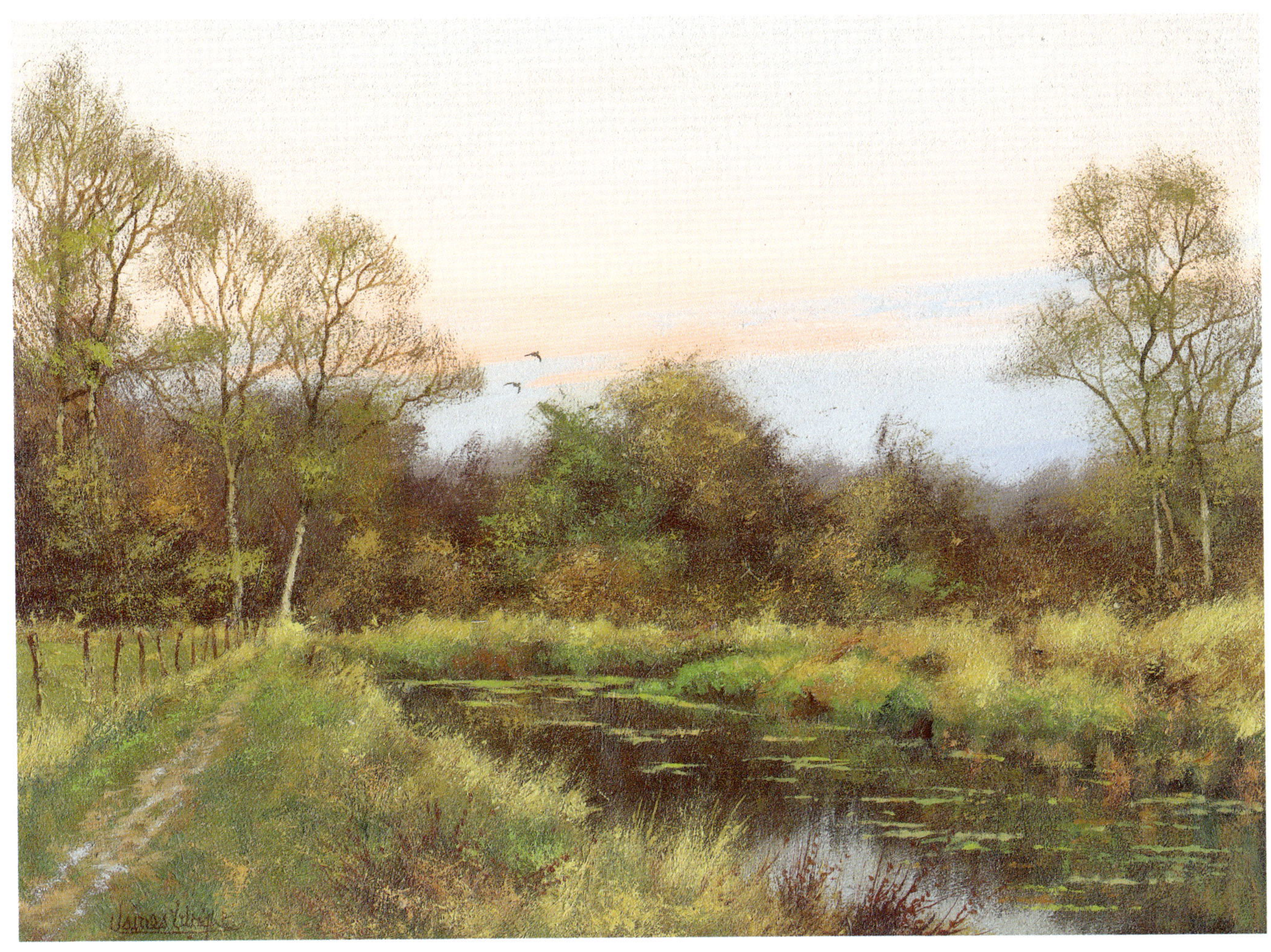

Shades of Autumn.

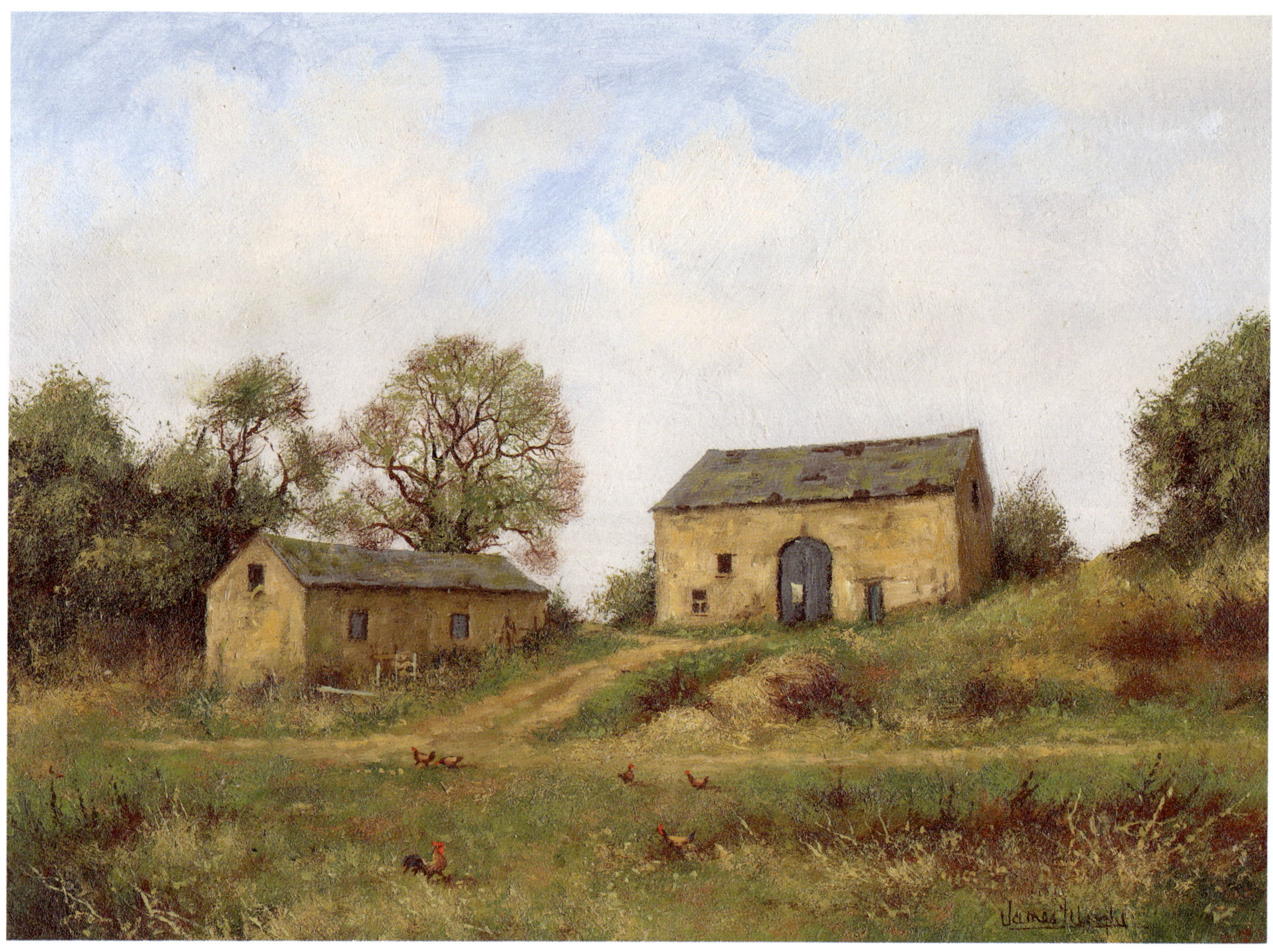

The Stone Barn.

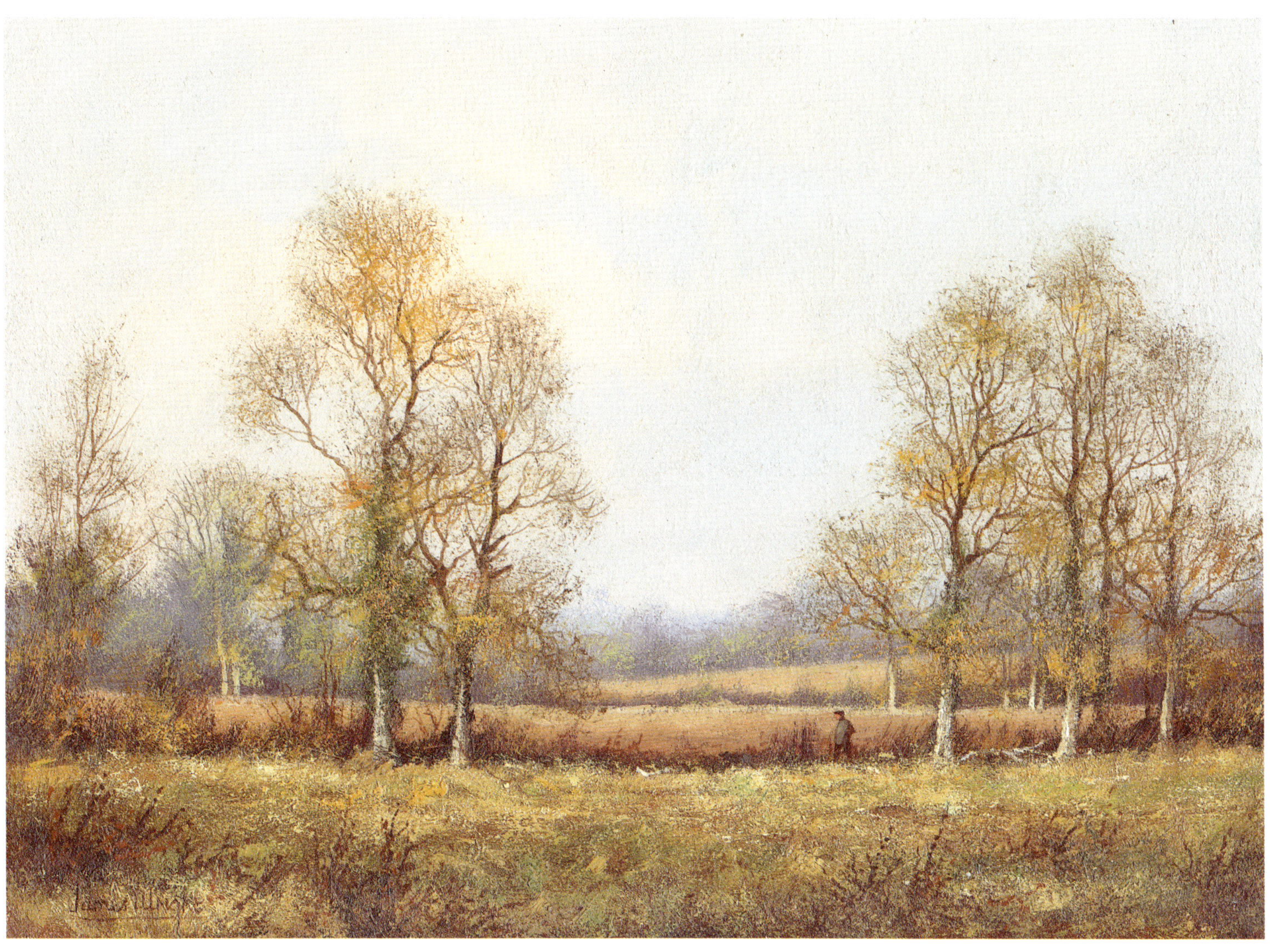

Clearing Skies.

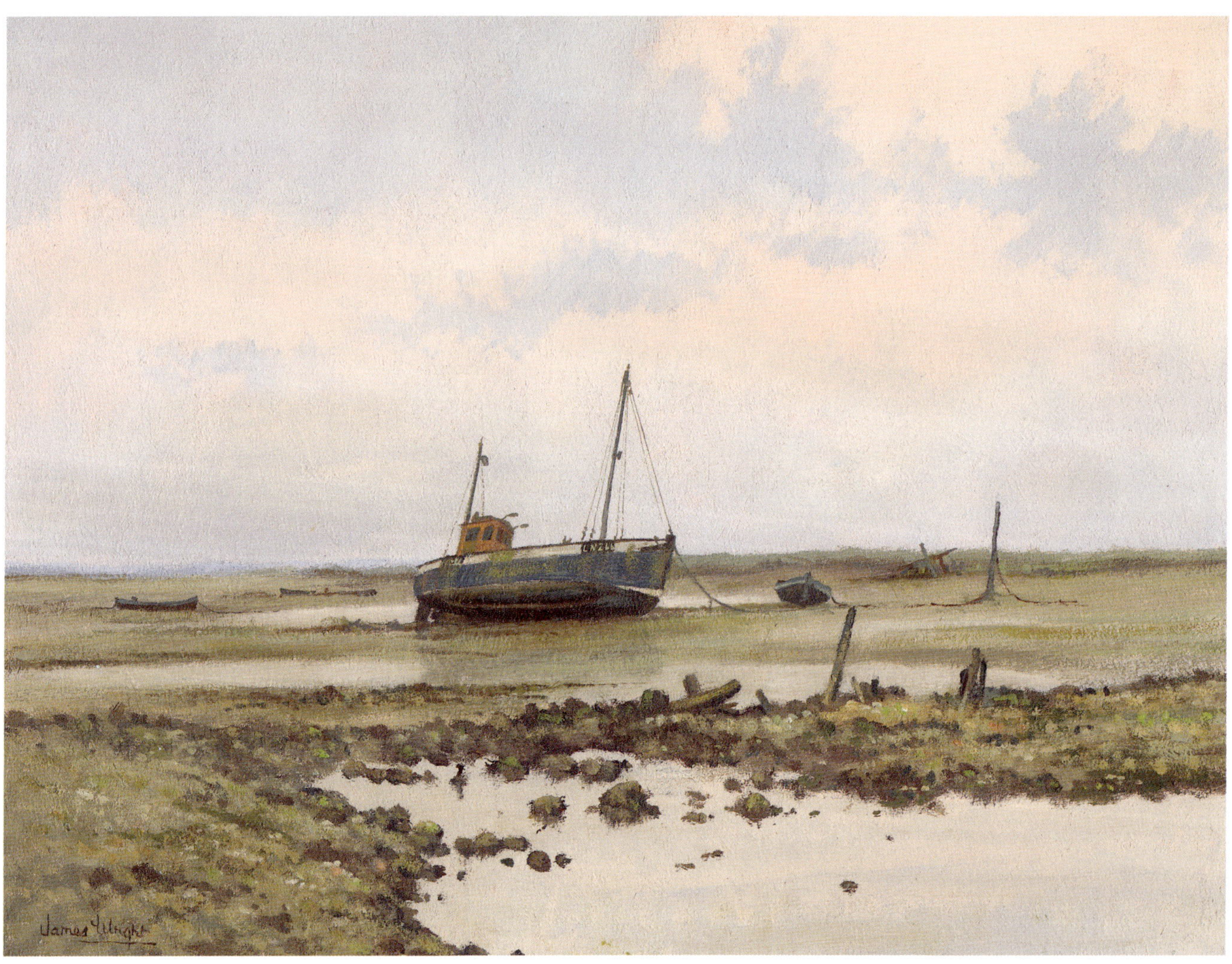

High and Dry, Brancaster Staithe.

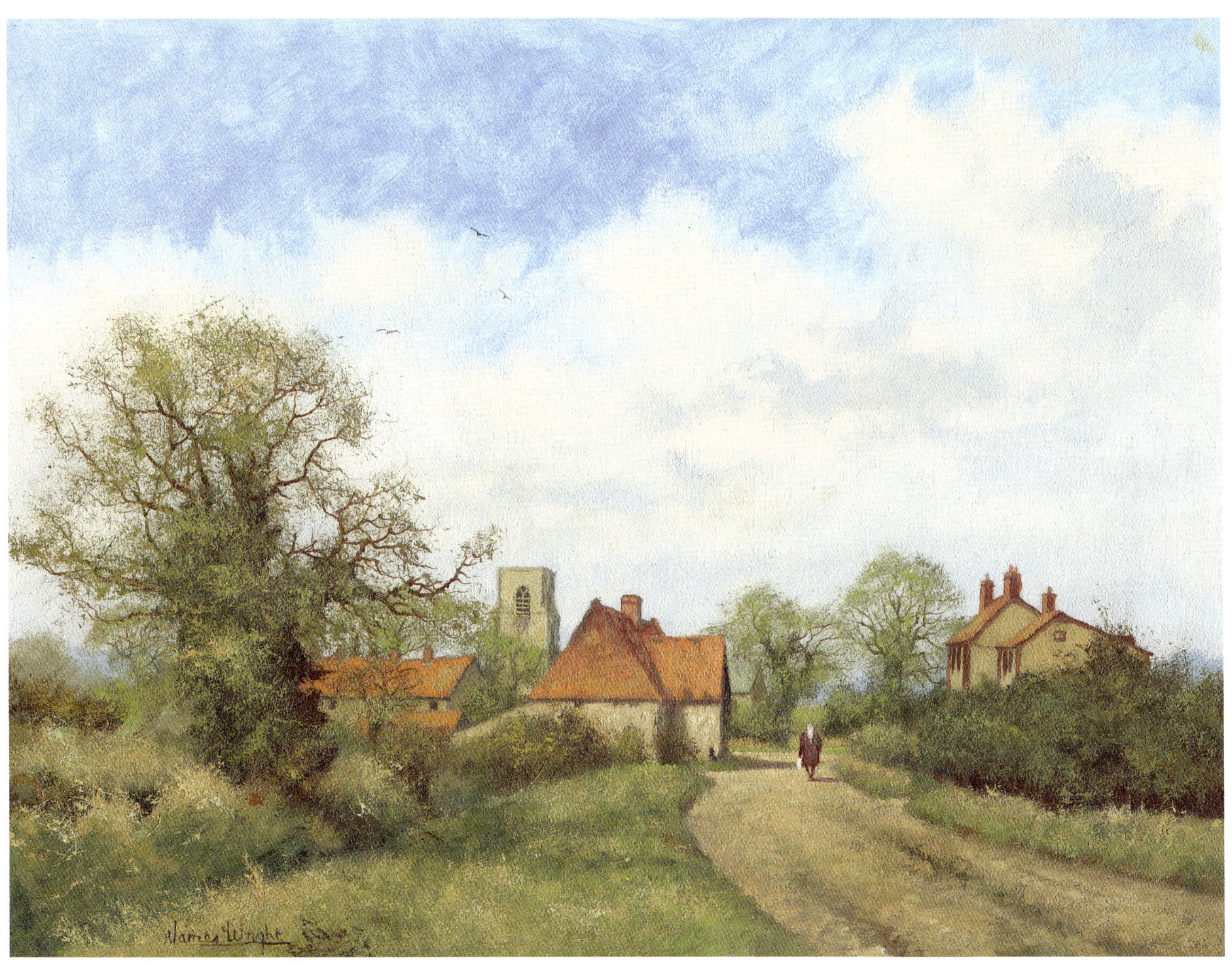

Saxlingham, Norfolk.

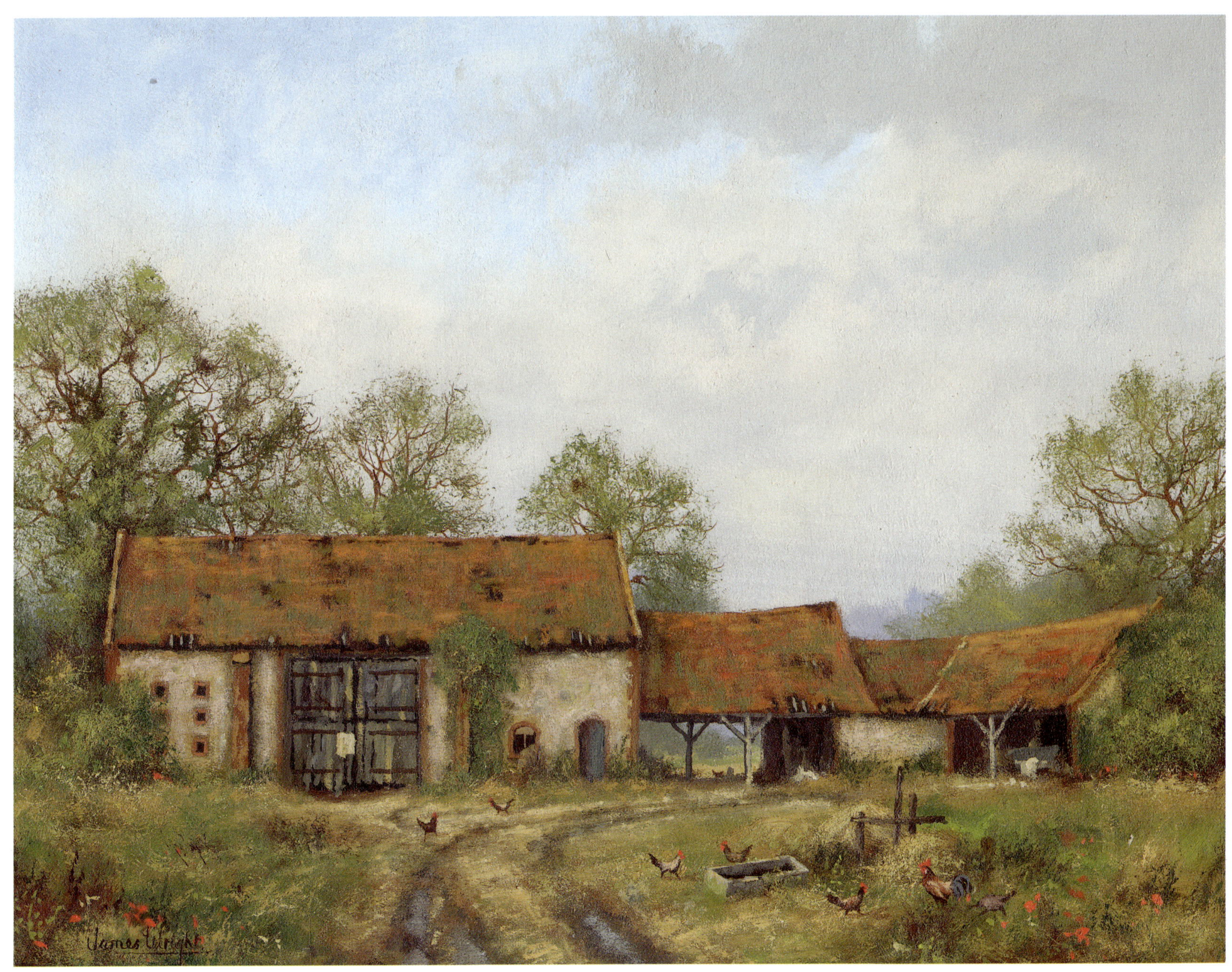

Barns at East Wynch, Norfolk.

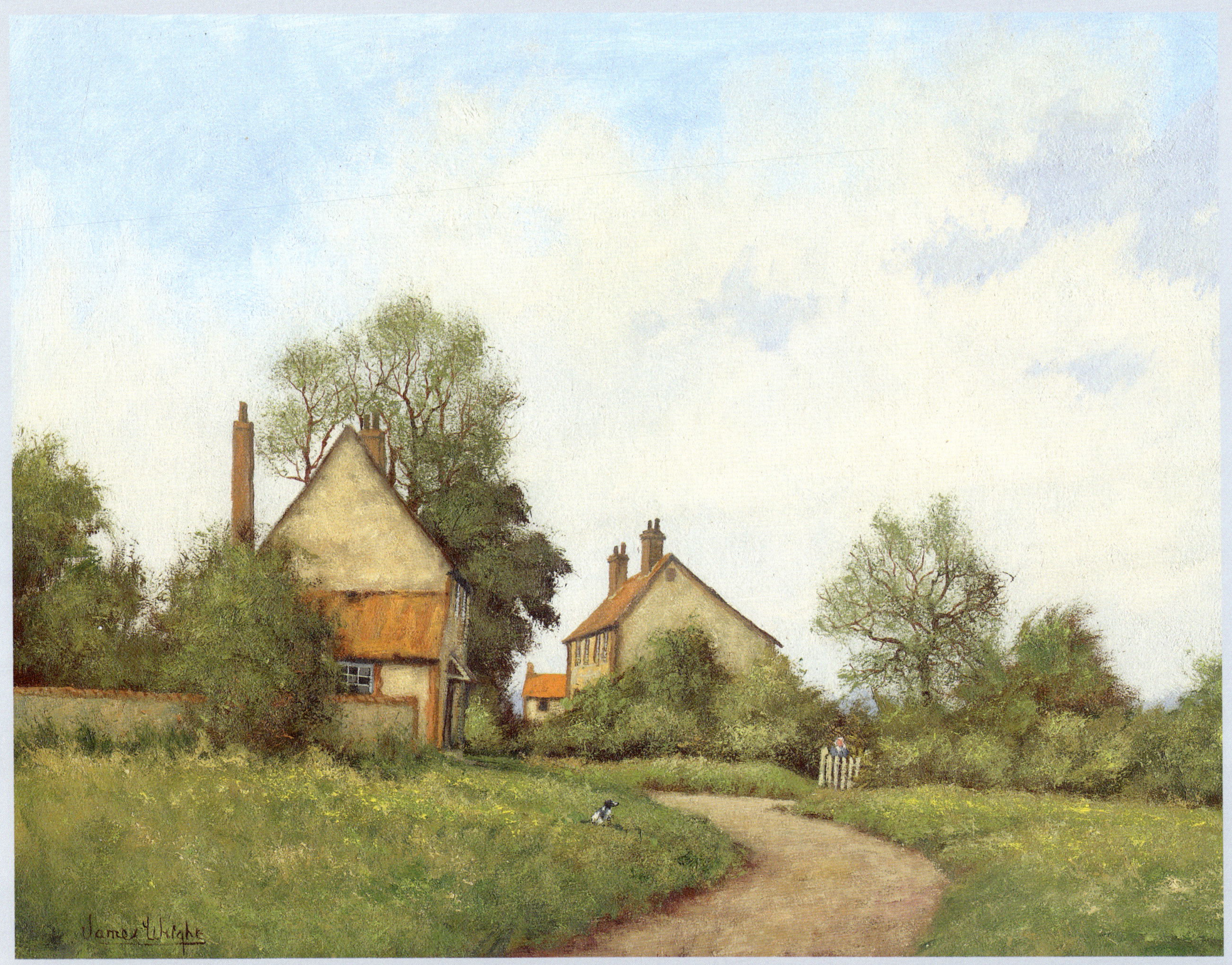

Great Walsingham, Norfolk.

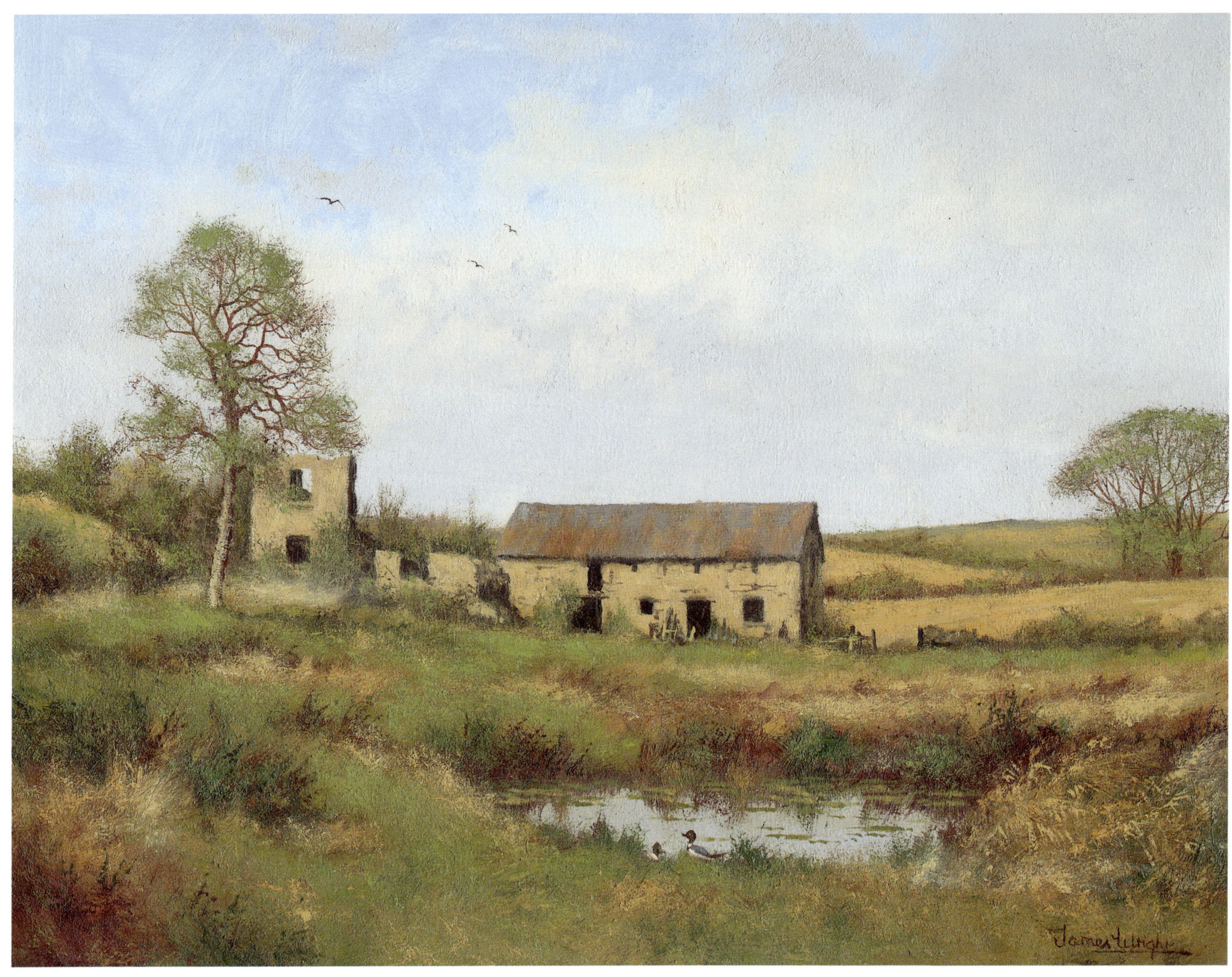

Bradford Mill, near Holsworthy, Devon.

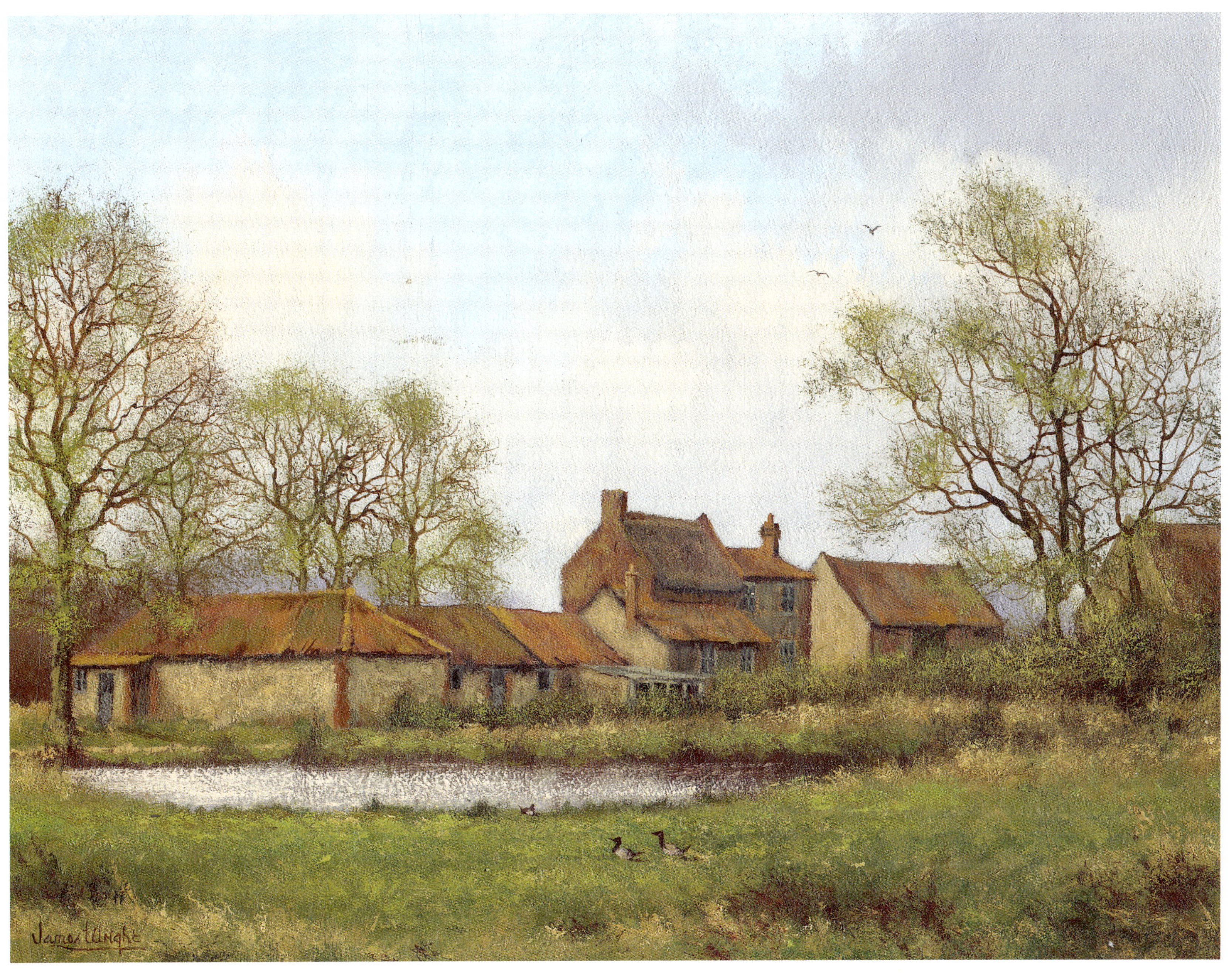

Farm Pond at Hanworth, Norfolk.

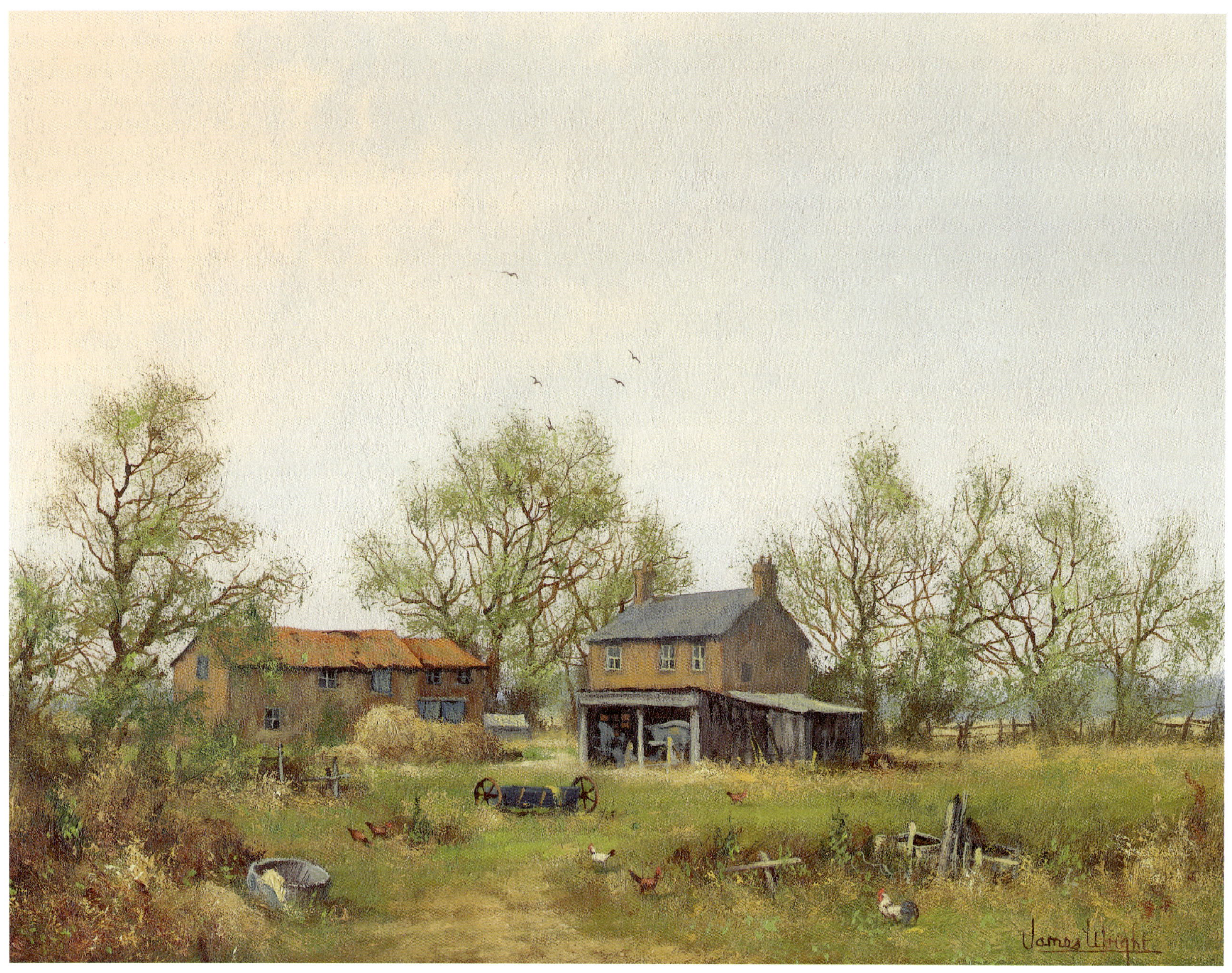

The Farm at Salters Lode, Norfolk.

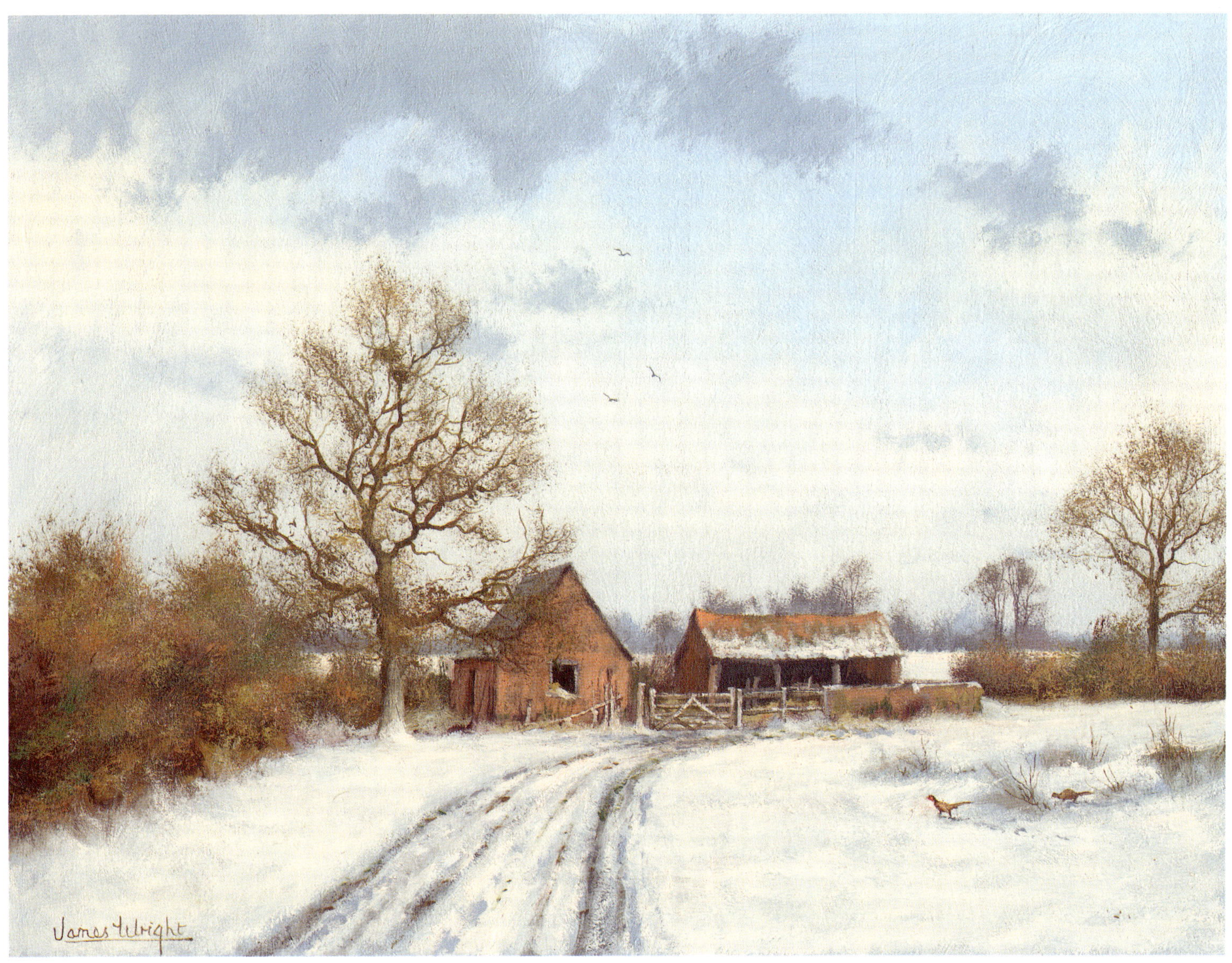

Winter's Carpet, Norfolk.

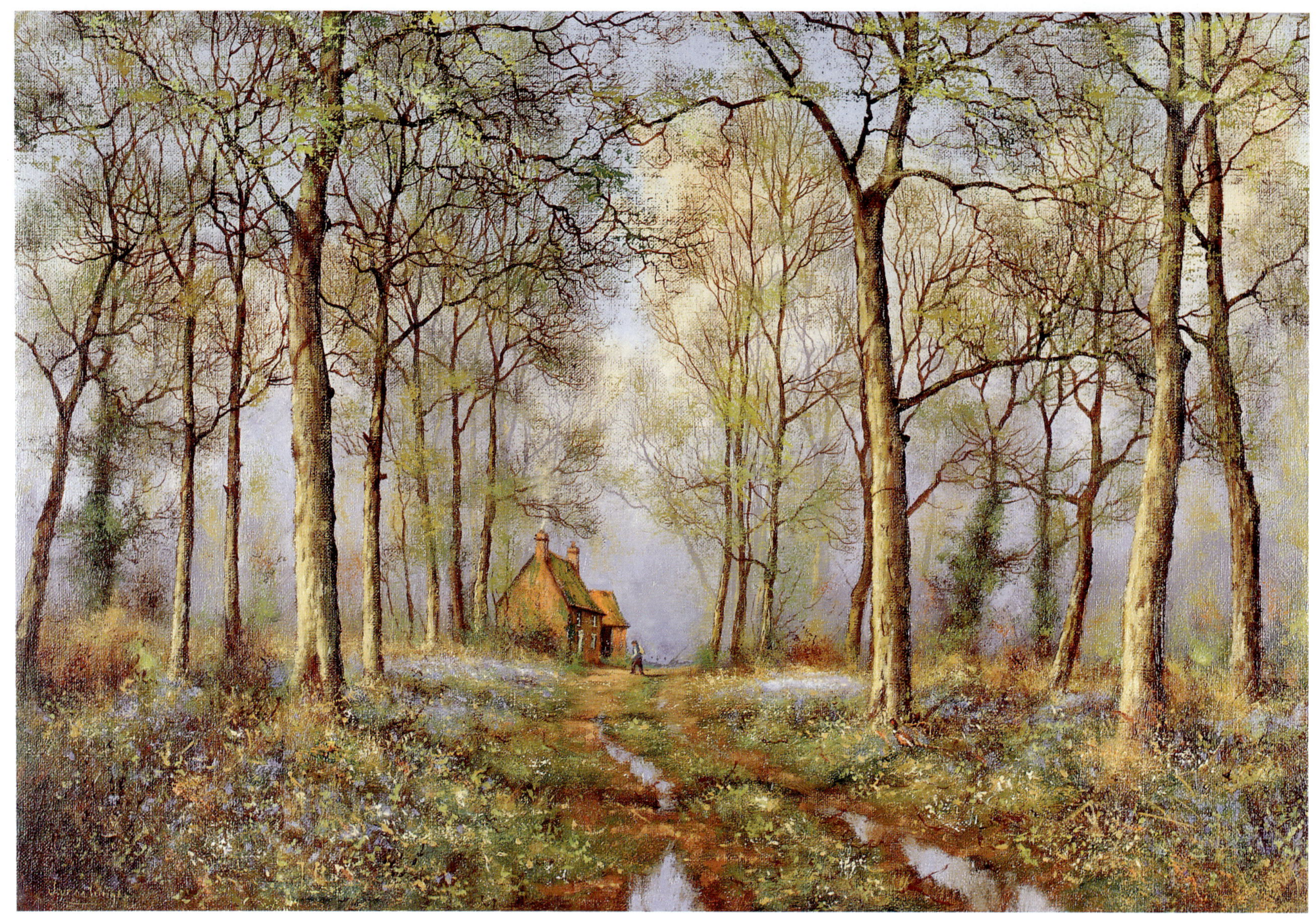

Poacher's Cottage.

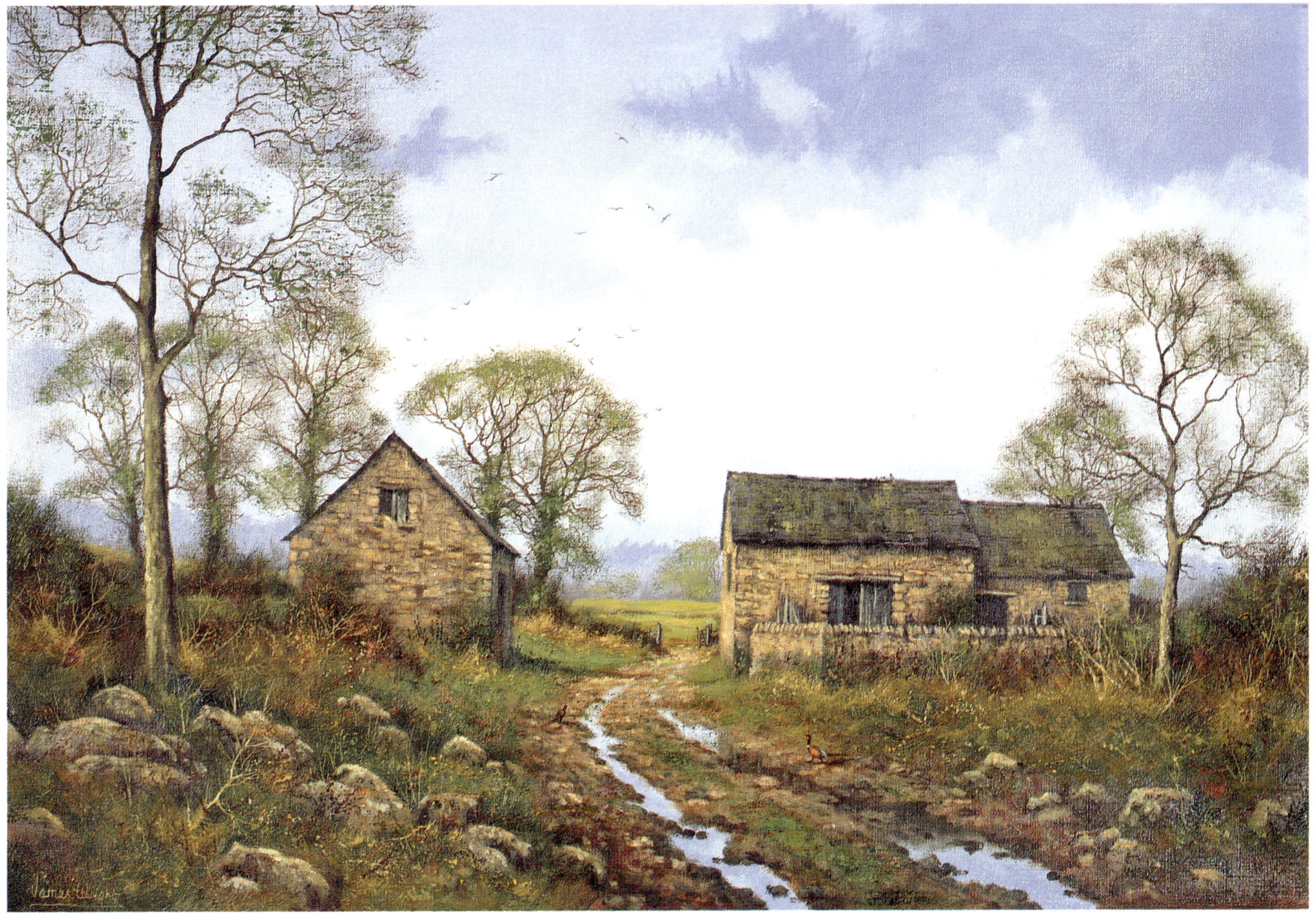

Stone Barns.

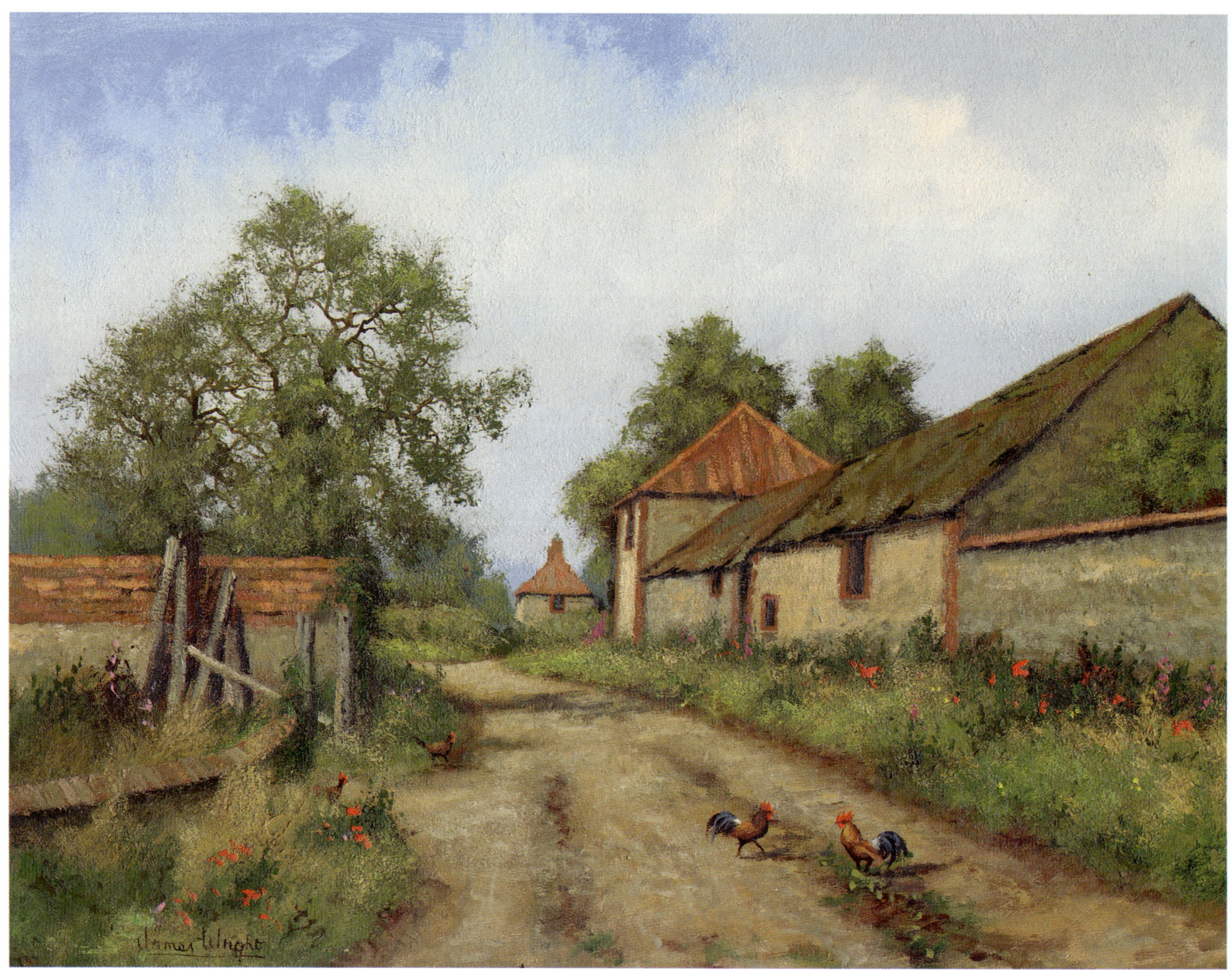

The Road to Great Walsingham, Norfolk.

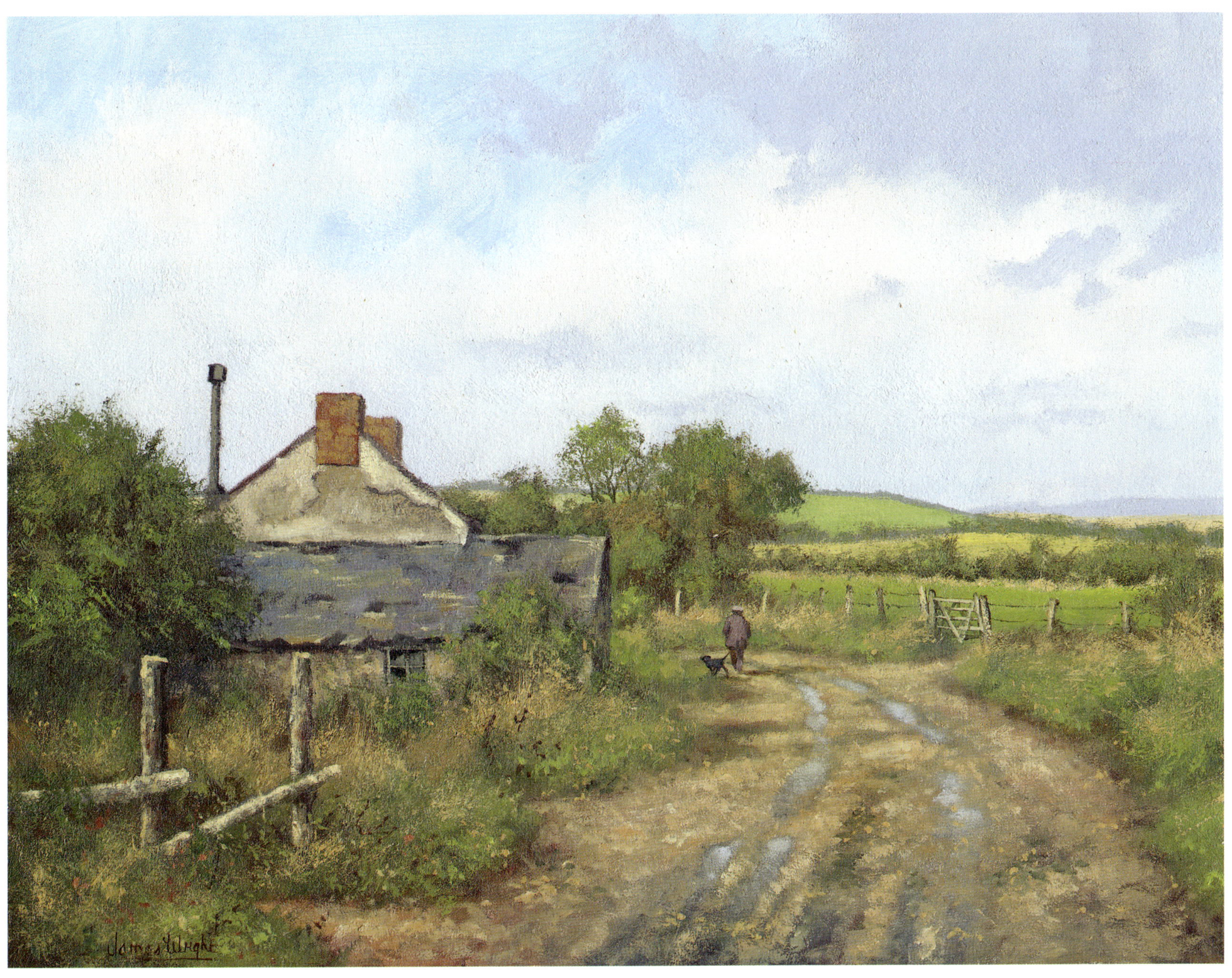

Cottage at Polzeath.

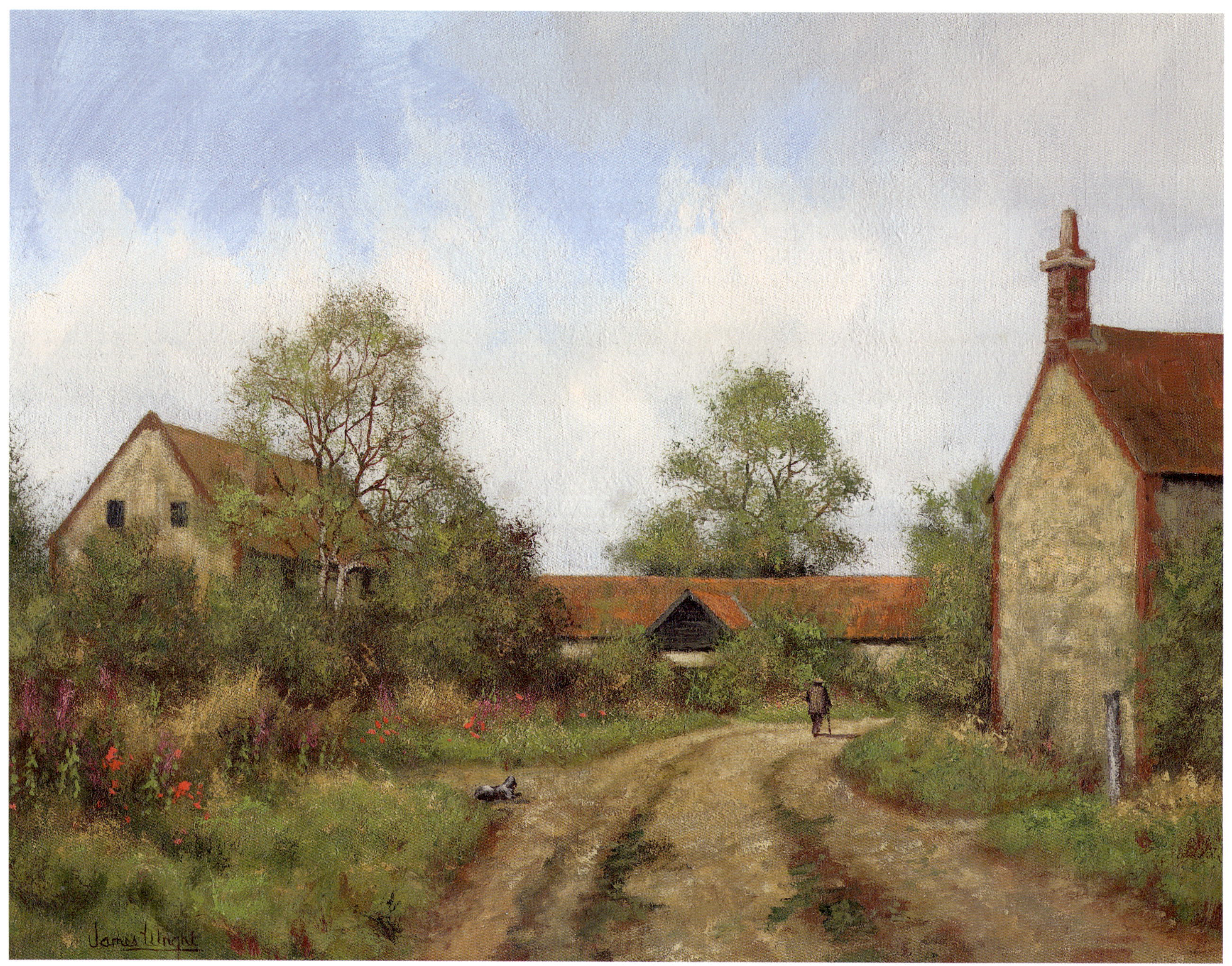

Stanhoe, Norfolk.

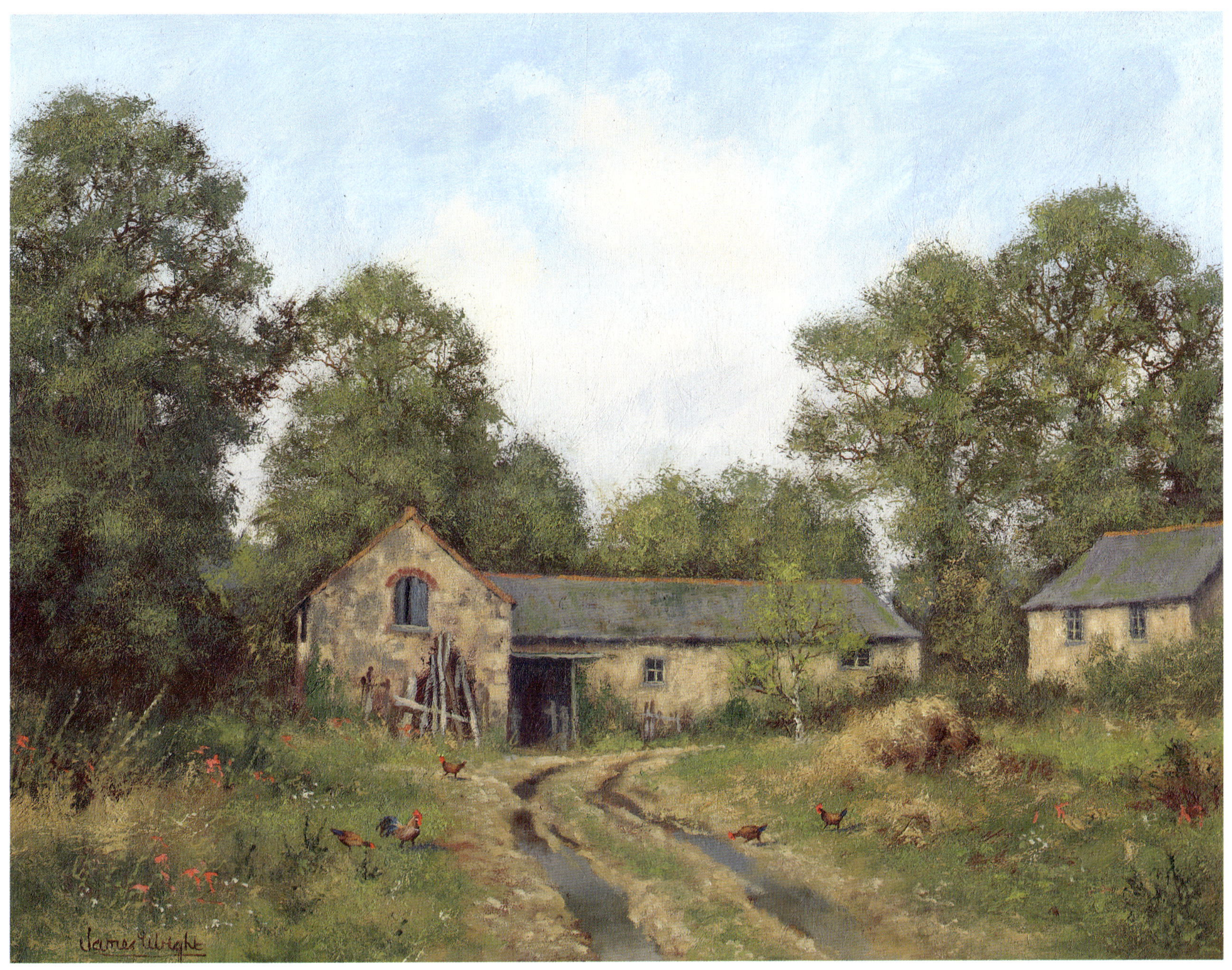

Rob's Barn near Yealmpton, Devon.

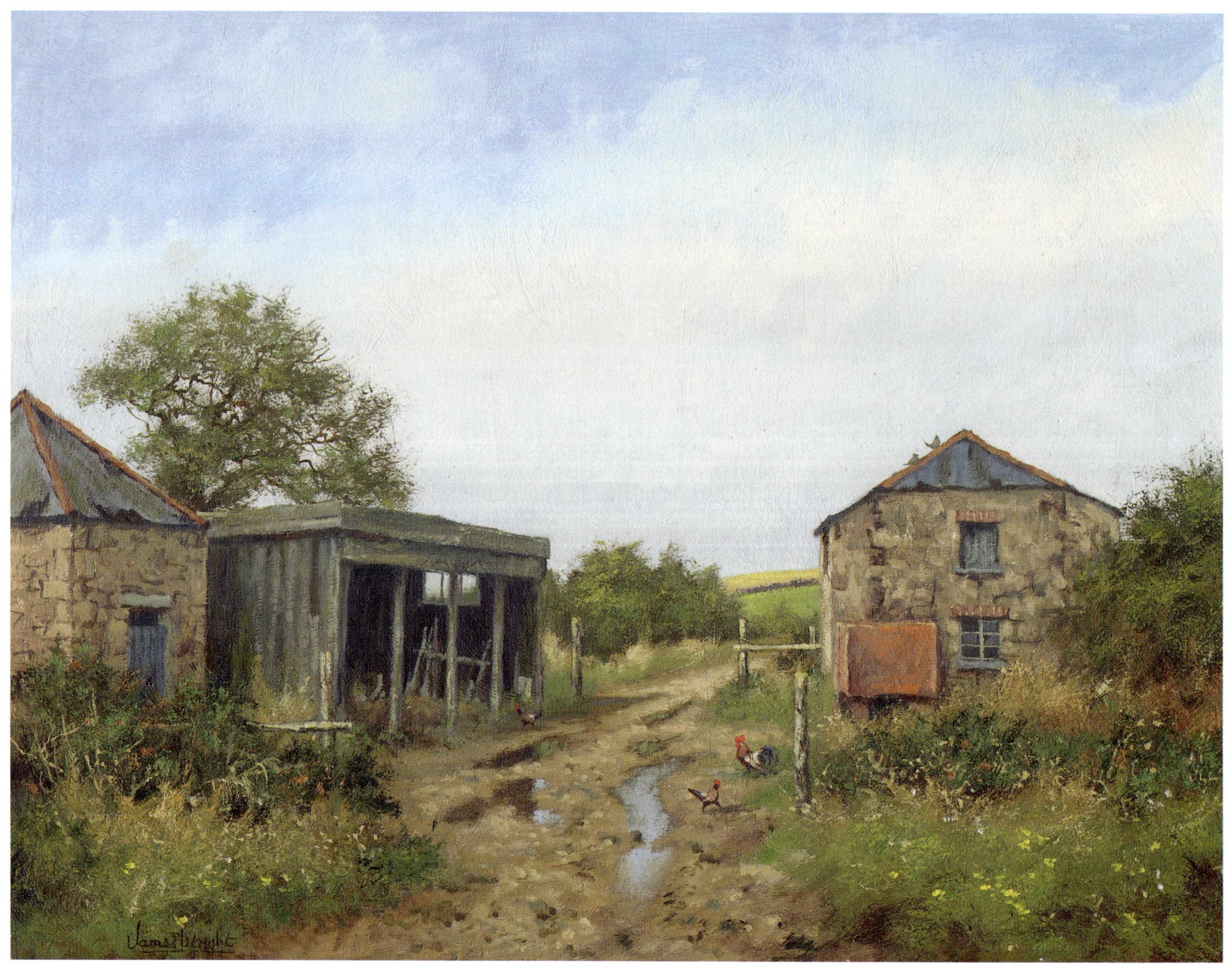

Farm, near Polzeath.

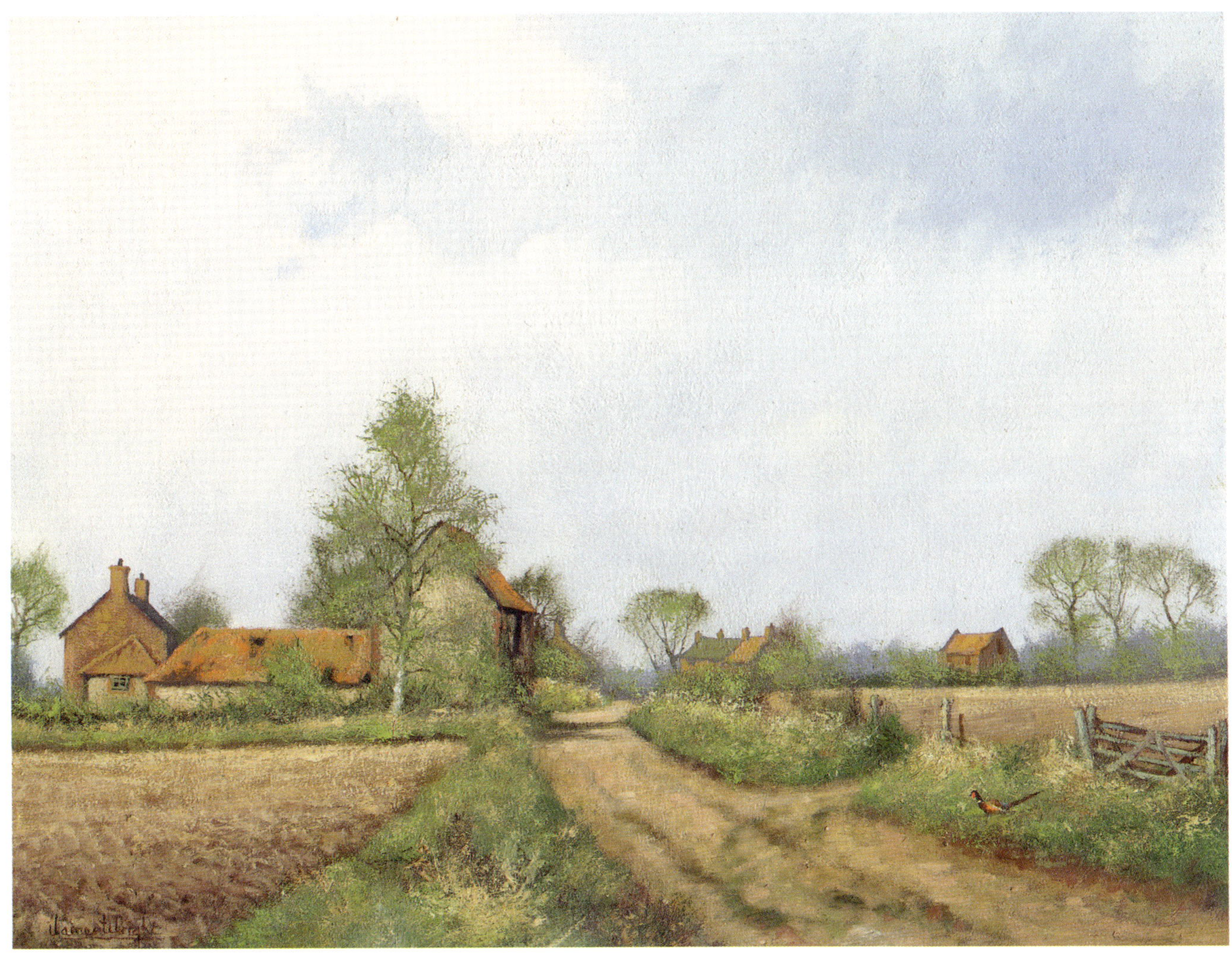

Clearing Skies near Hindringham, Norfolk.

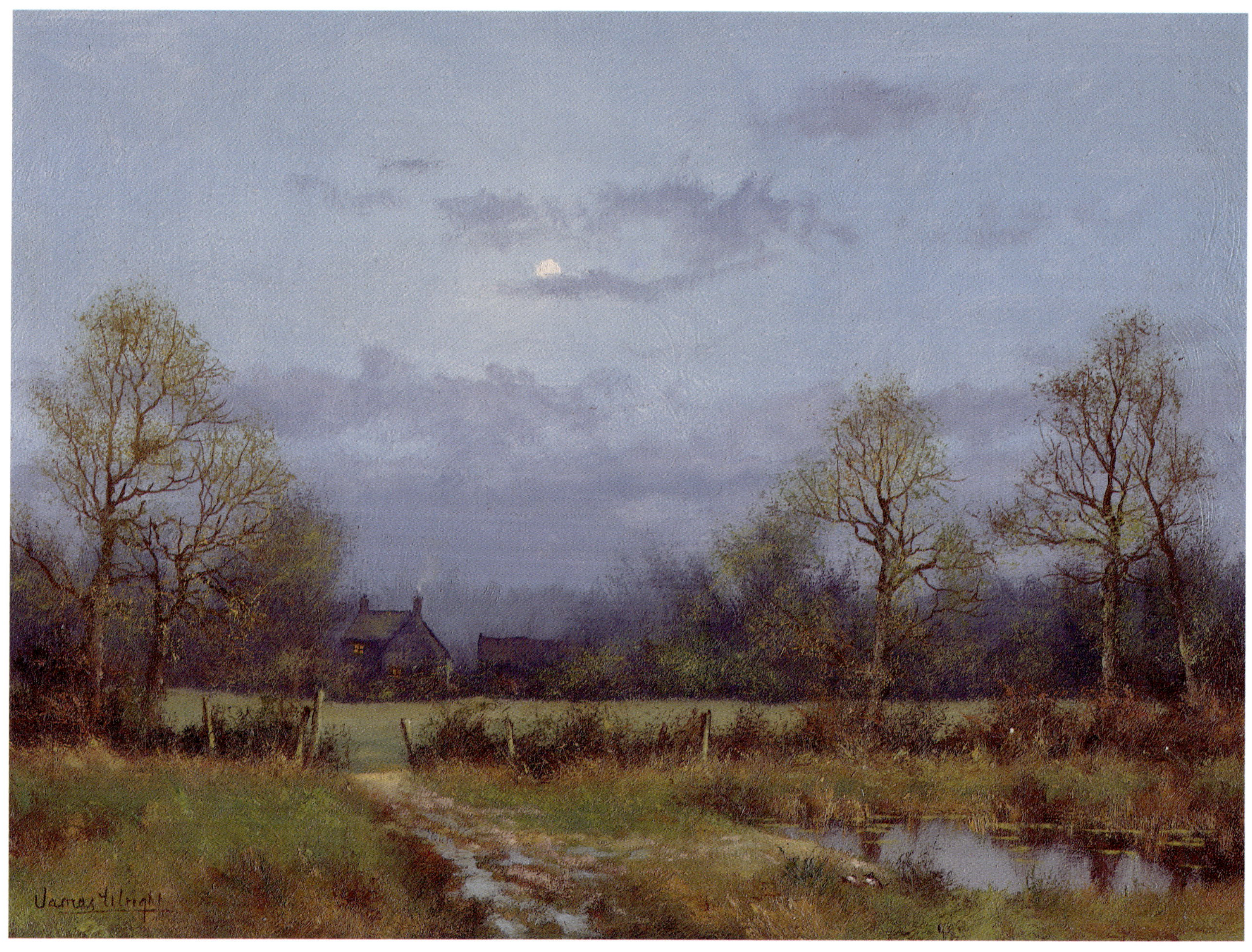

Autumn Moon.

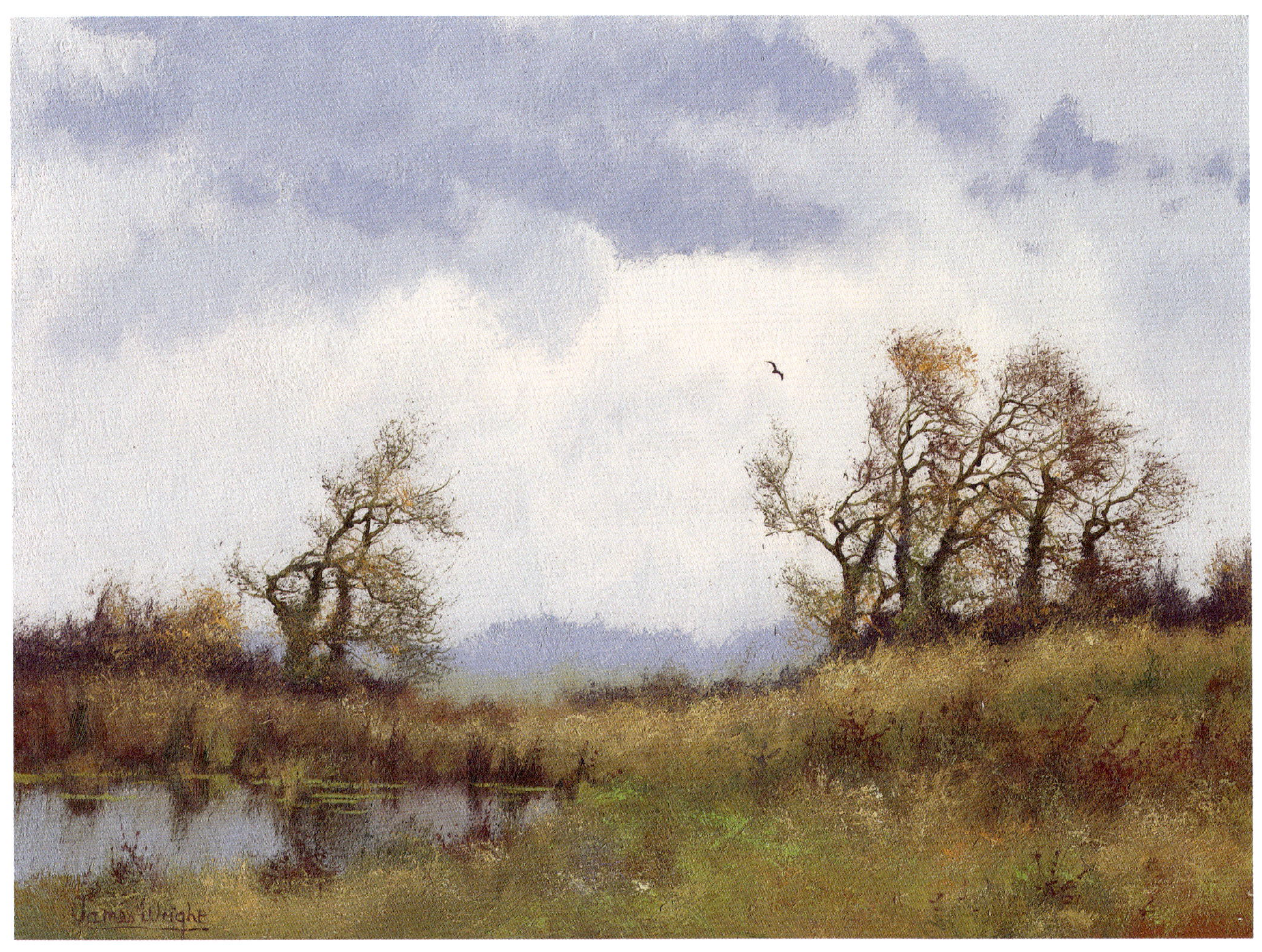

A Moorland Pond.

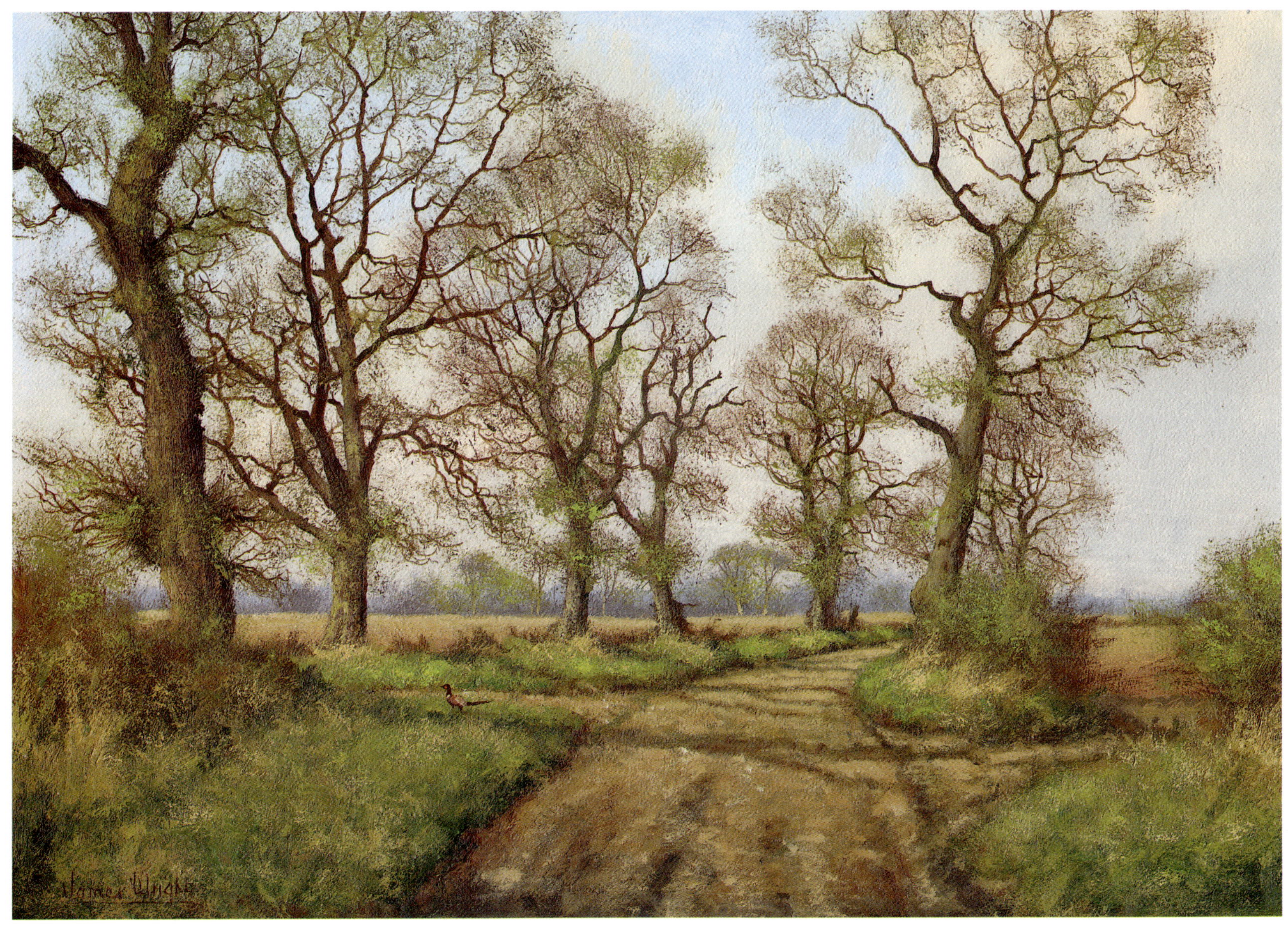

The Road to Hindringham, Norfolk.

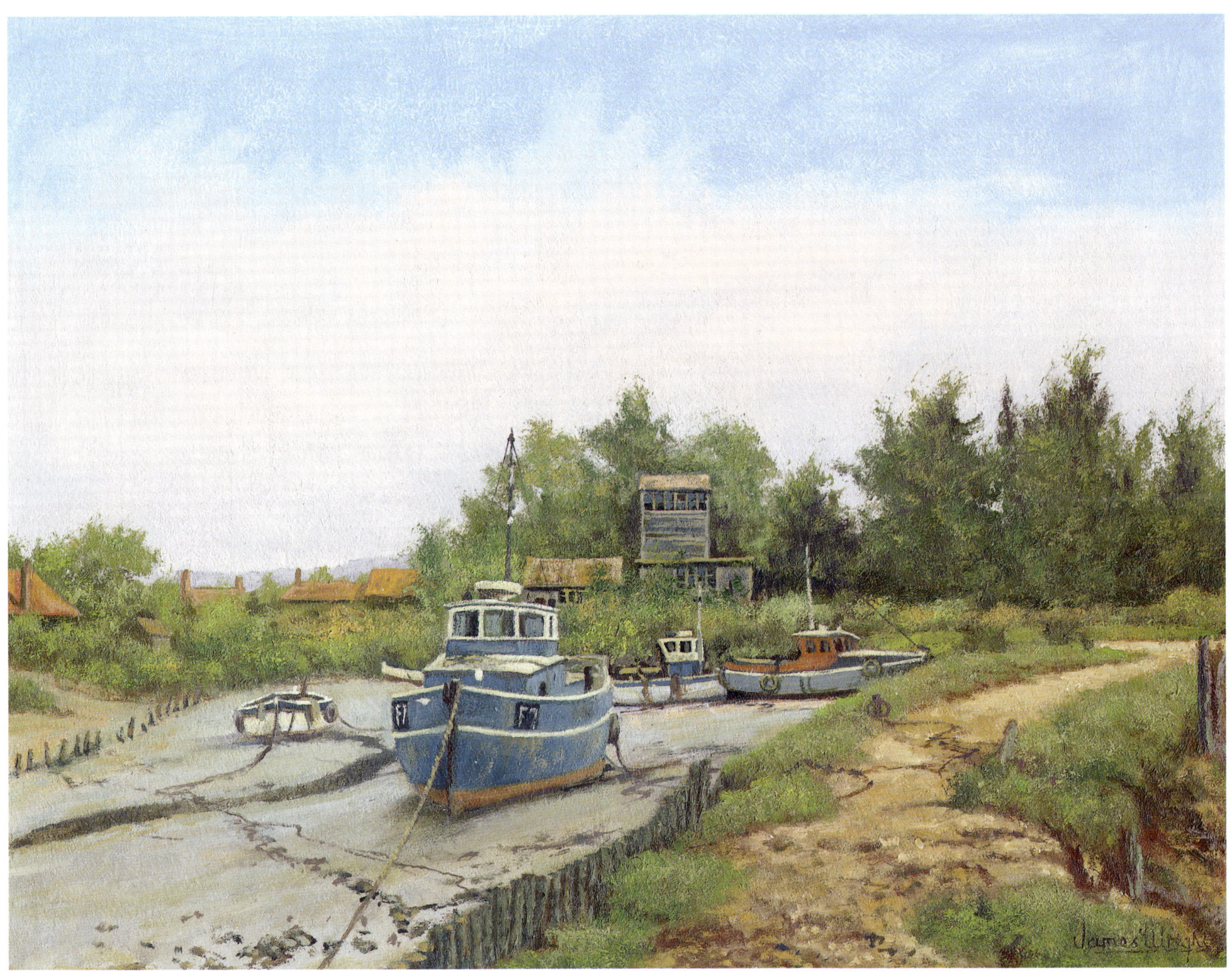

Brancaster Staithe, Norfolk.

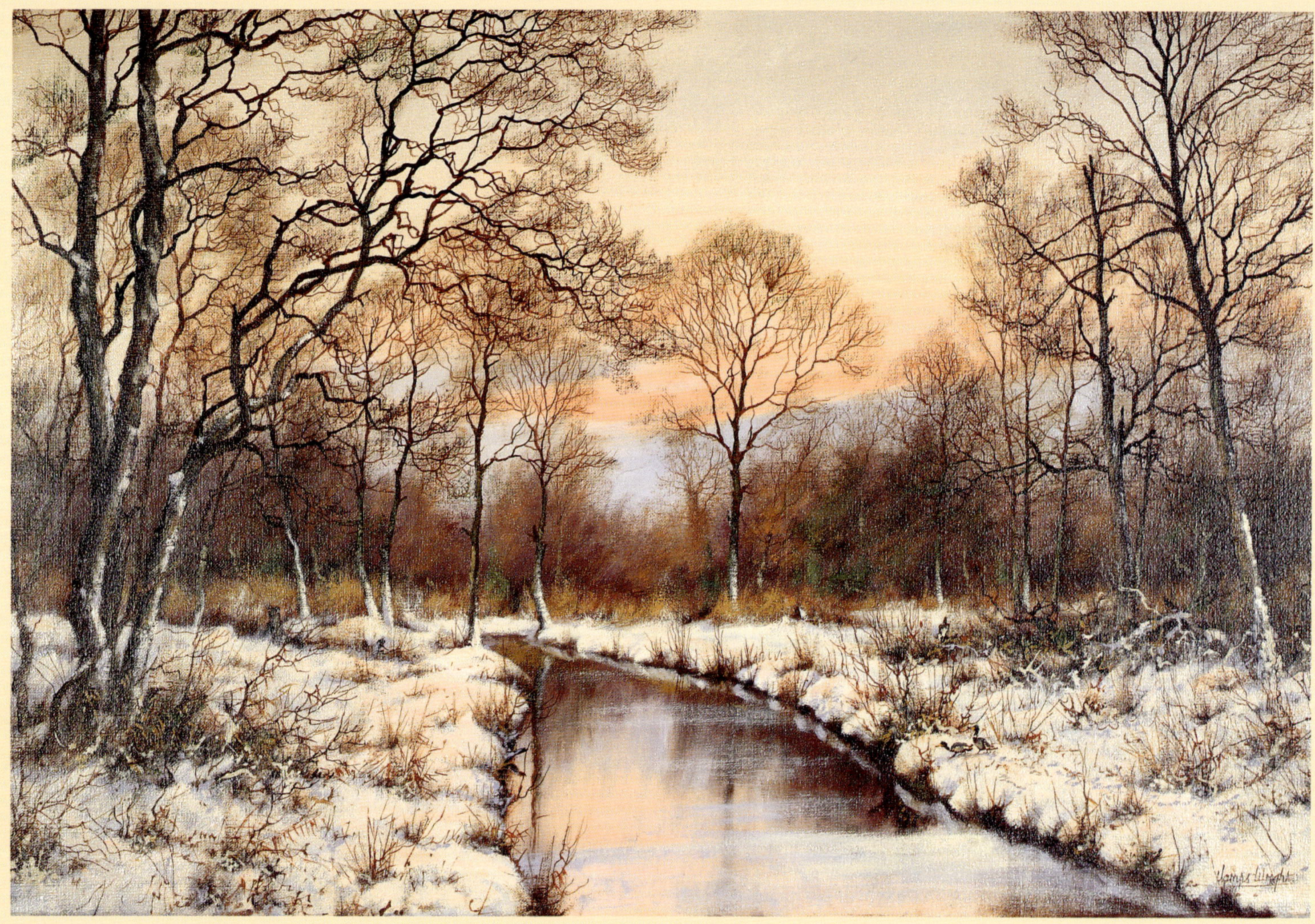

Winter Stream, Thetford.

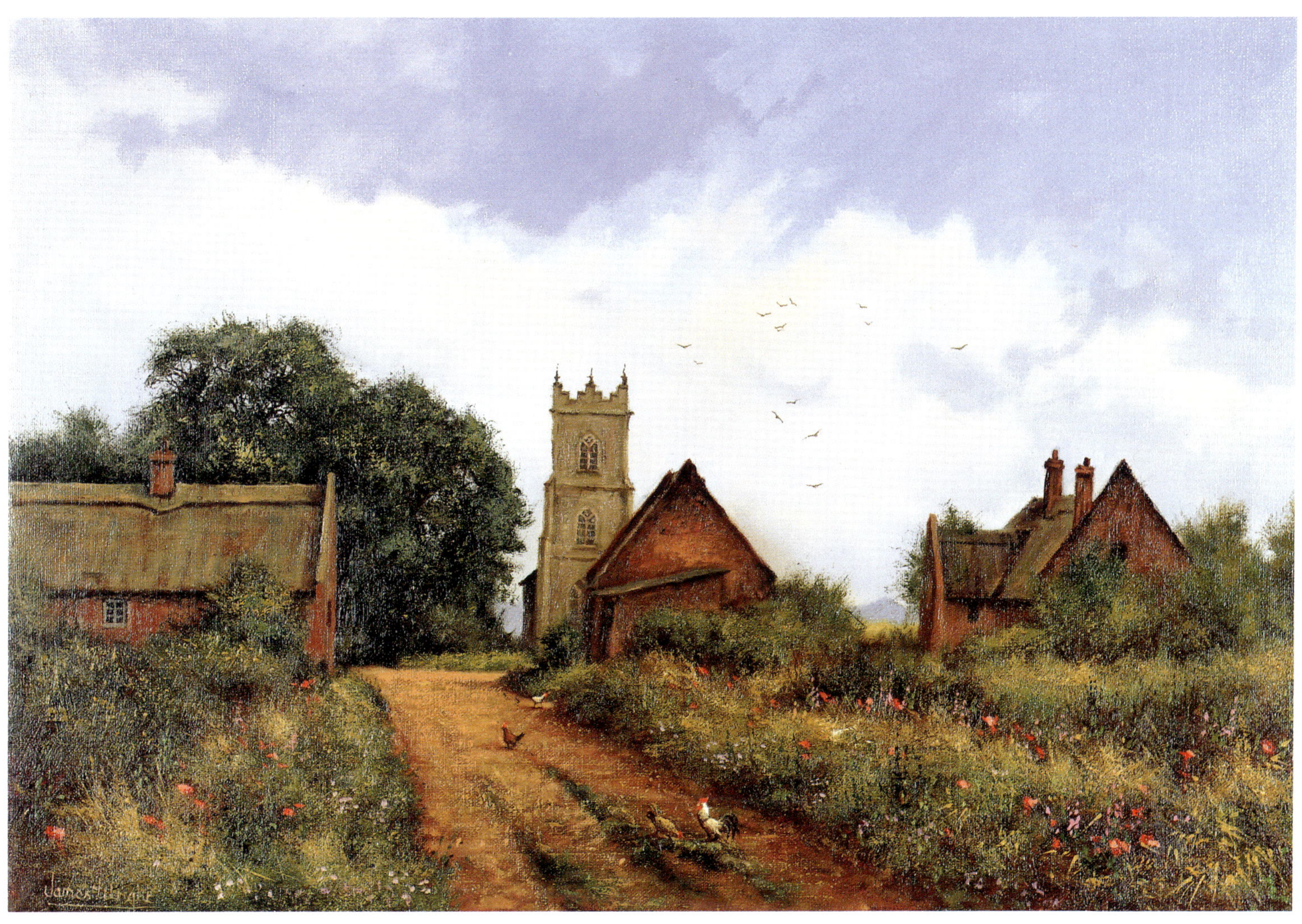

Wickhampton.

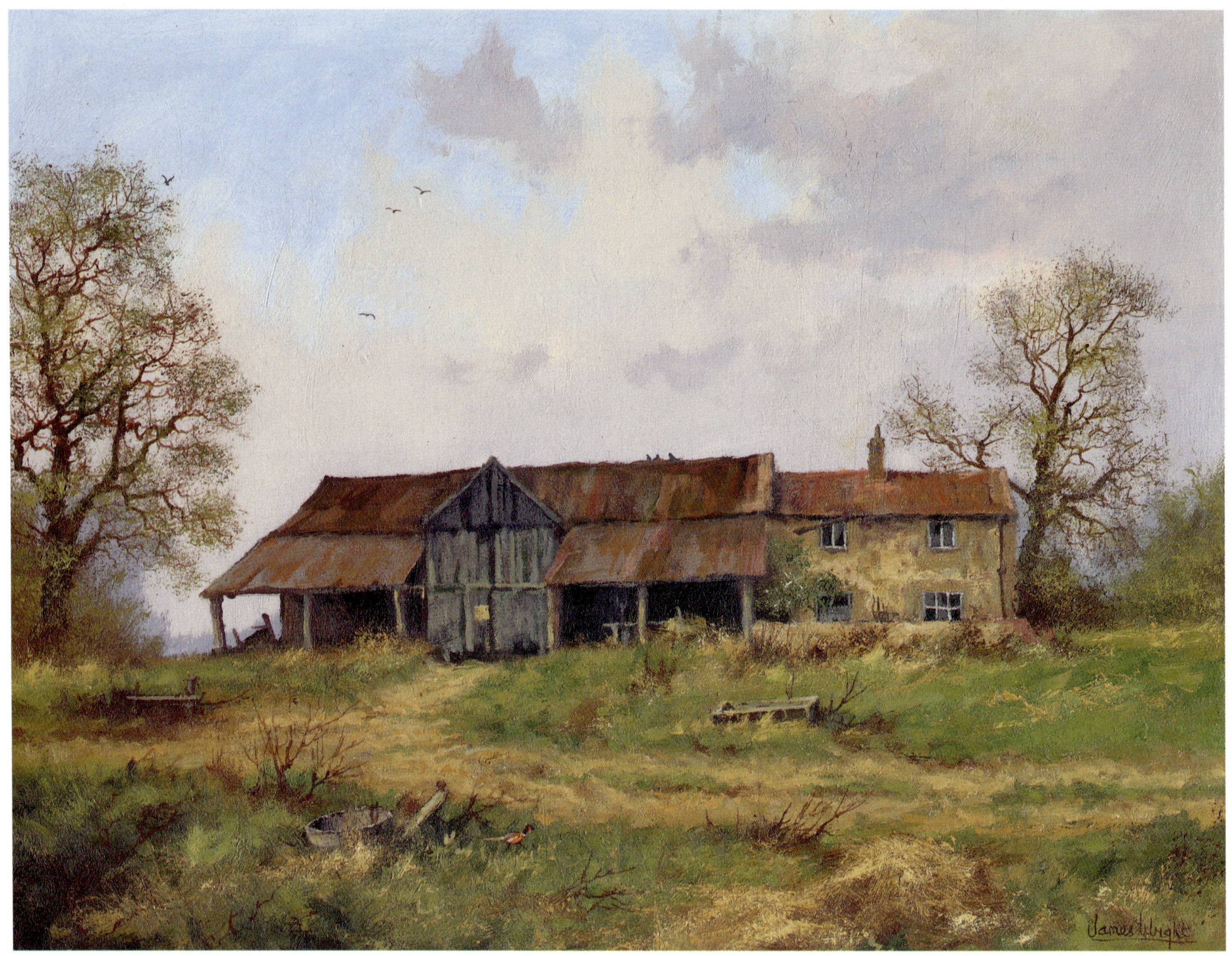

Derelict Farm.

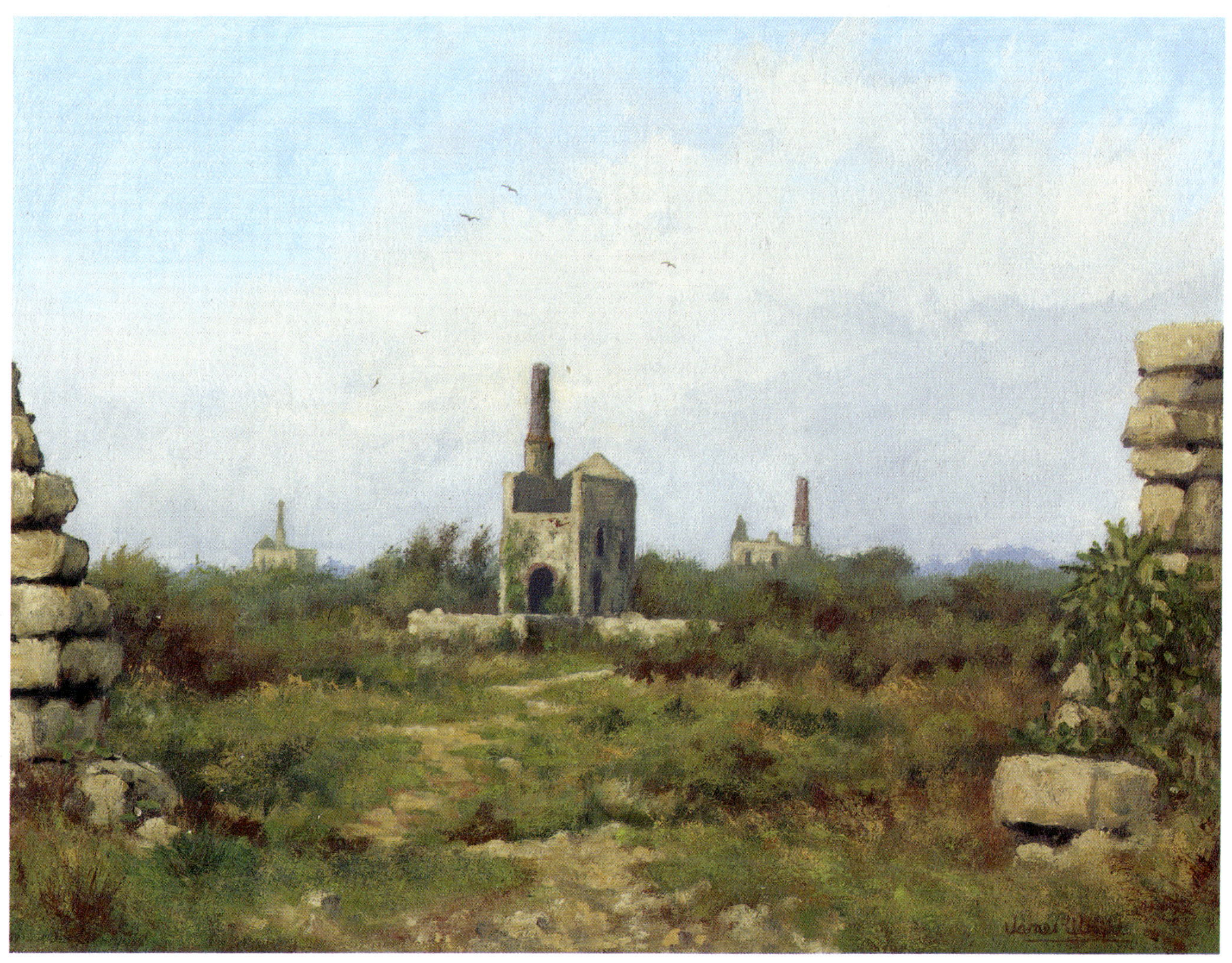

Old Tin Mines near Redruth, Cornwall.

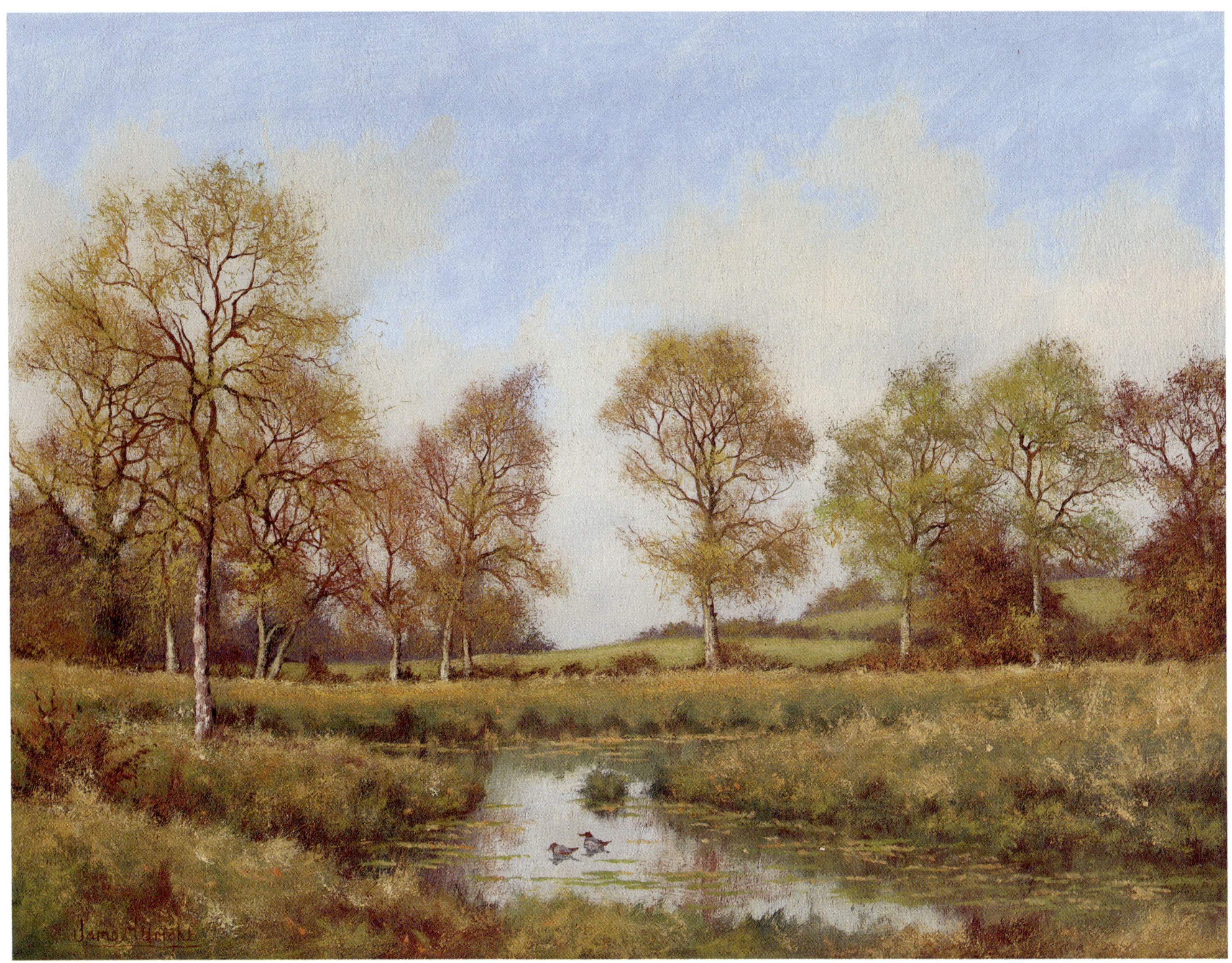

The Pond on Bracebridge Heath, Lincoln.

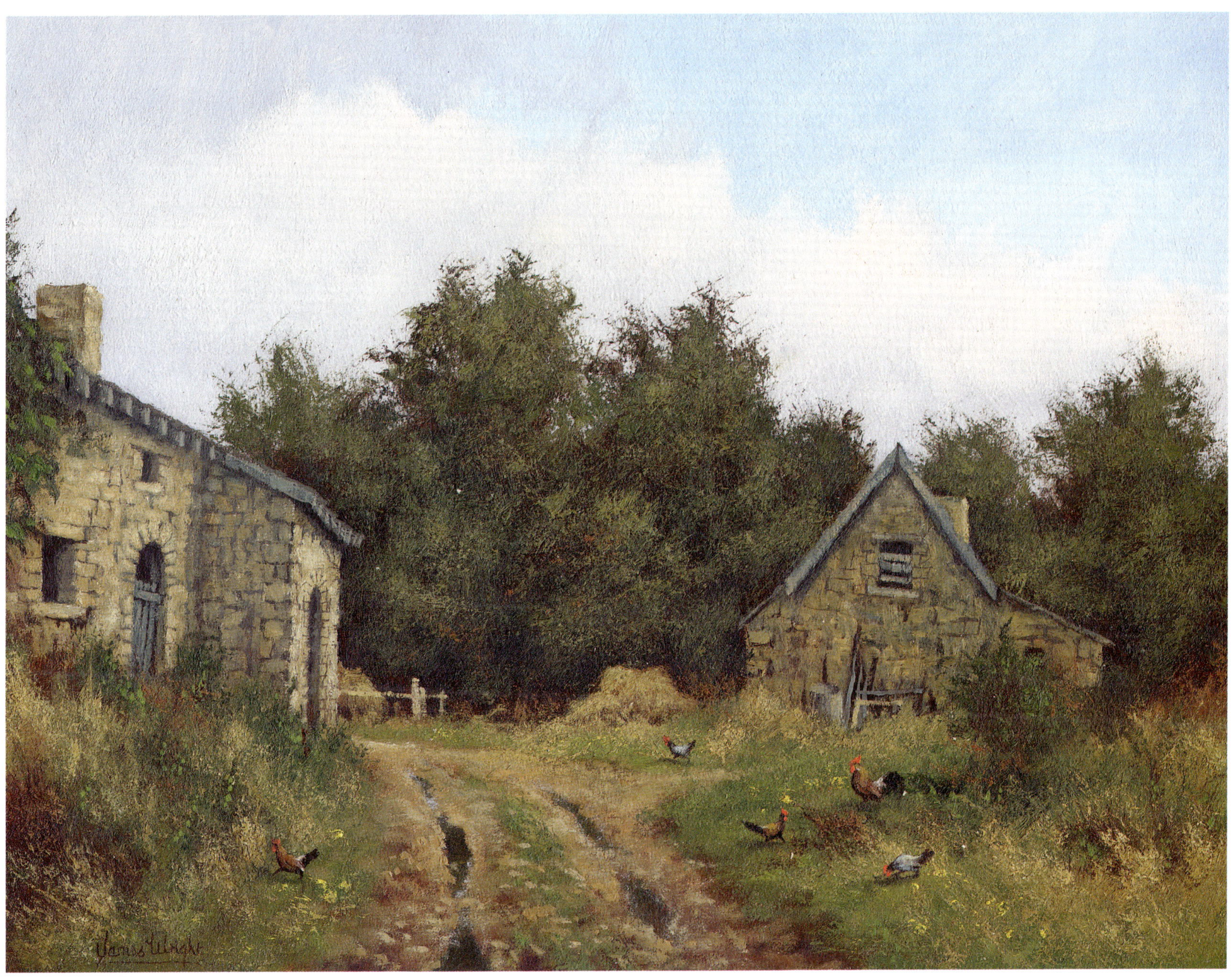

French Farm, Brittany.

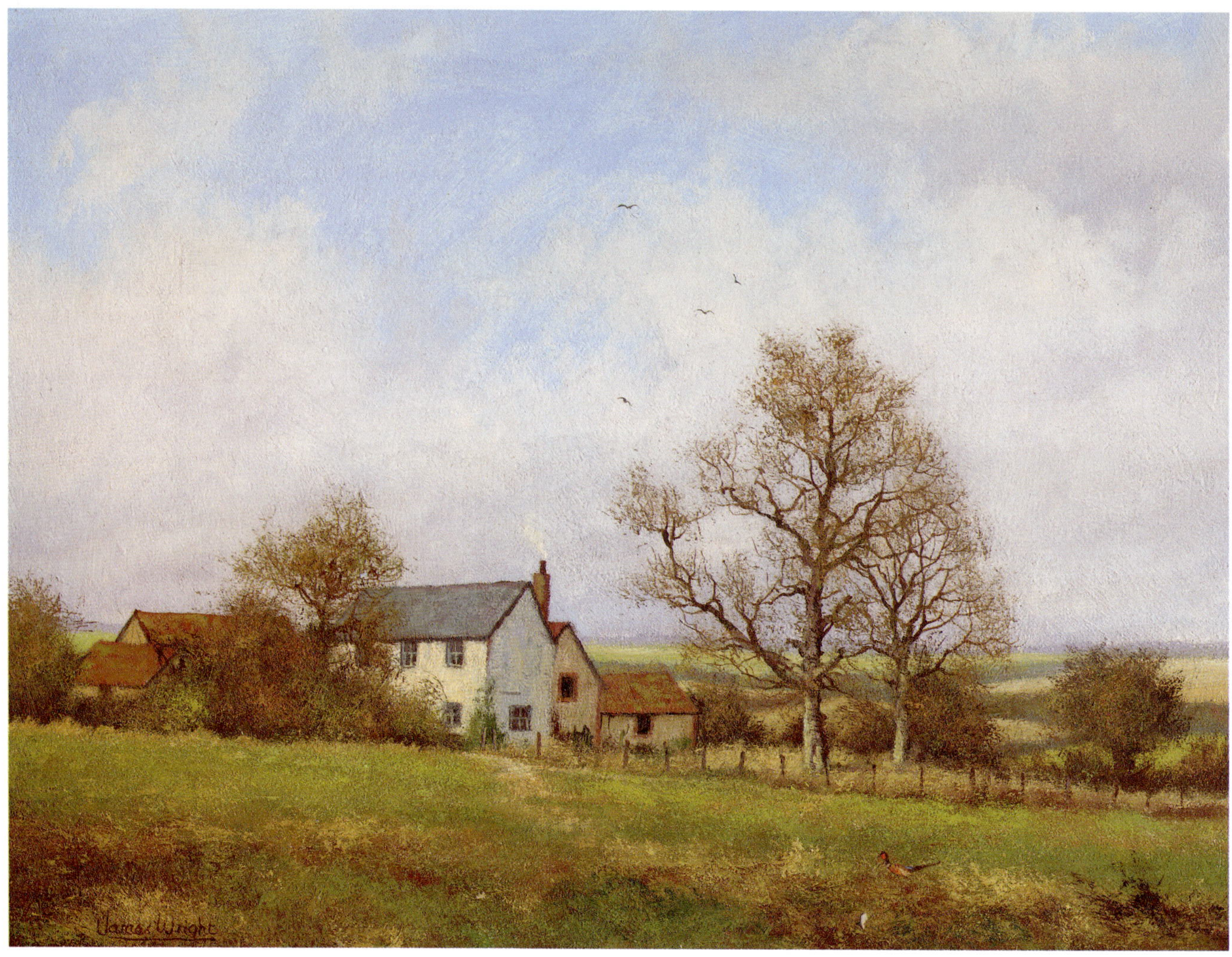

Hill Farm, Norfolk.

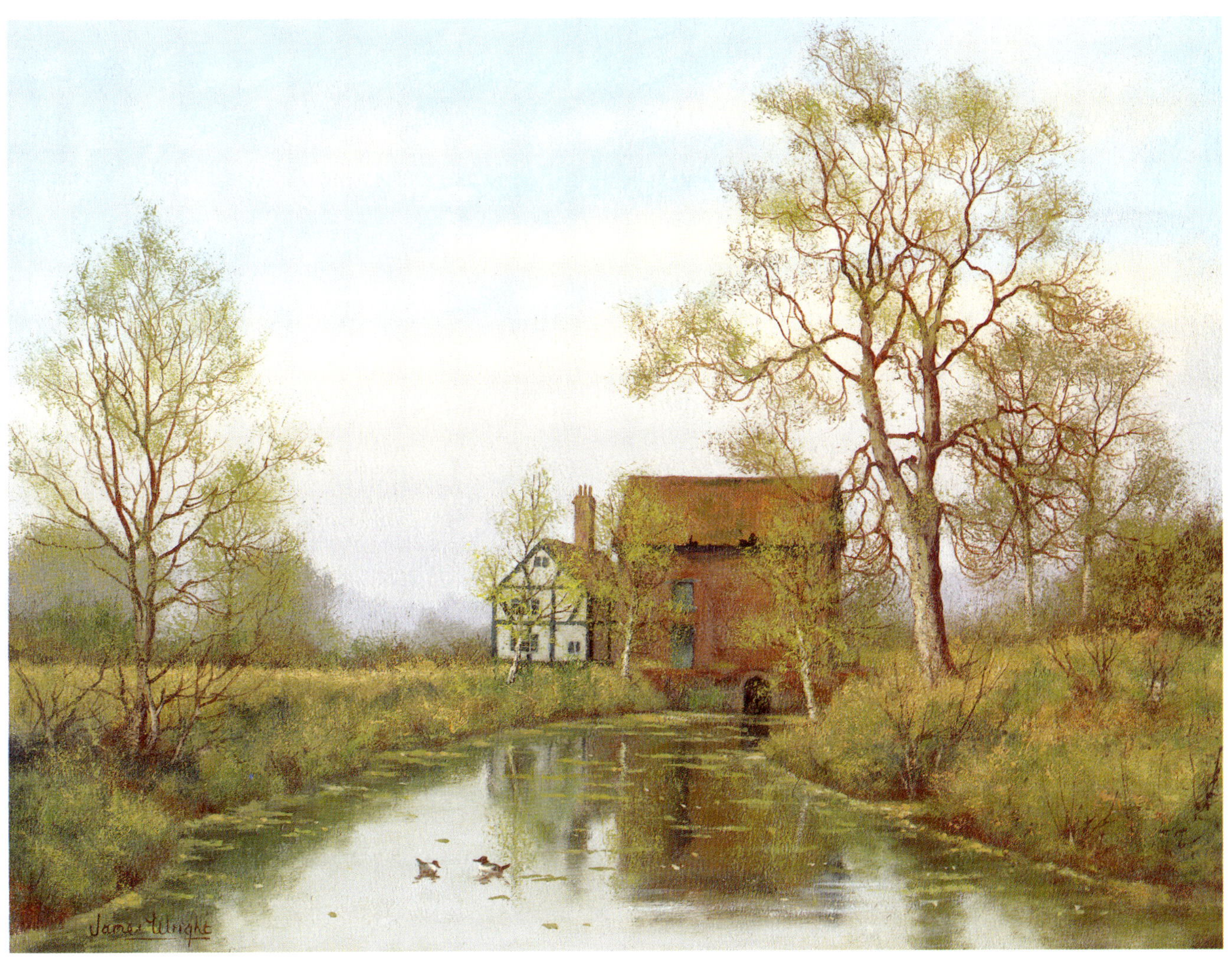

Brockdish Mill, Suffolk.

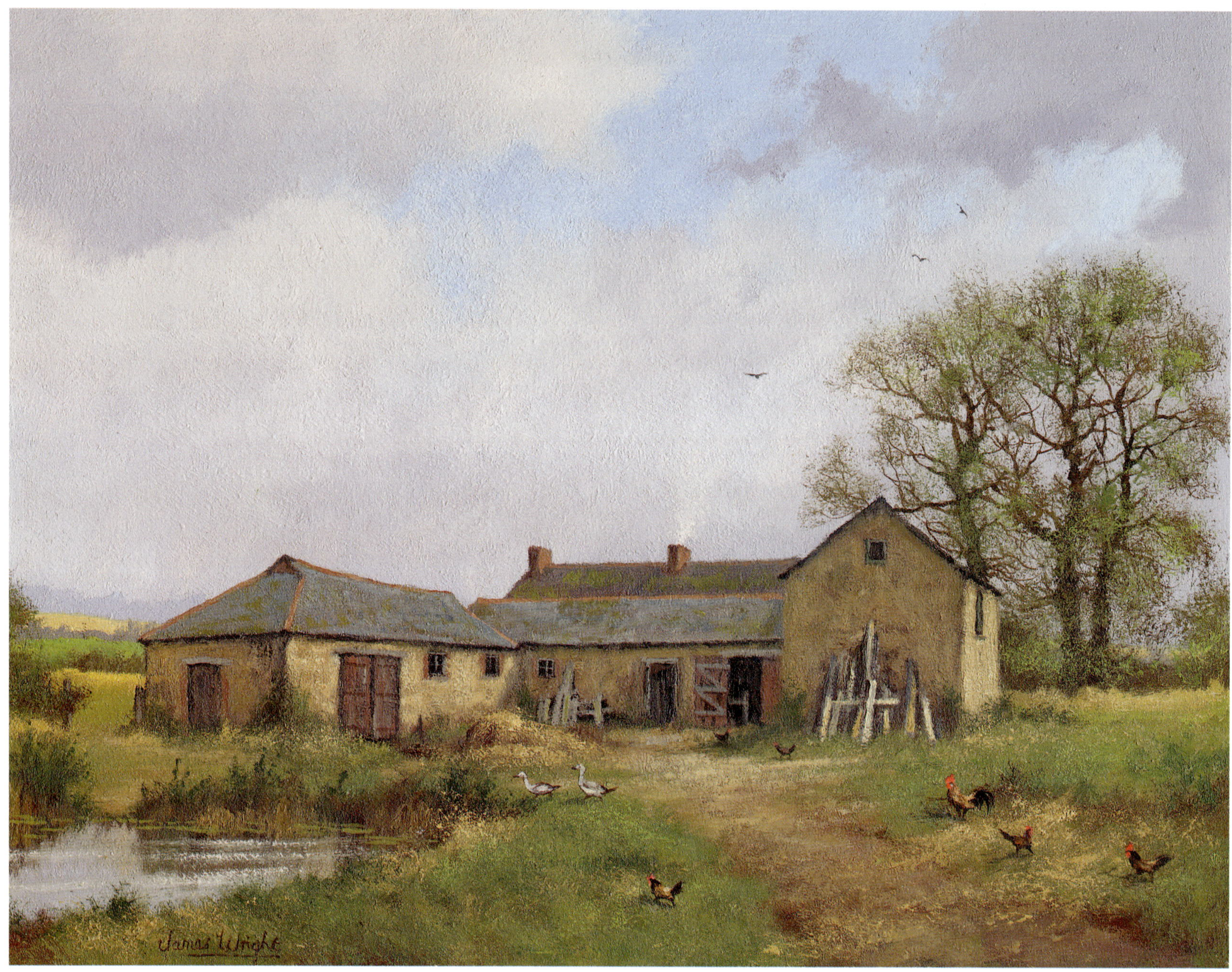

A Devon Farm.

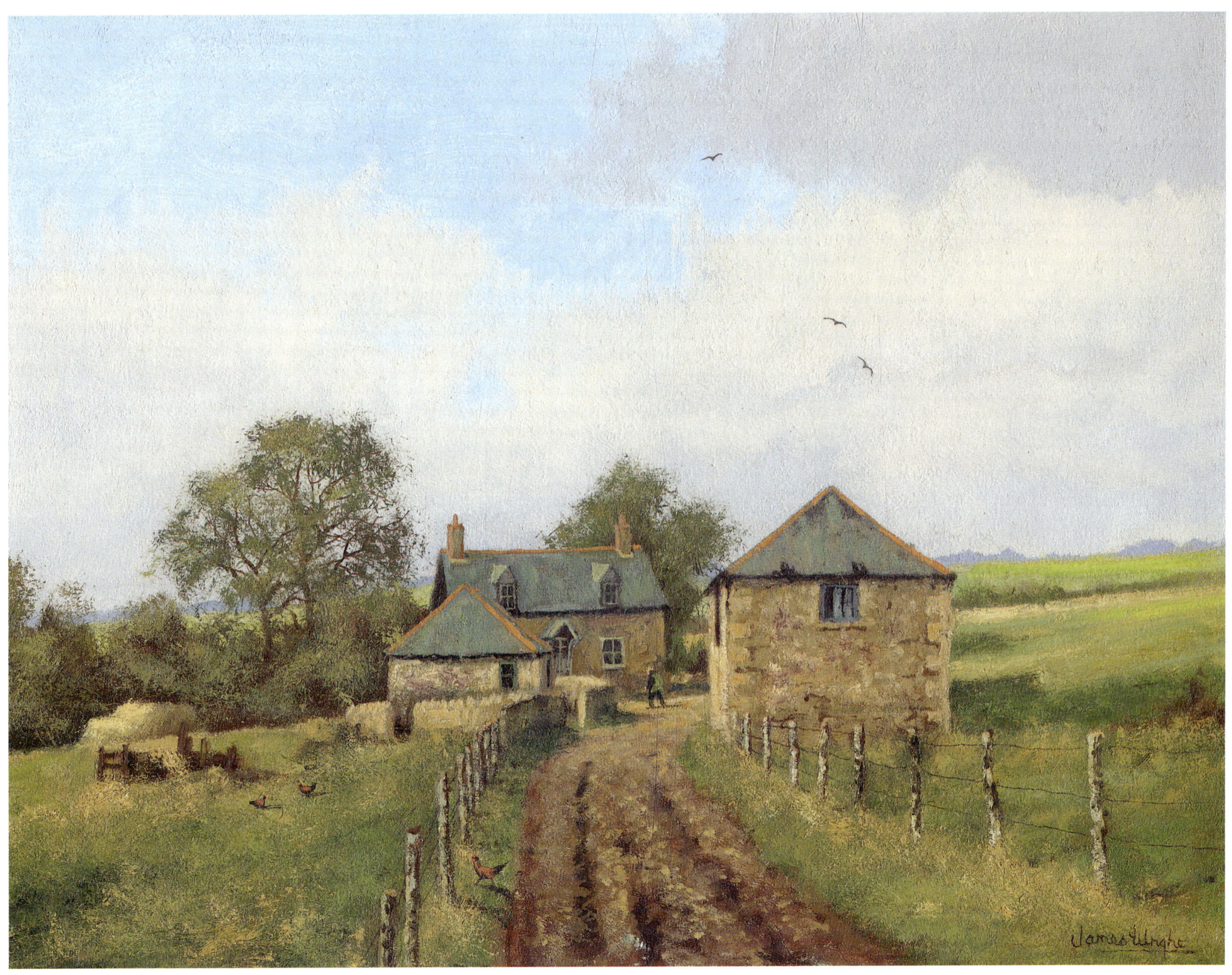

A Farm in Cornwall.

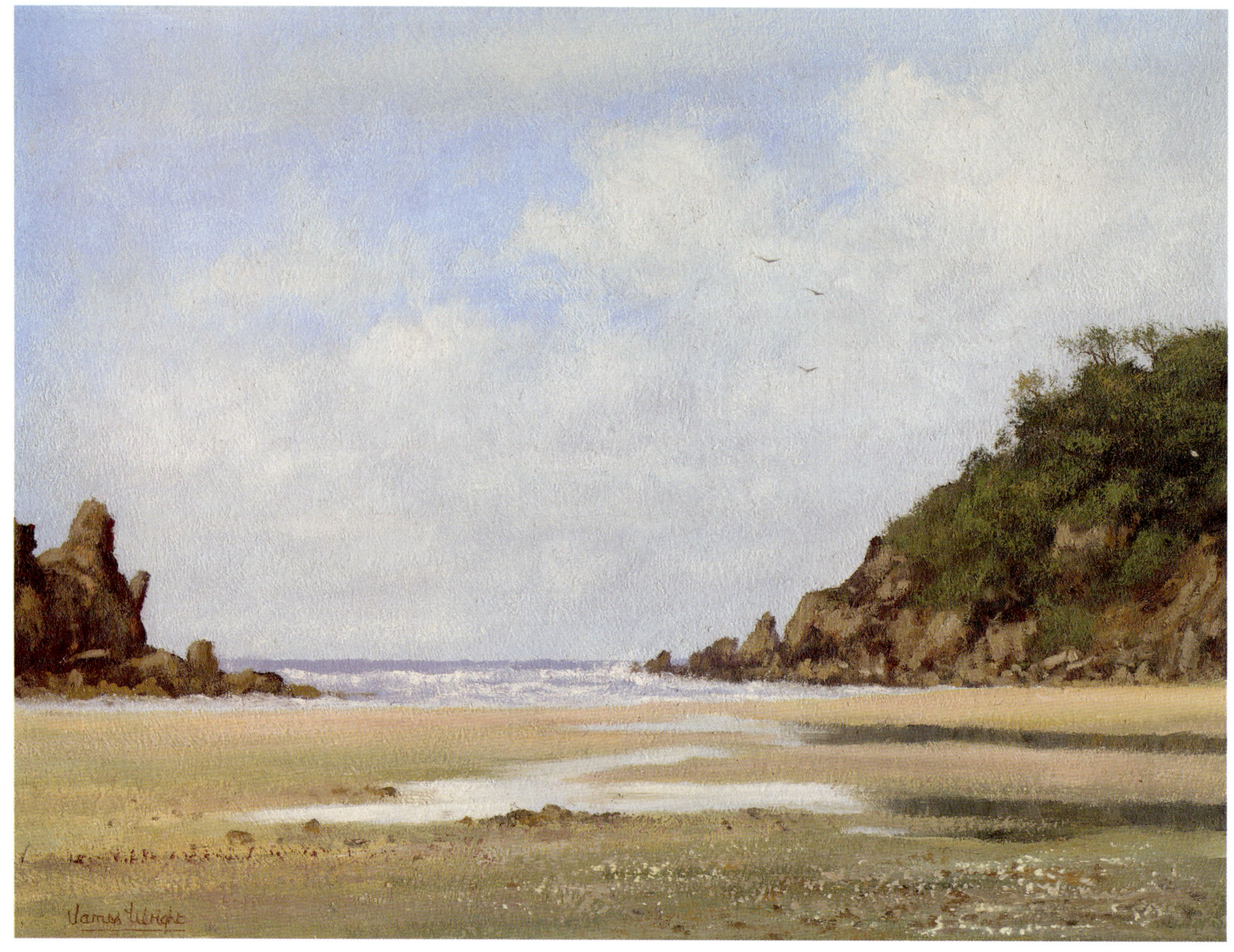

Mothecombe Beach, Devon.

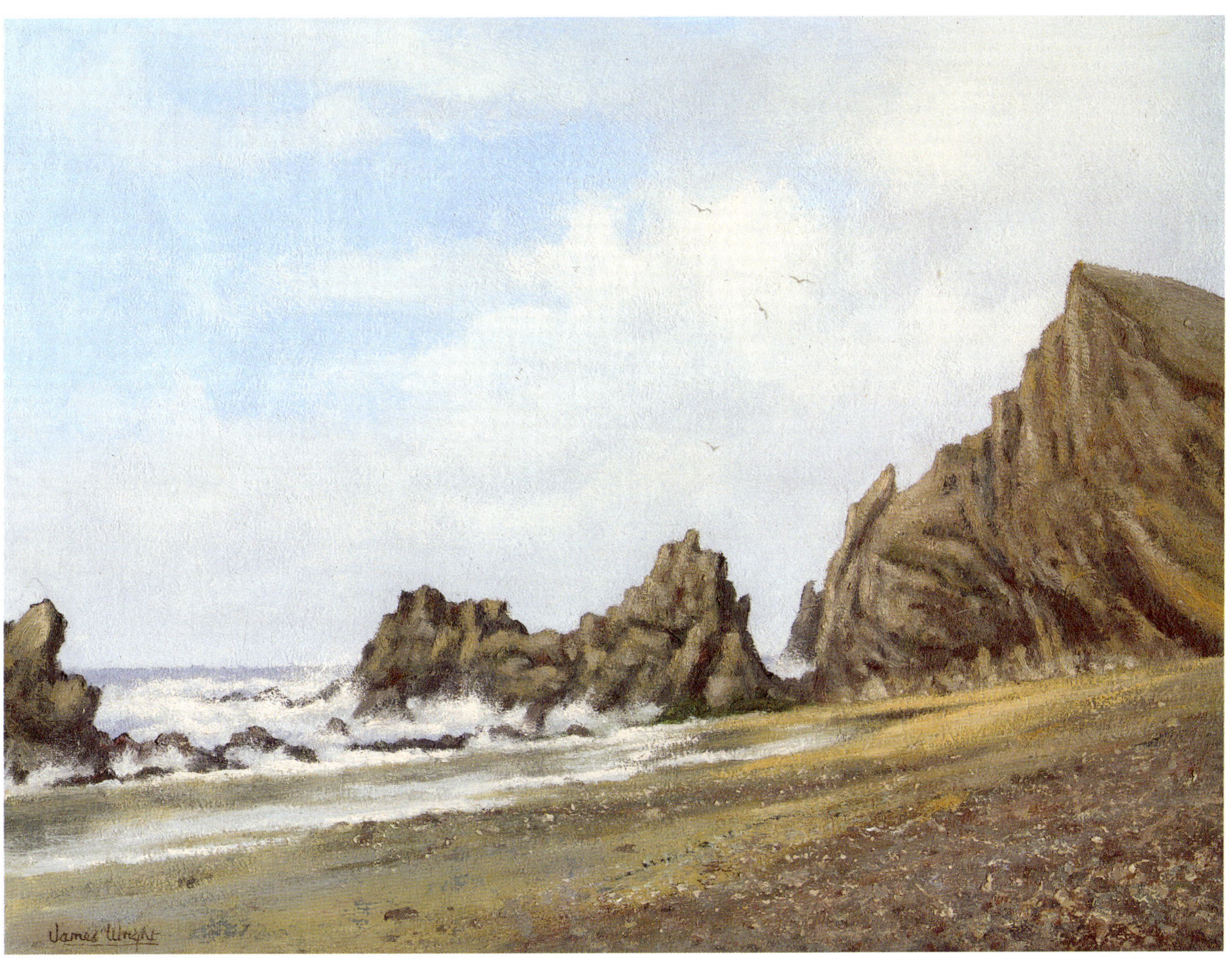

The Beach, Sandymouth, Devon.

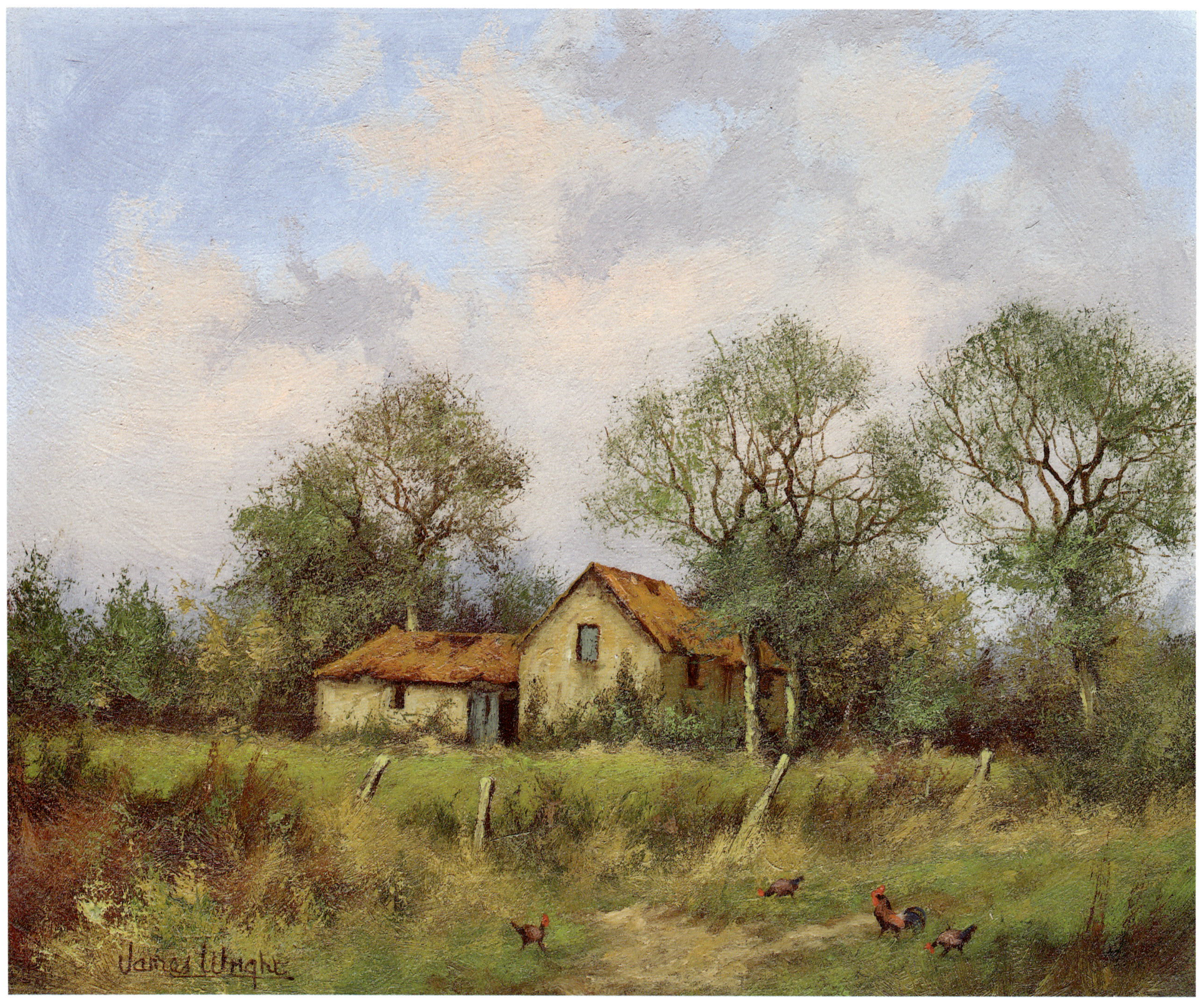
James Wright

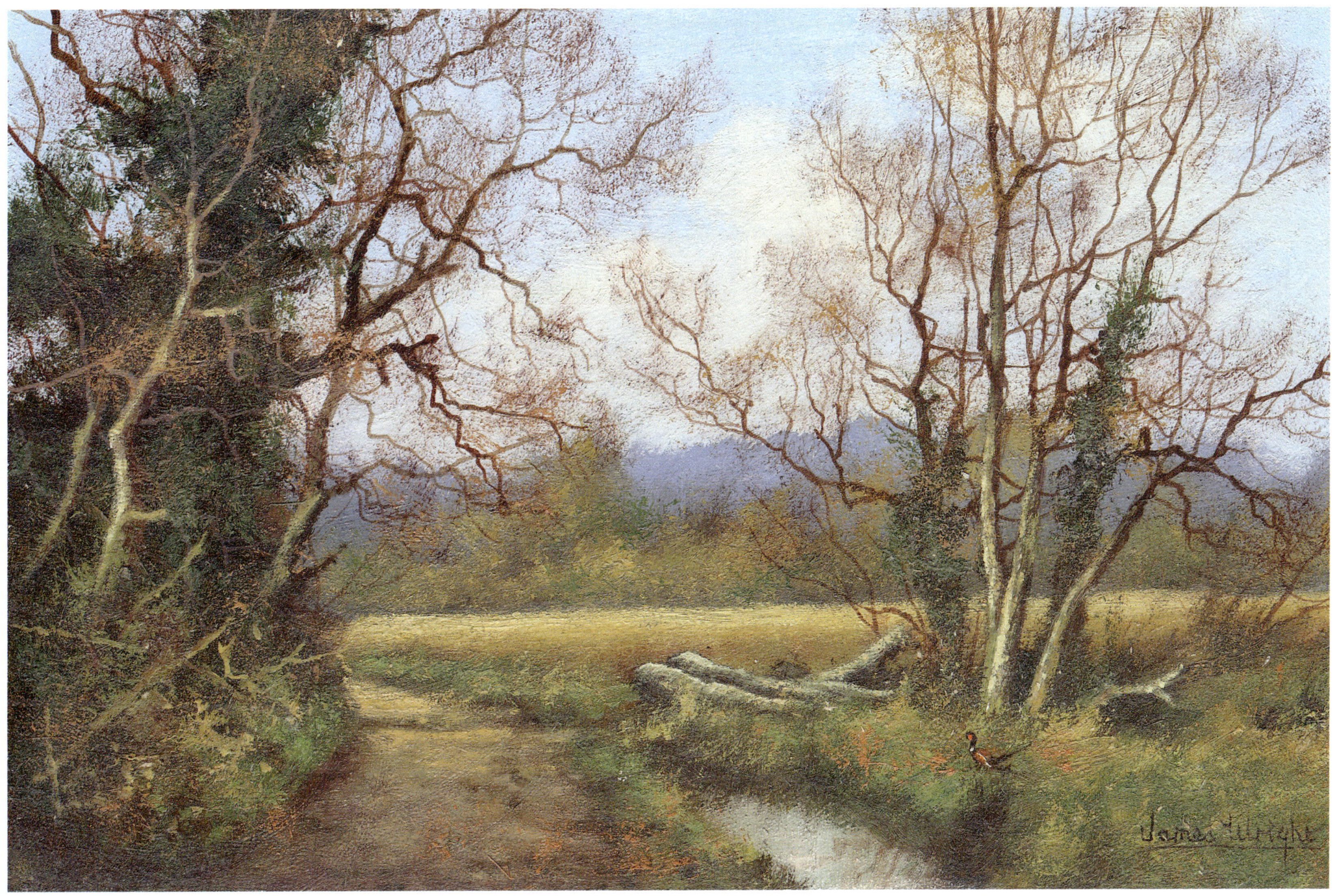

The Path to Salhouse Broad.

Opposite: *Mel's Barn.*

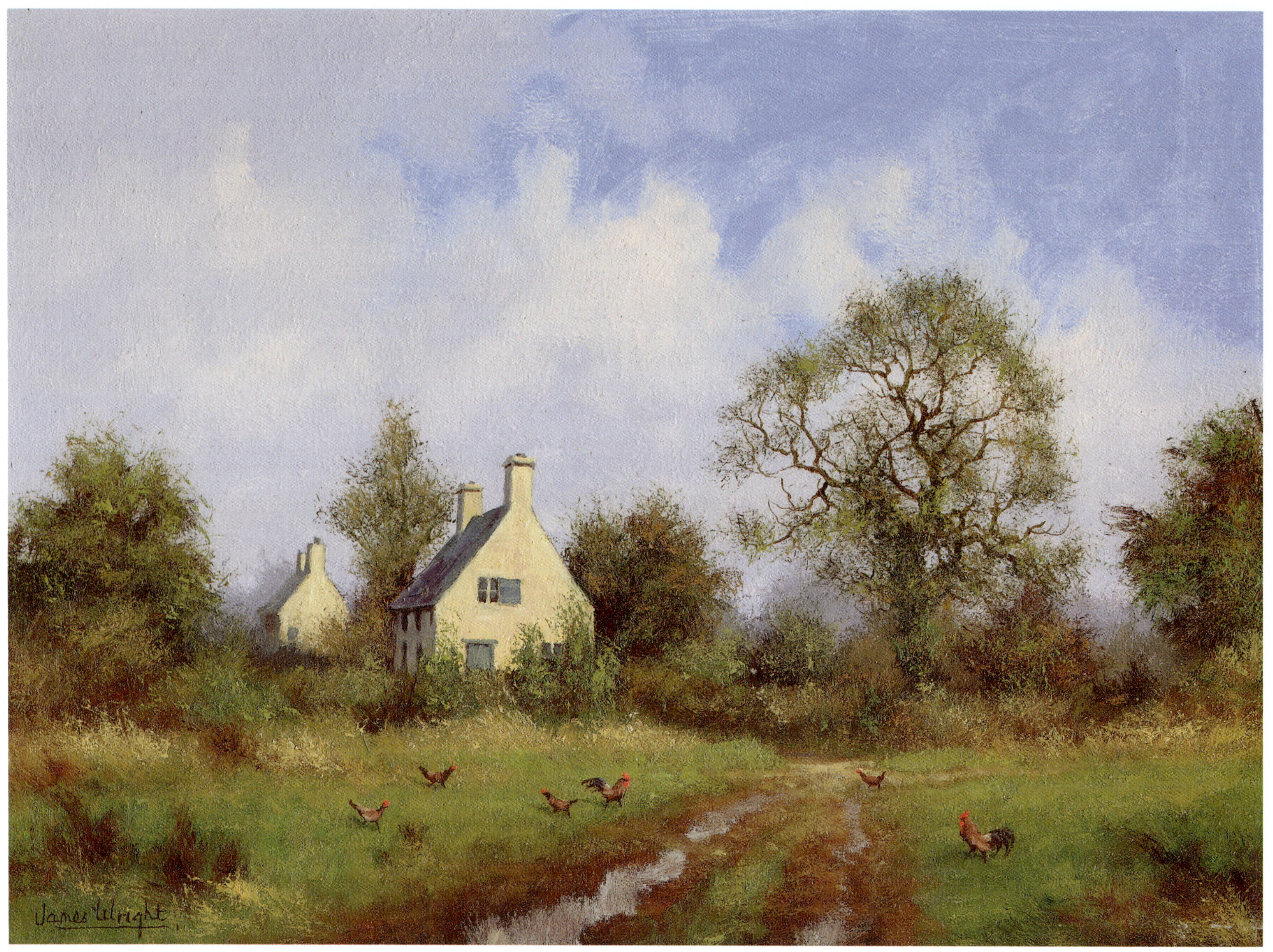

Cottages.

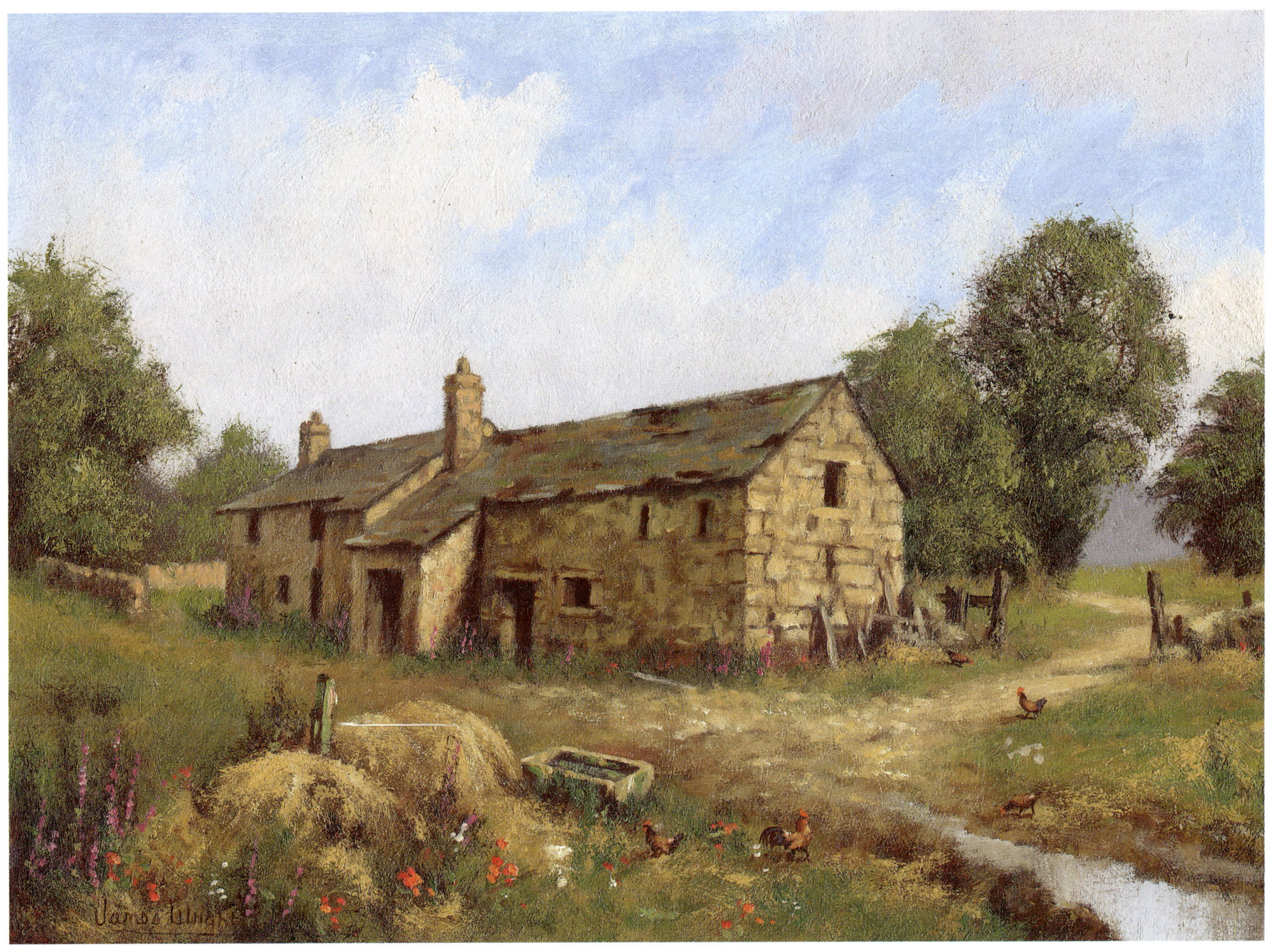

The Longhouse.

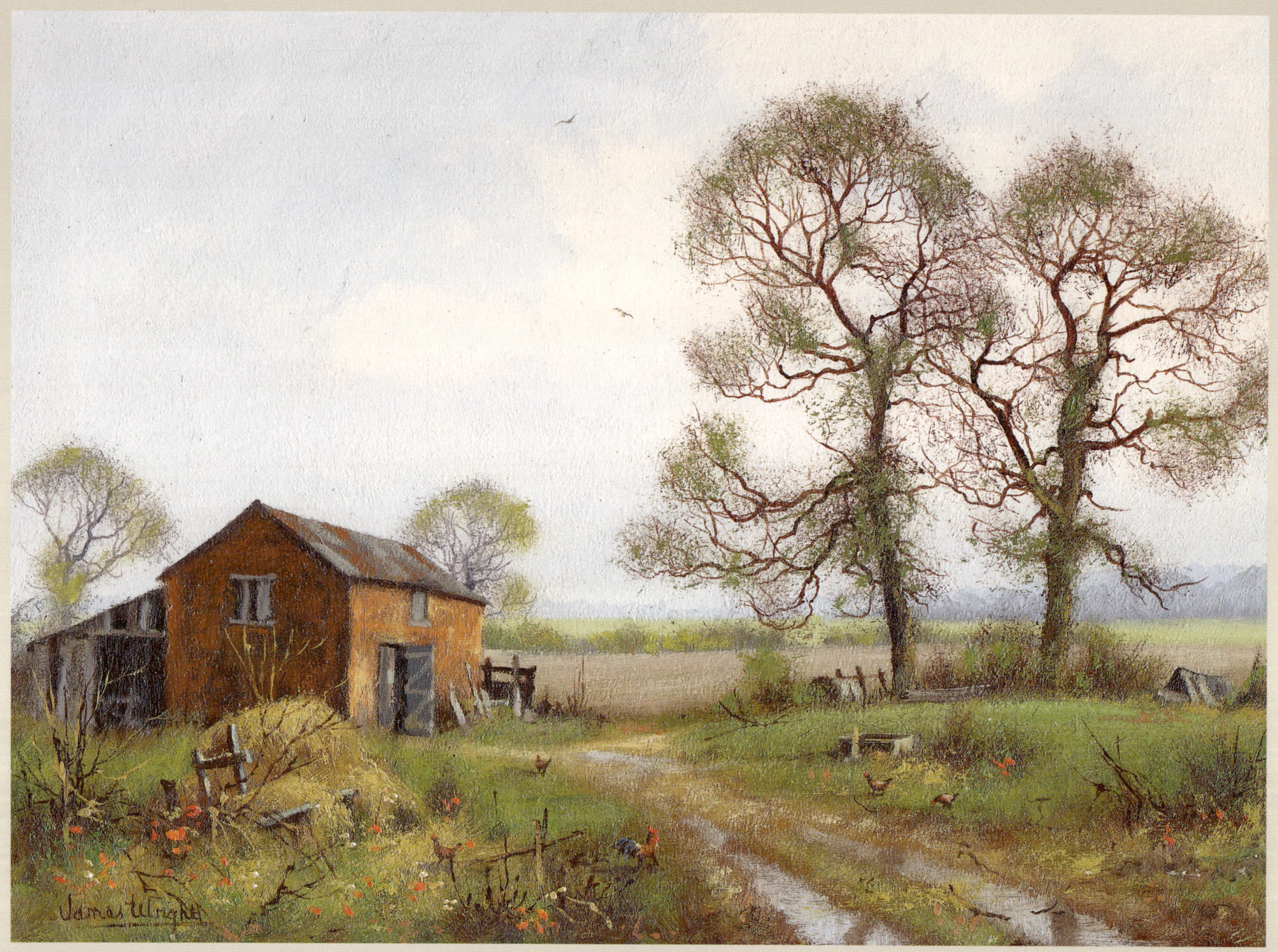

Barn near Kings Lynn.

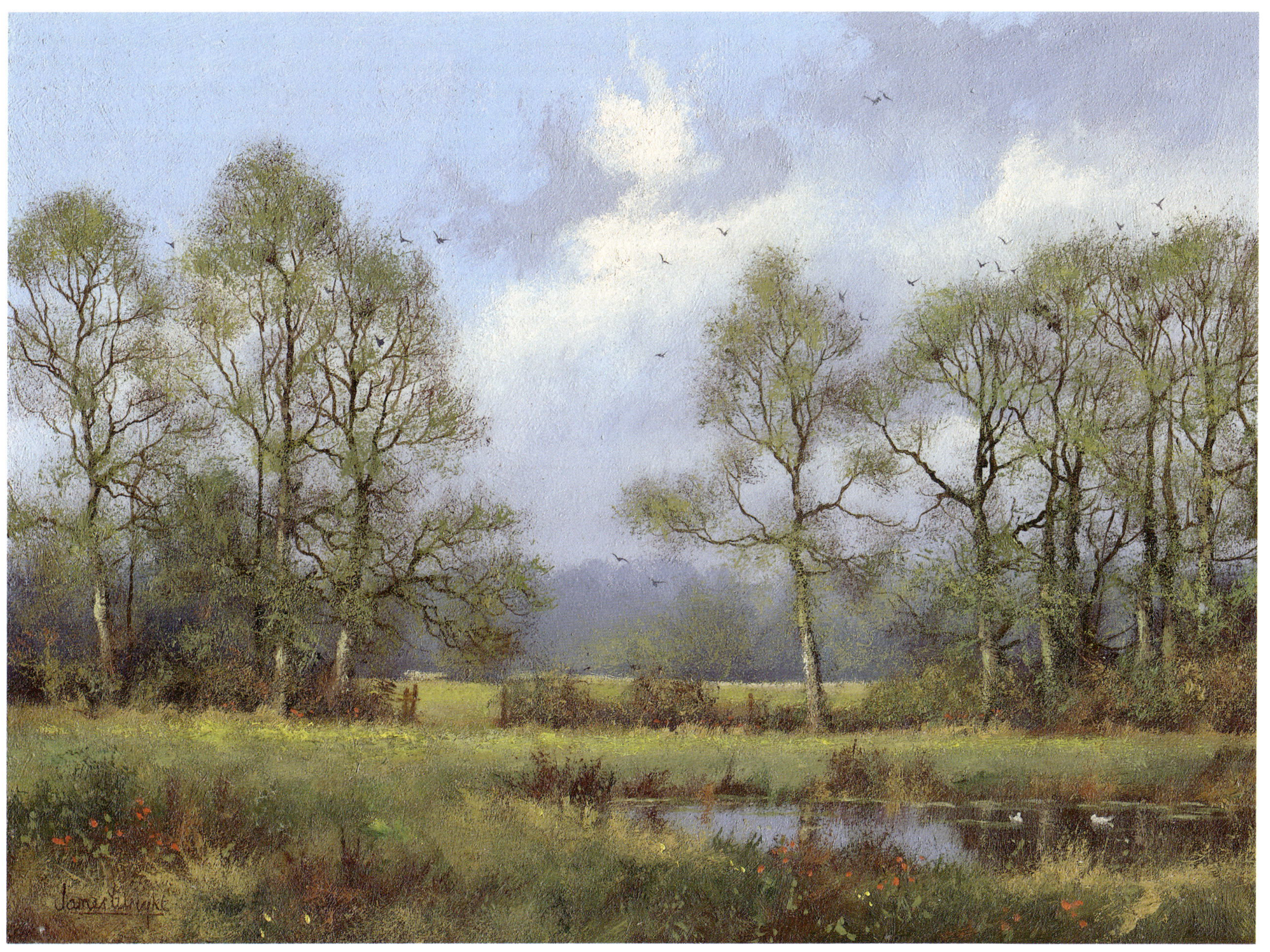

Morgans Pond.

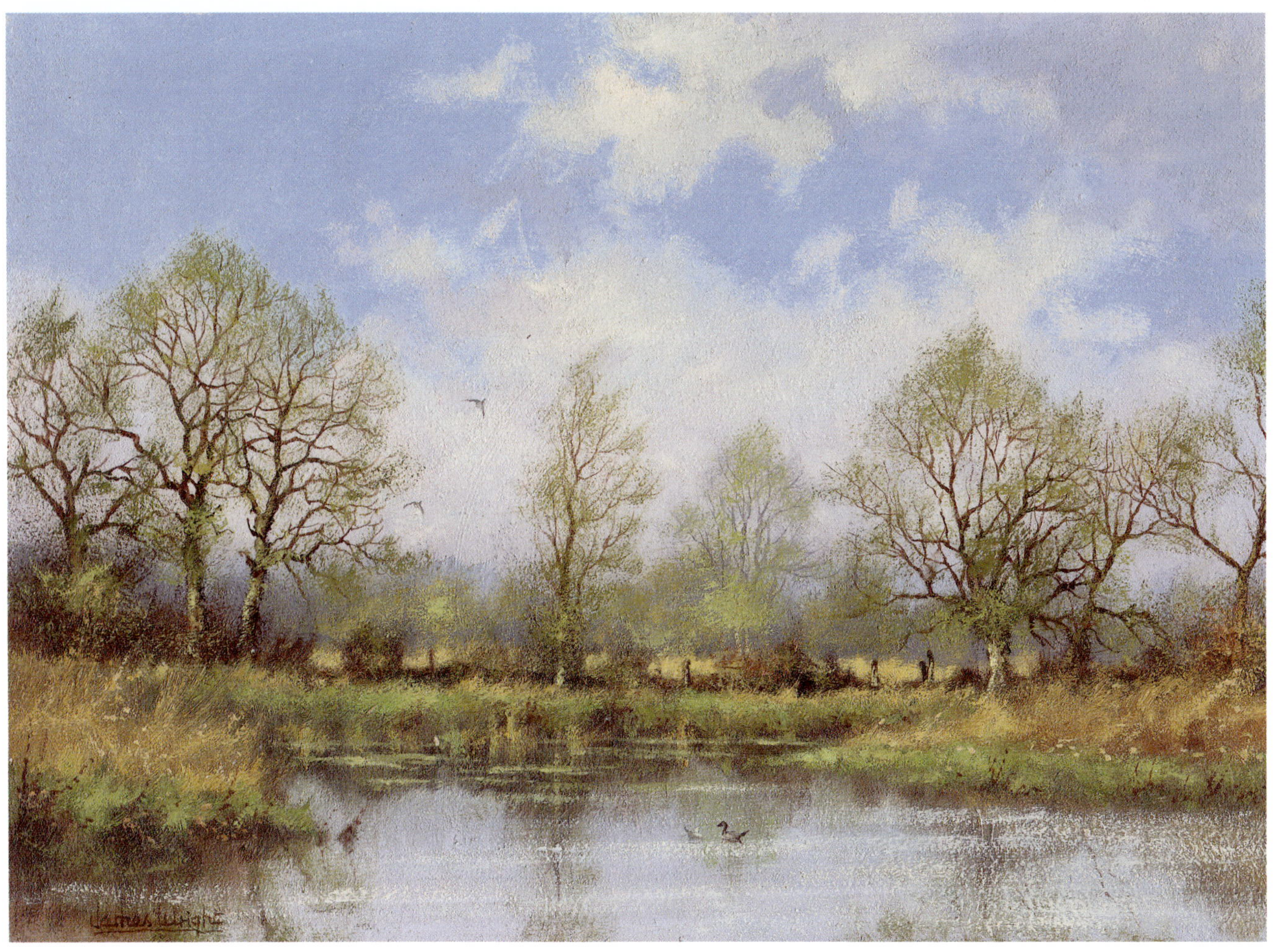

The River at Easton.

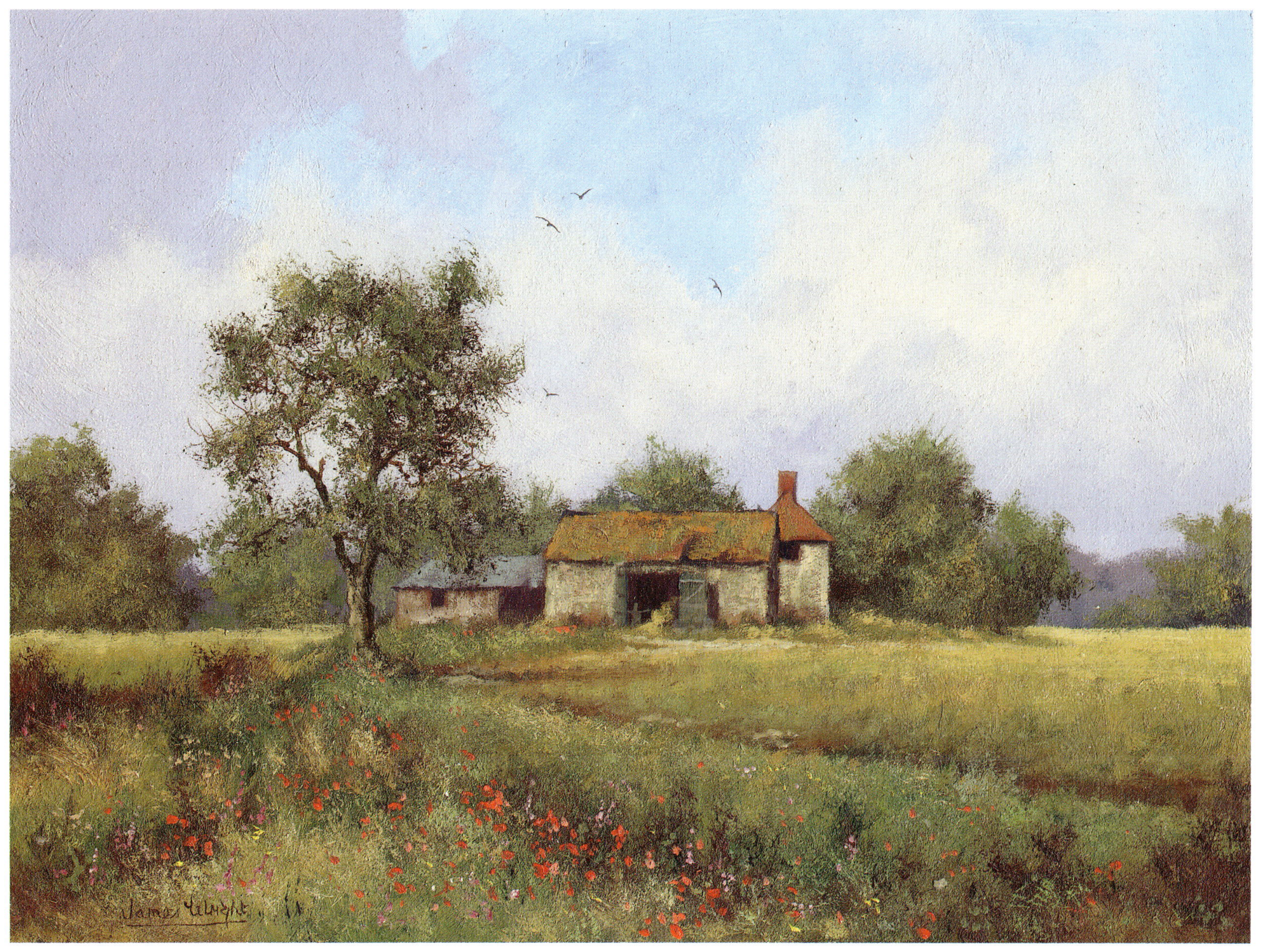

Tumbledown Farm.

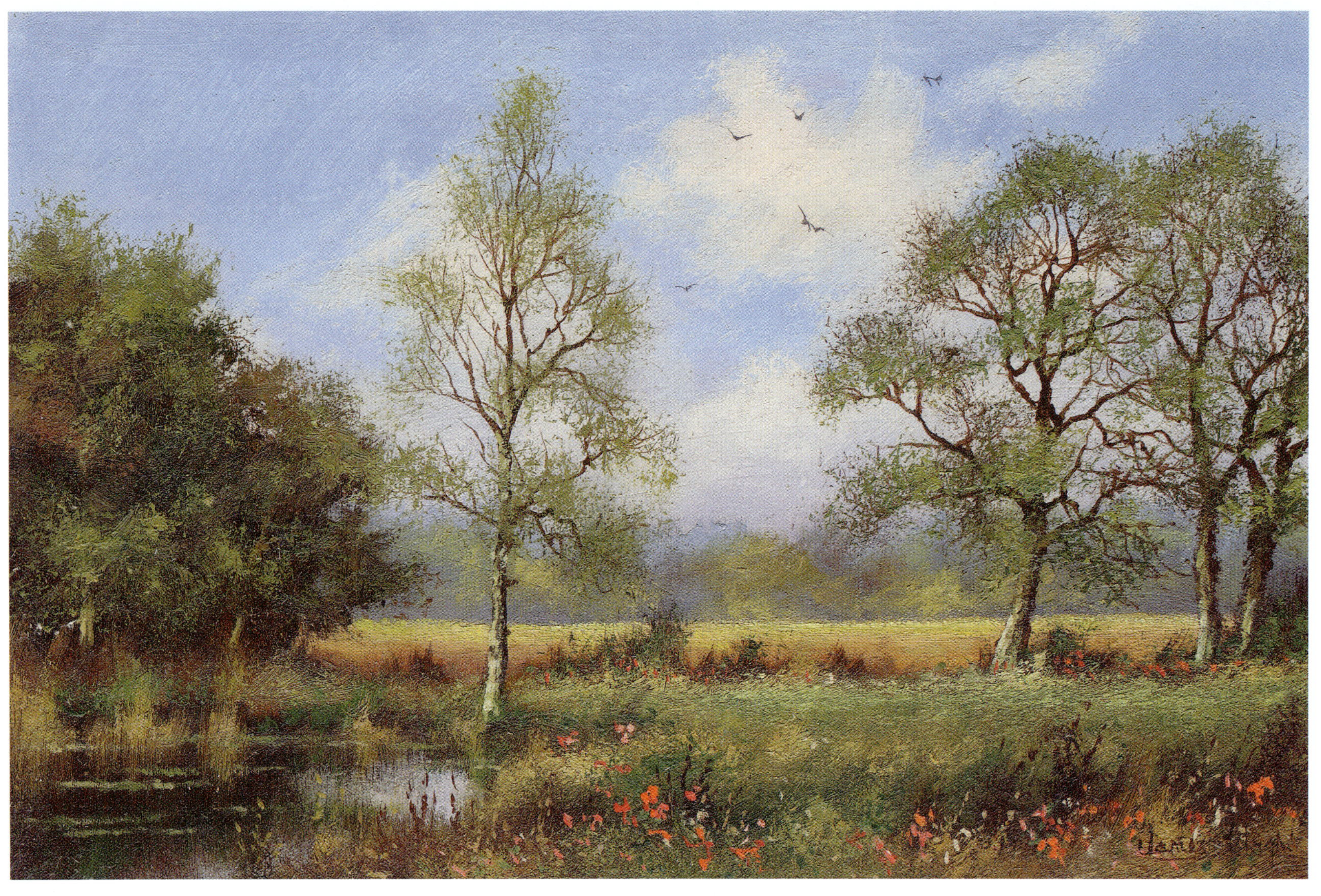

The Watering Hole.

Opposite: *Essex Farm.*

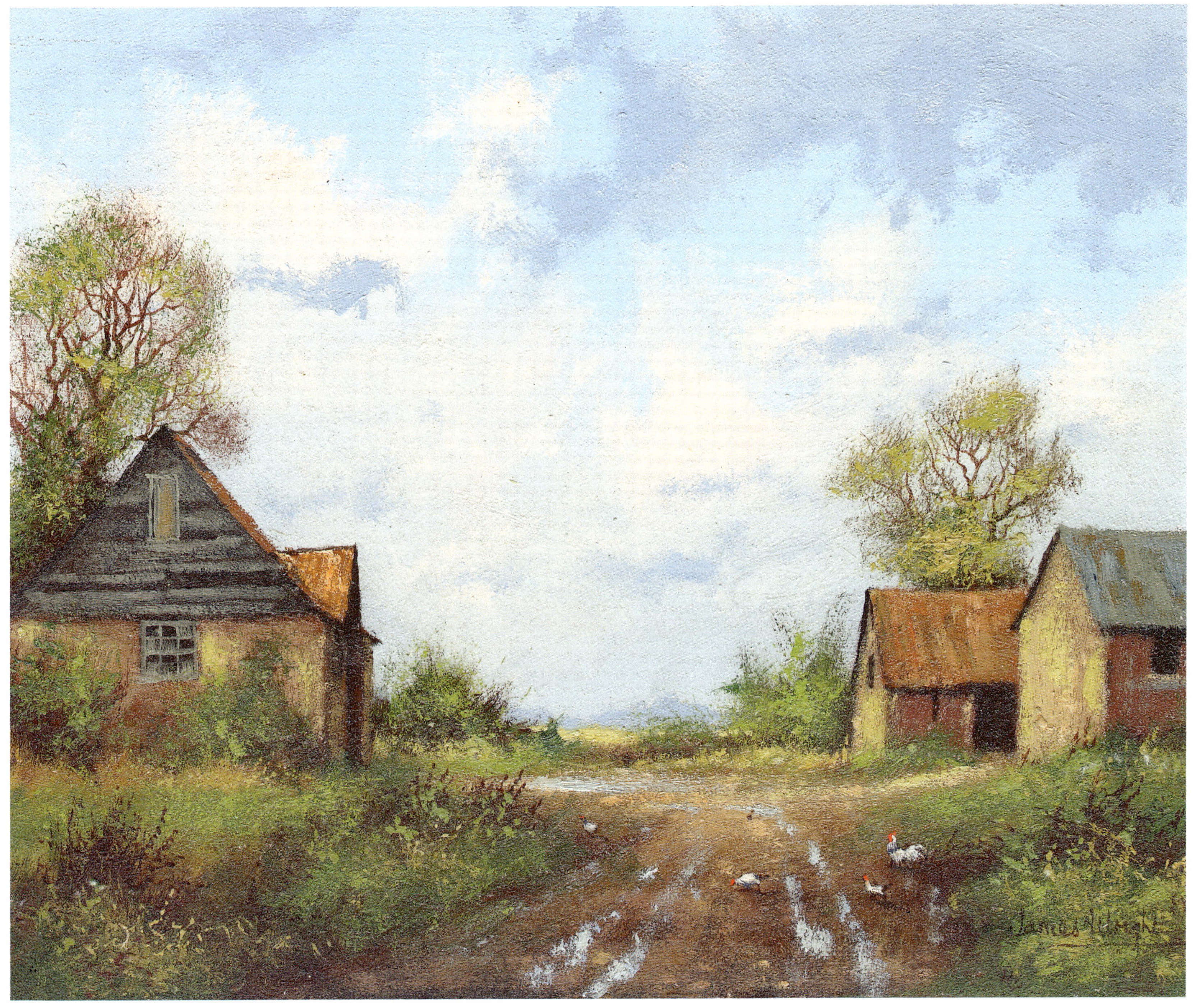

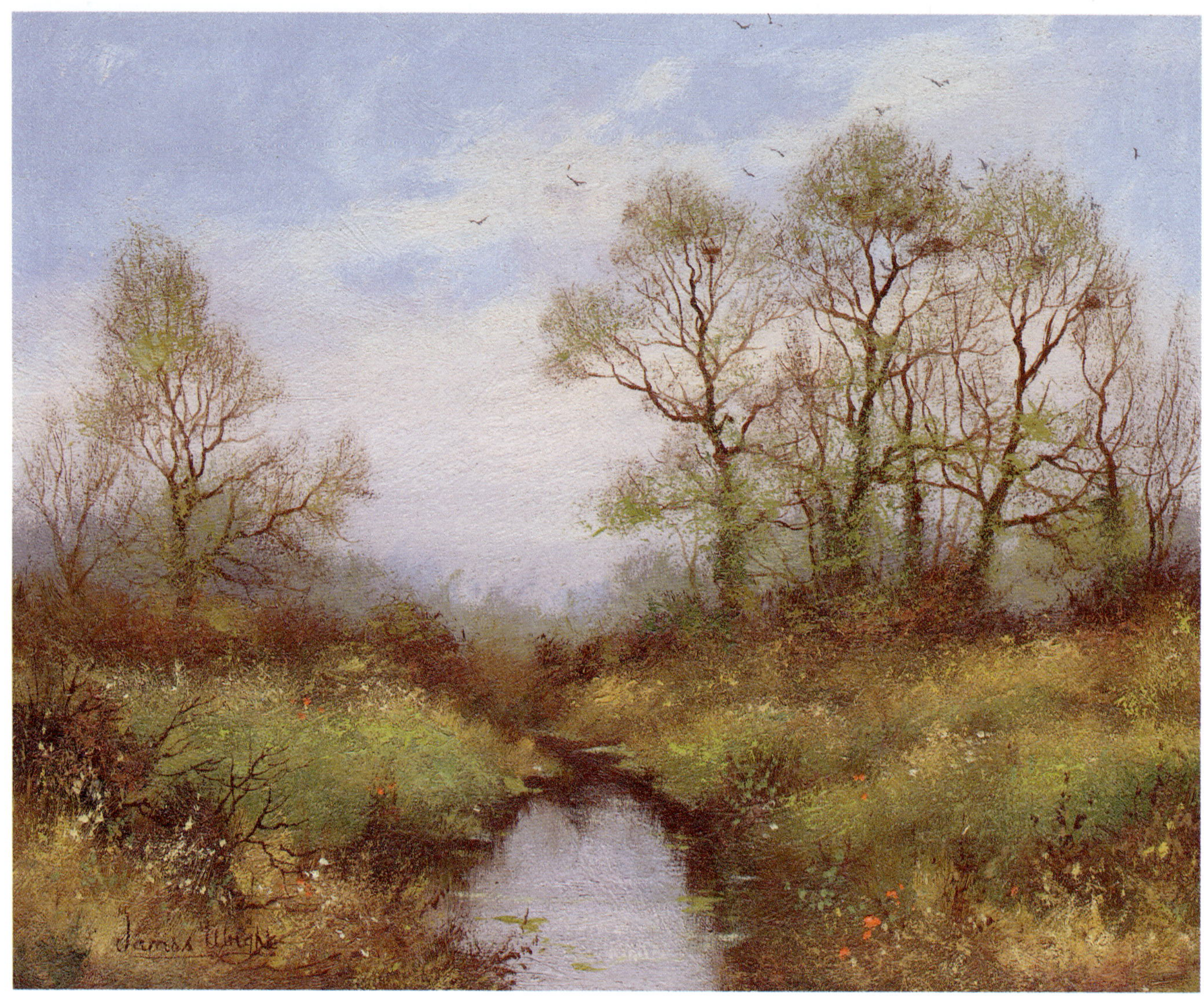

The Babbling Brook.

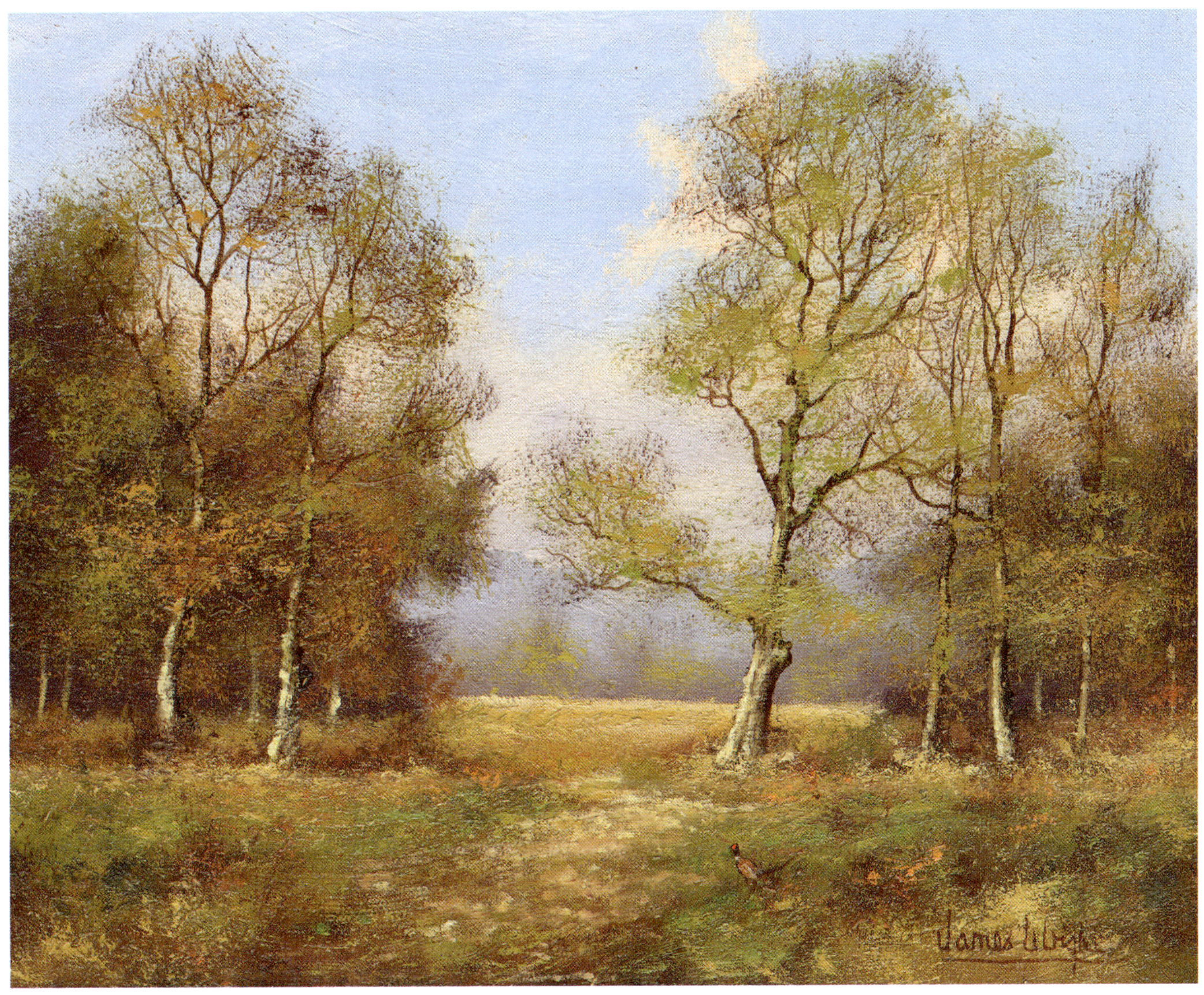

The Edge of the Woods.

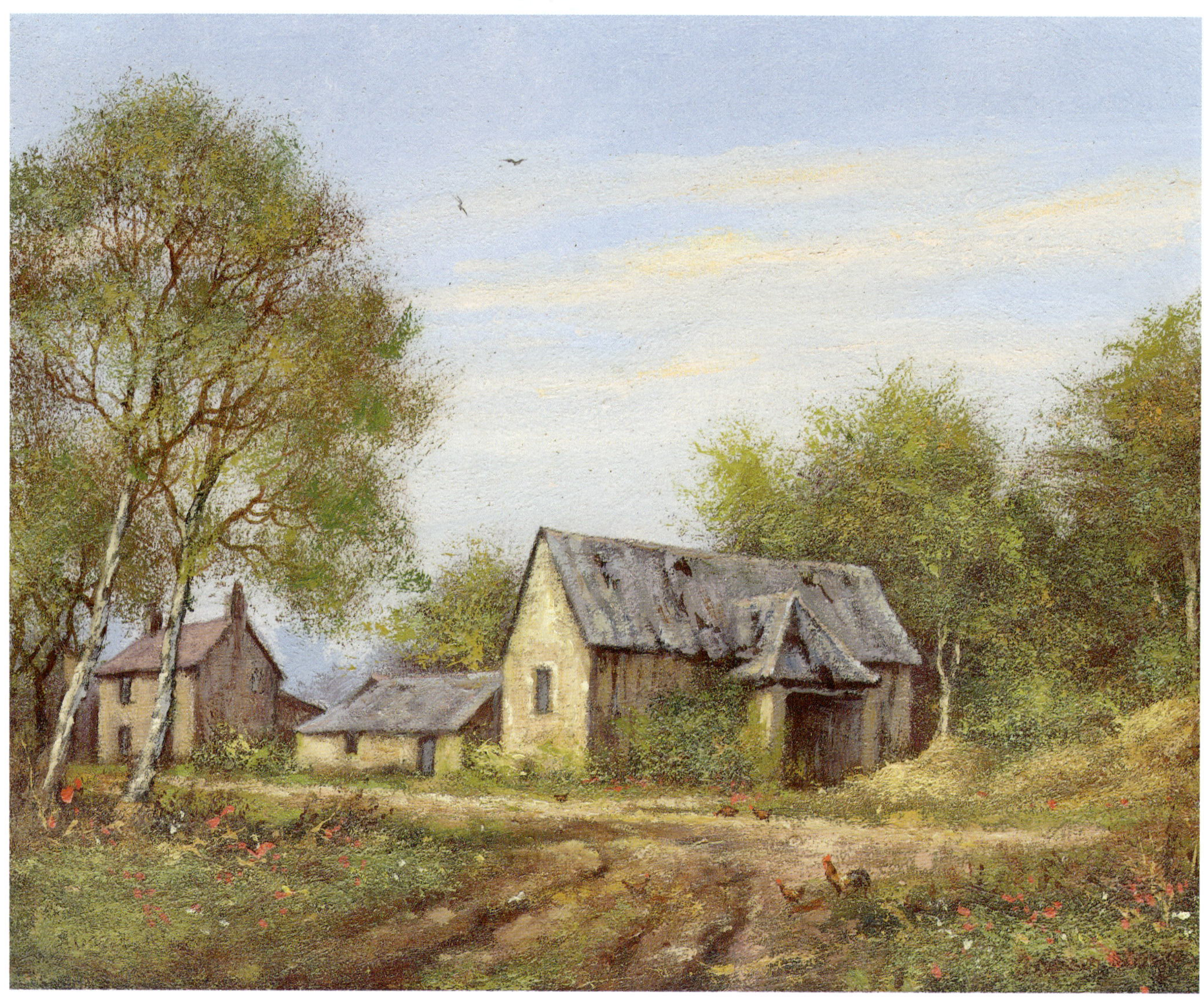

Cart Tracks and Barn.

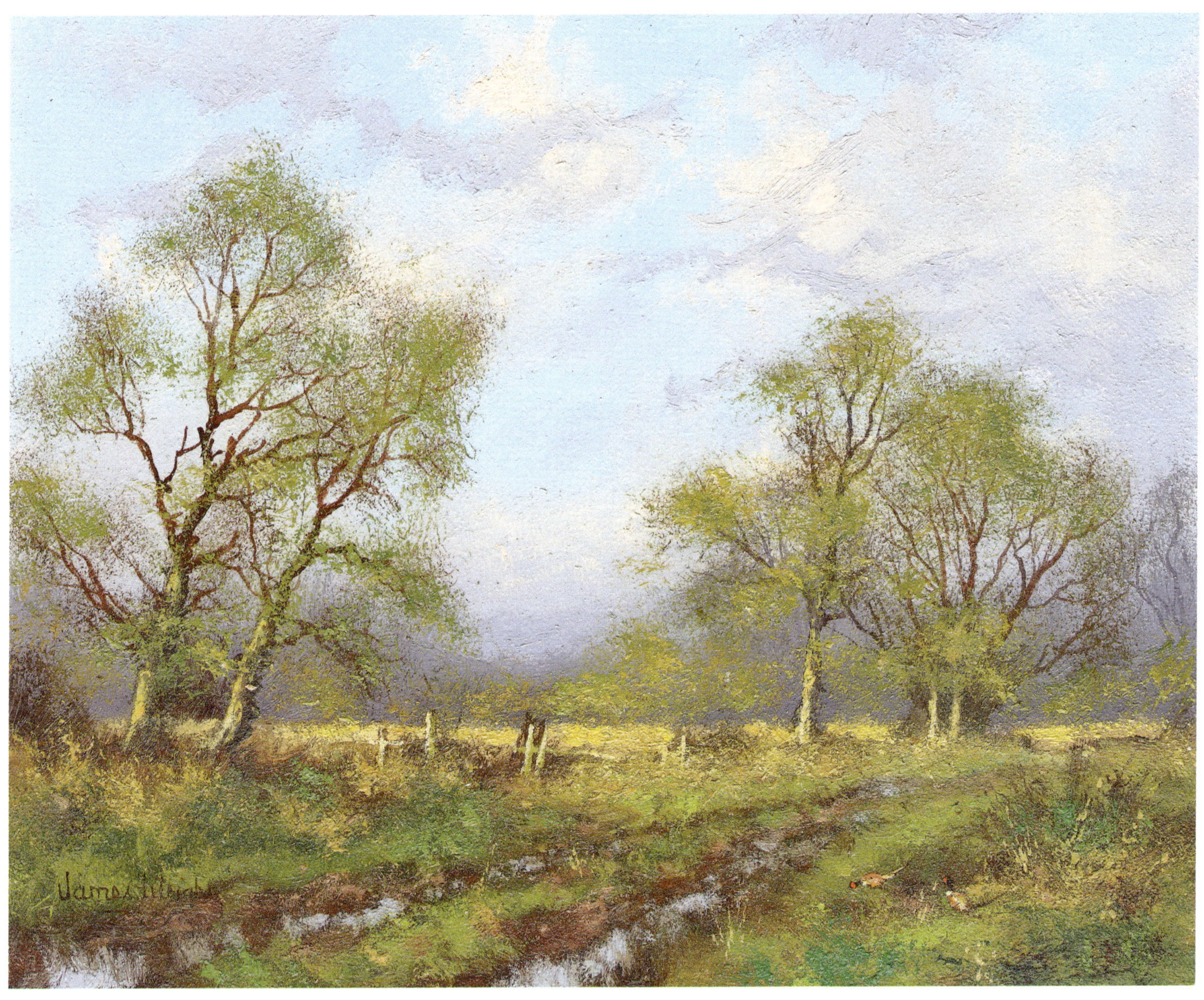

More Showers.

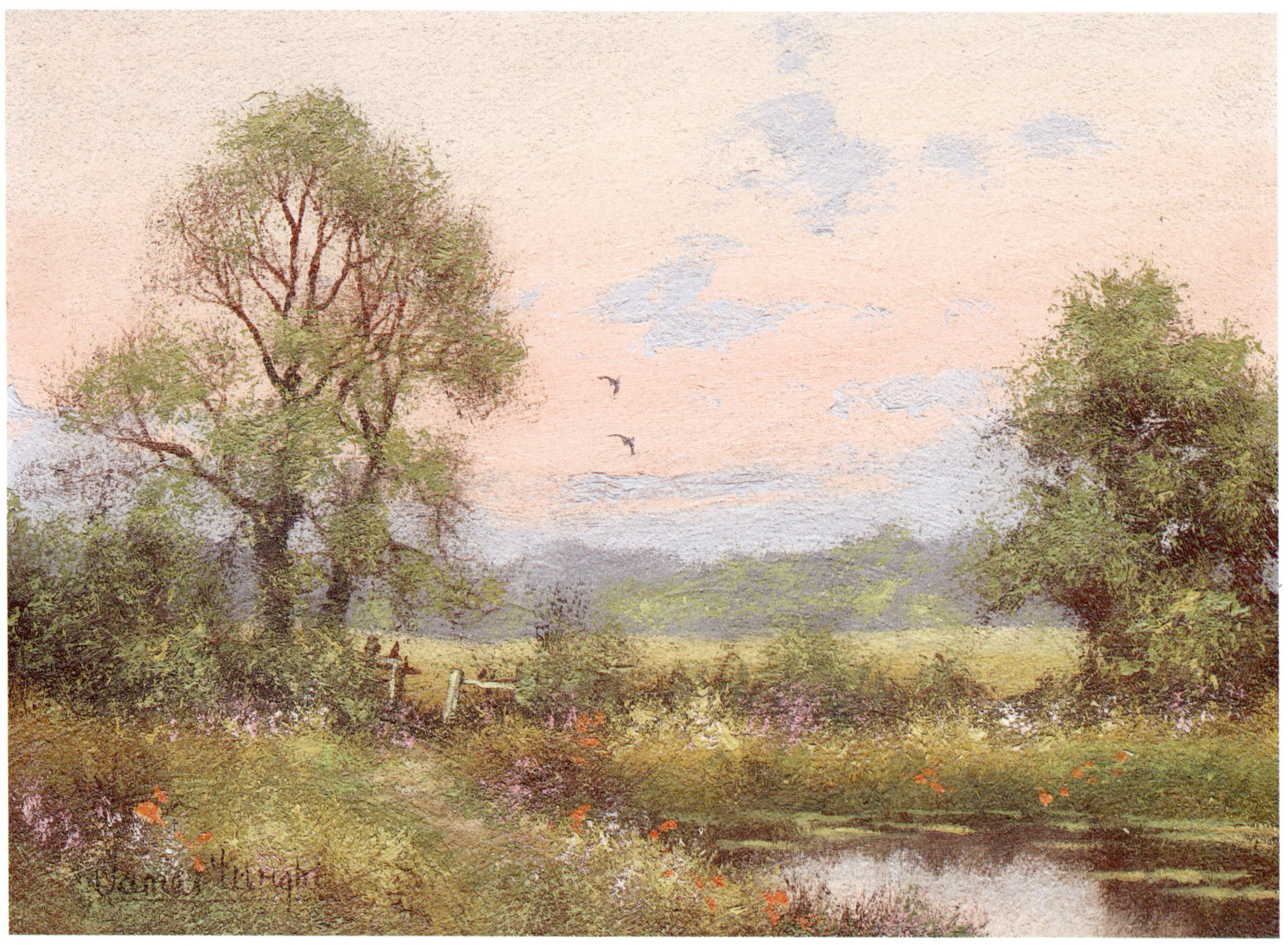

Evening Light.

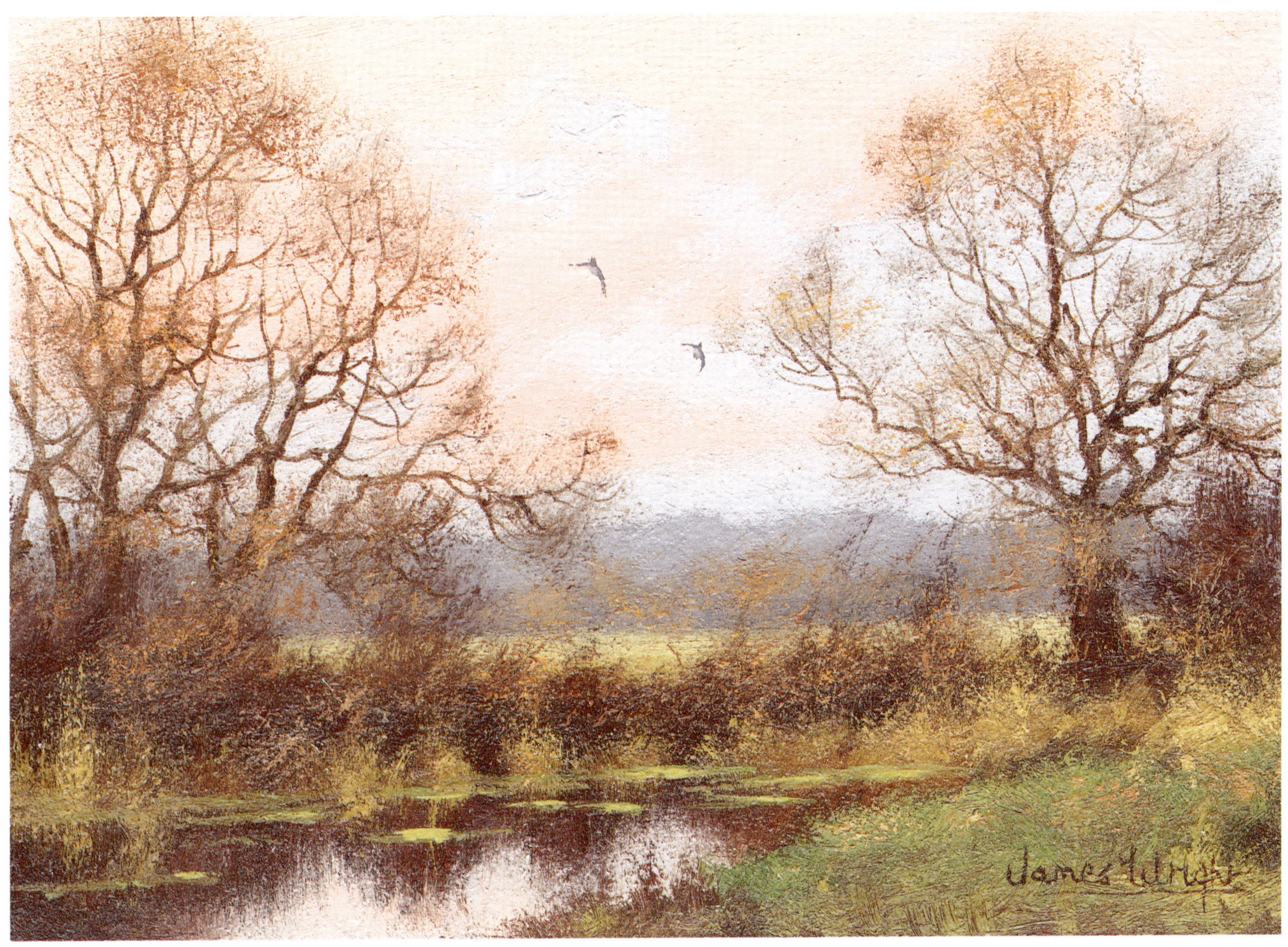

The Flight Pond.

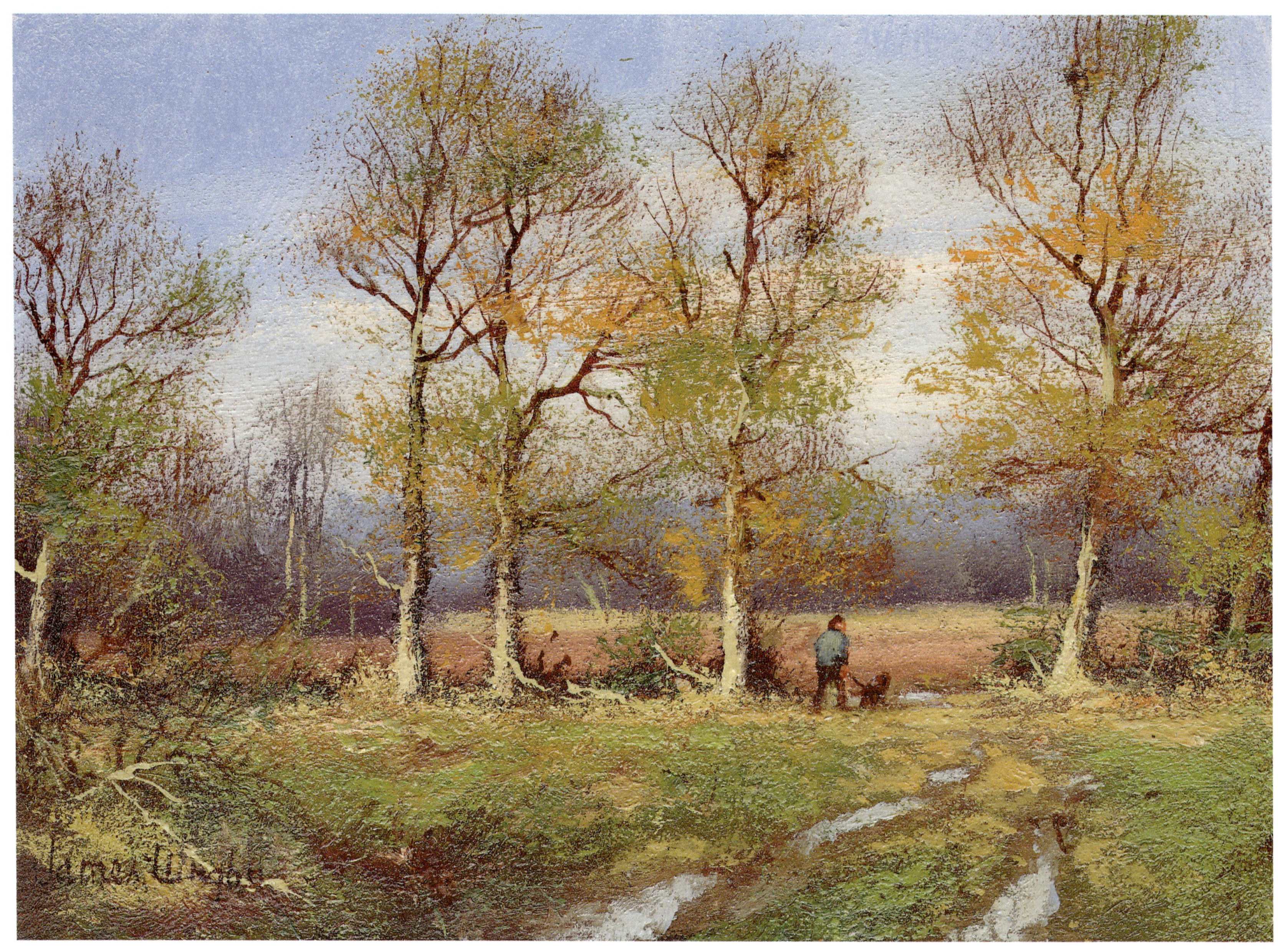

An Autumn Stroll.

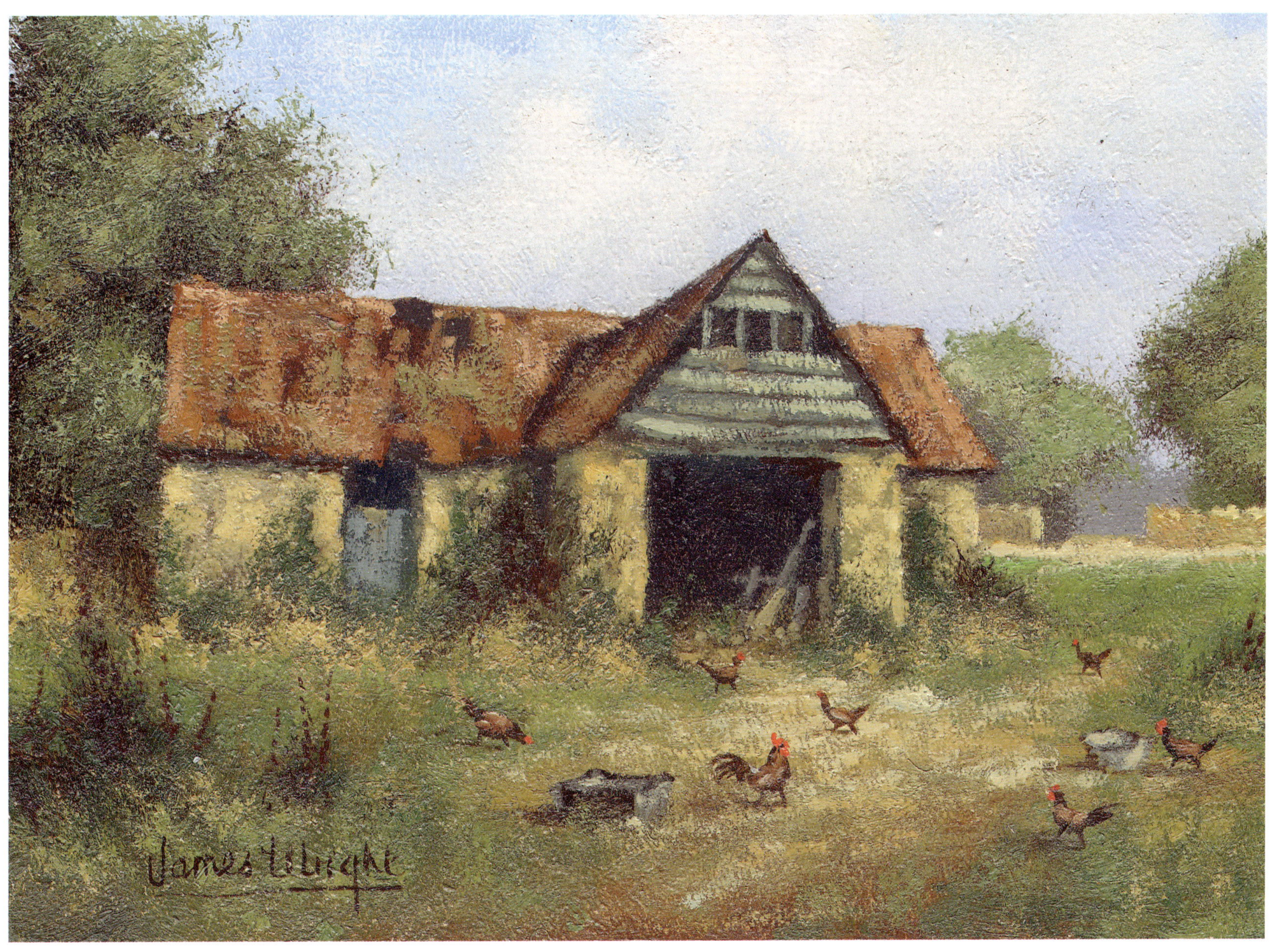

Old Barn and Chickens.

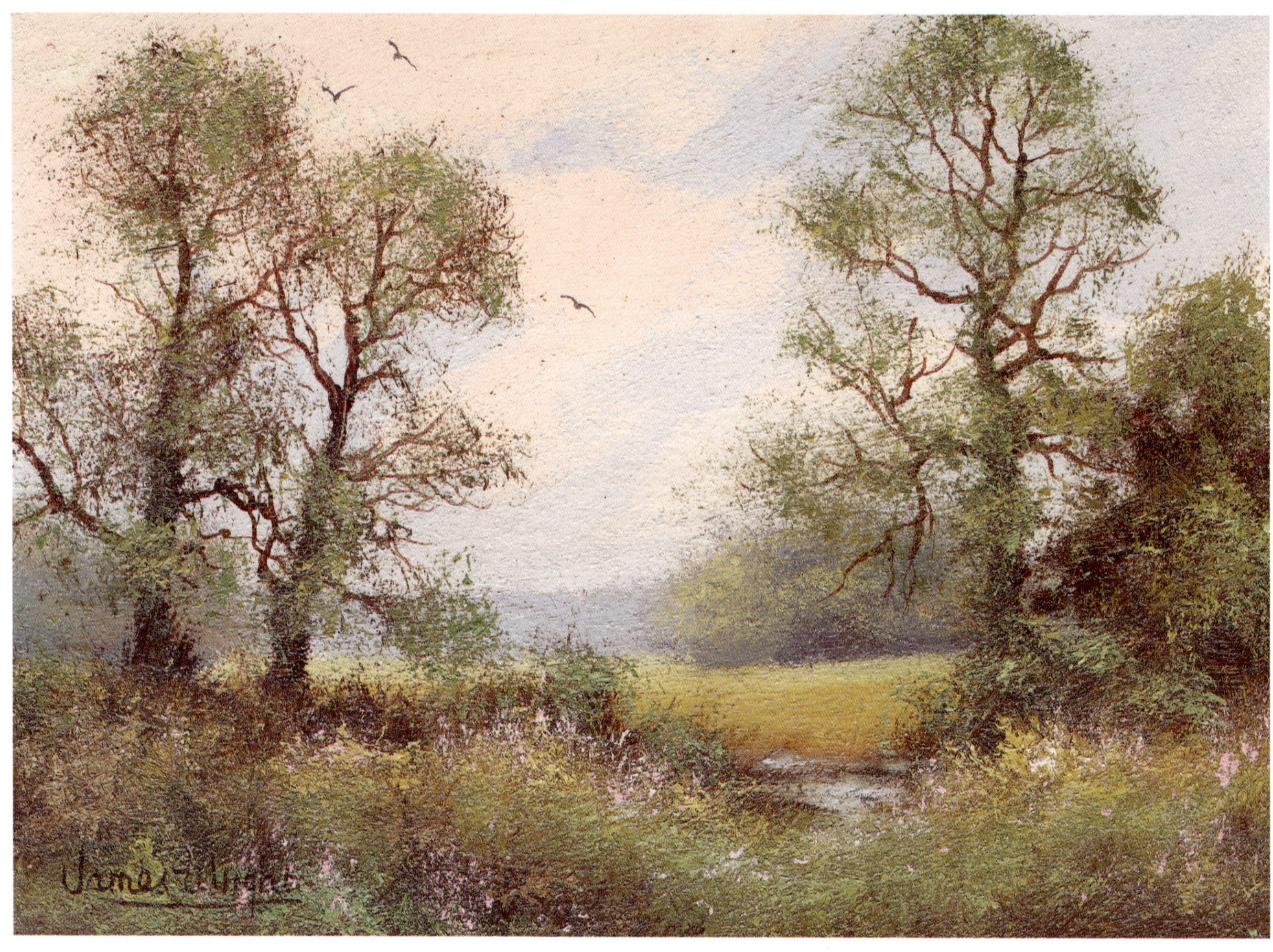

Spring Landscape.

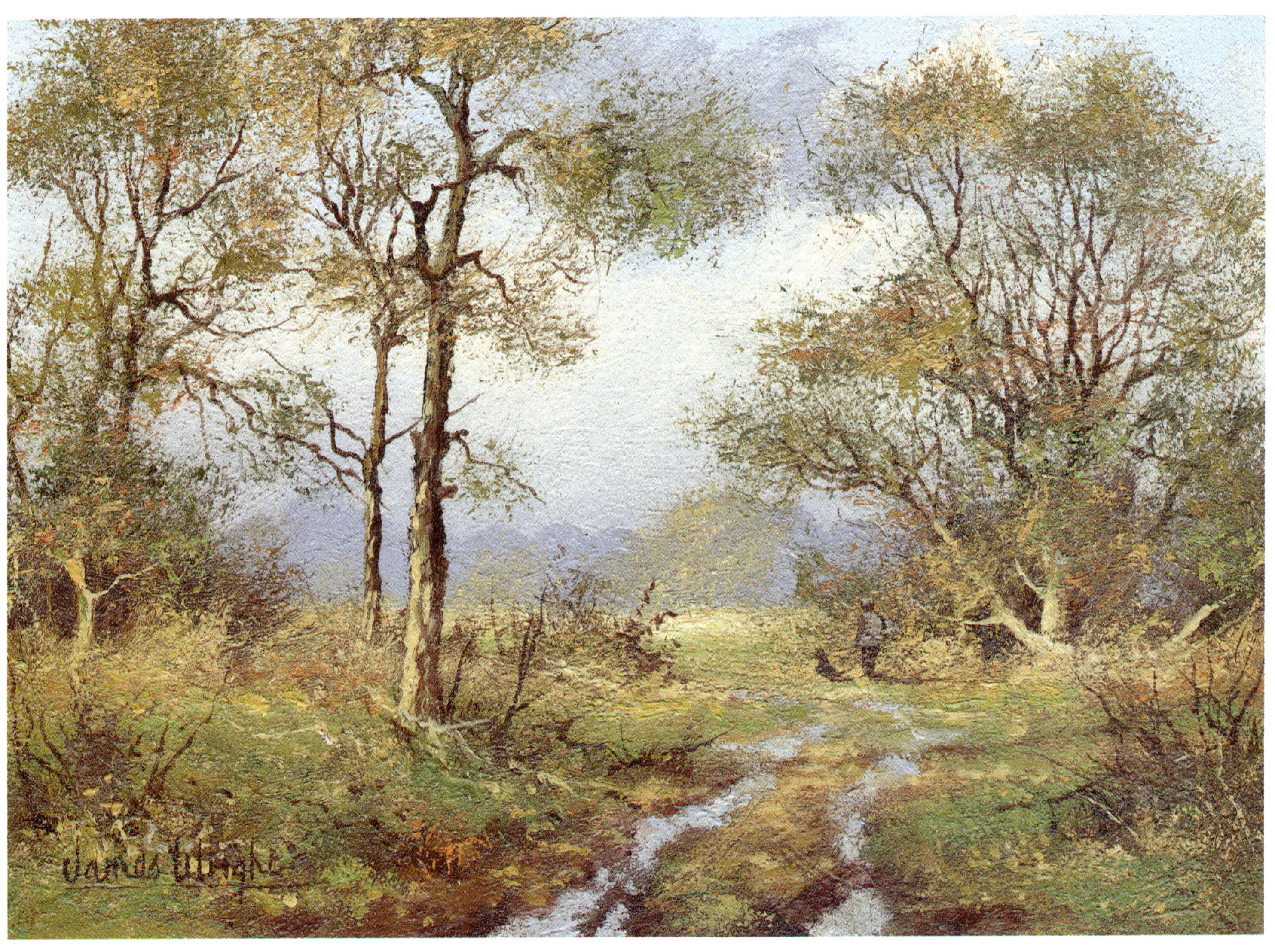

Walking the Dog.

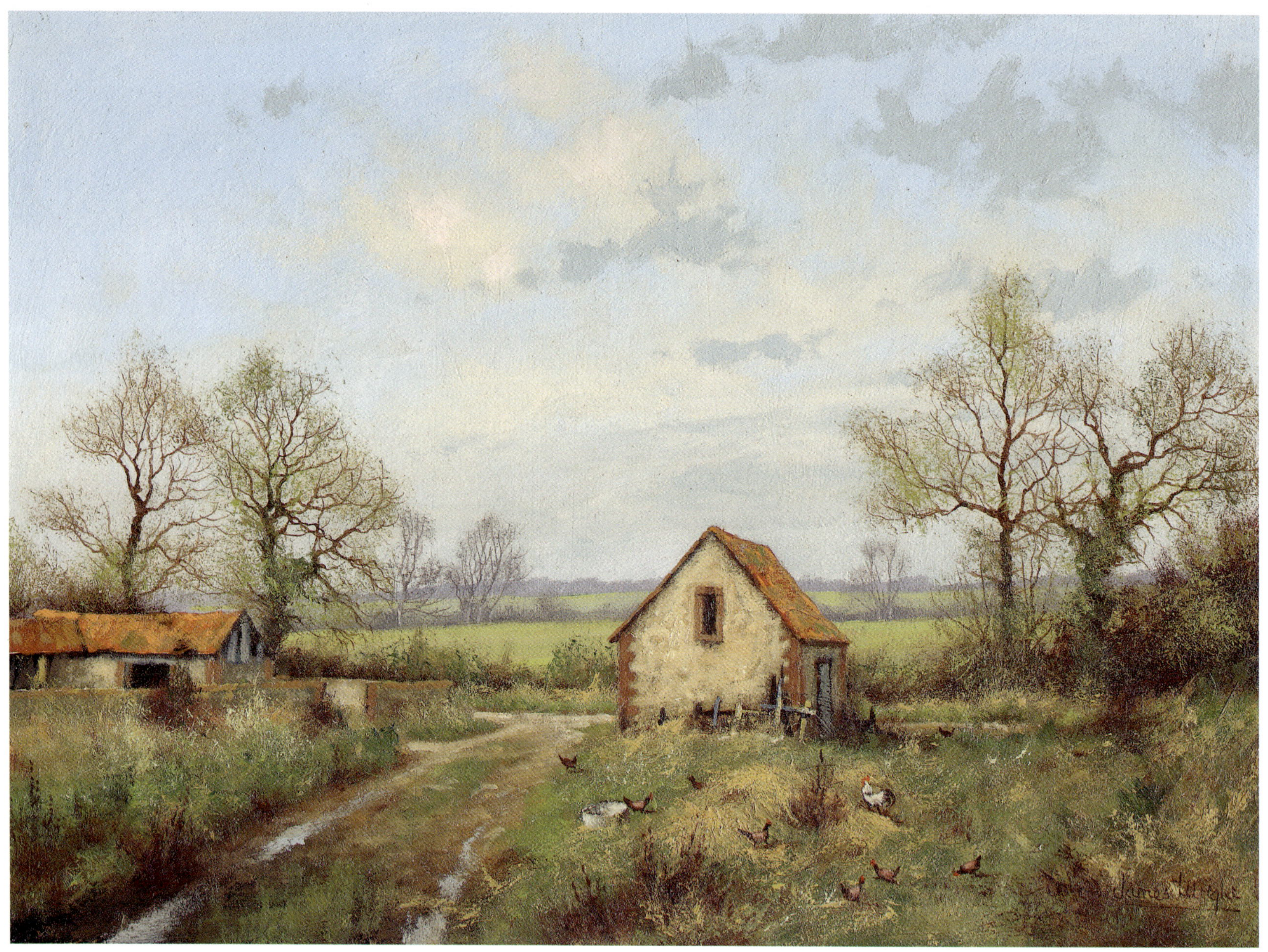

Farm Buildings, Thrapston.

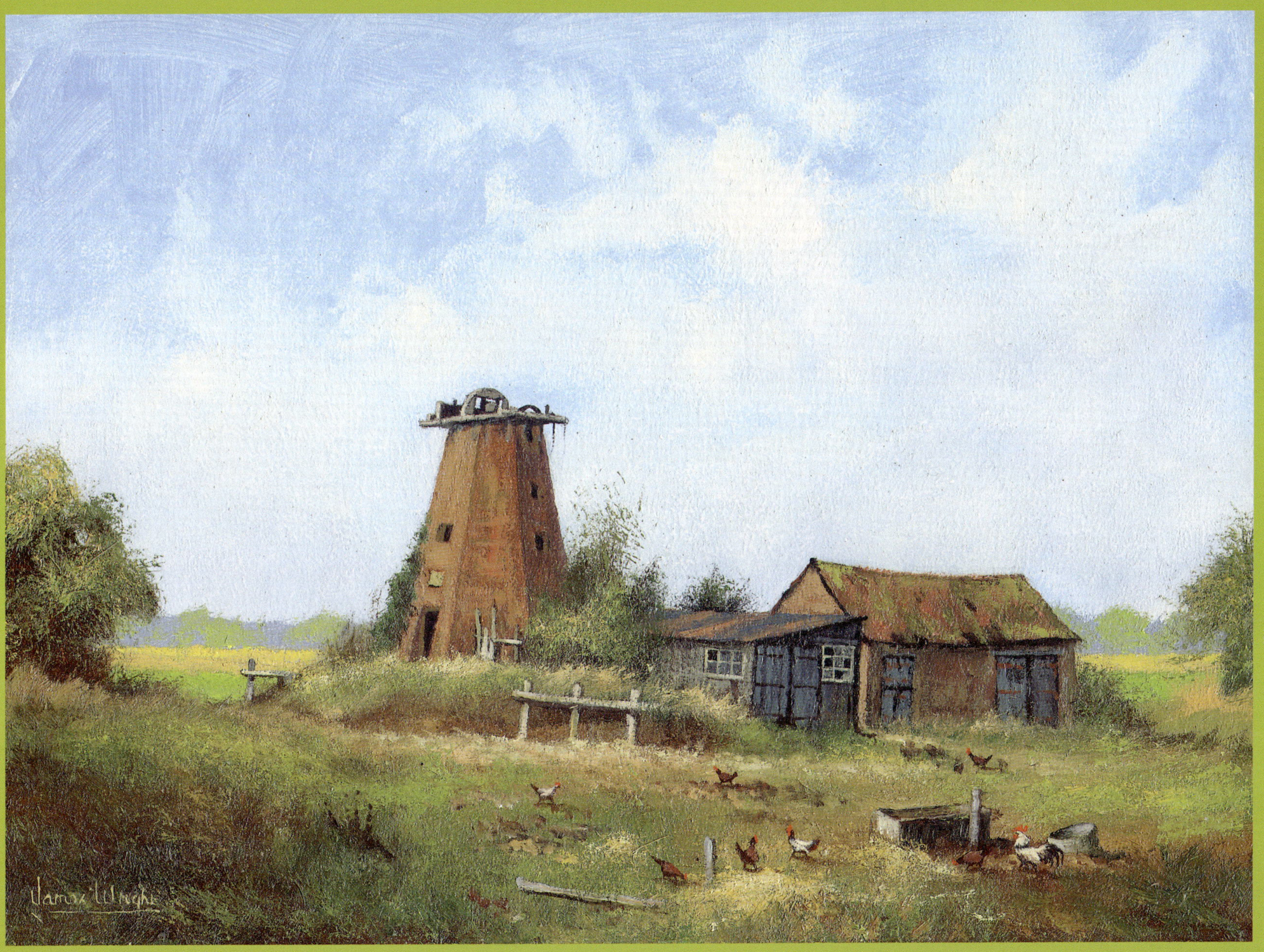

Lutton Mill.

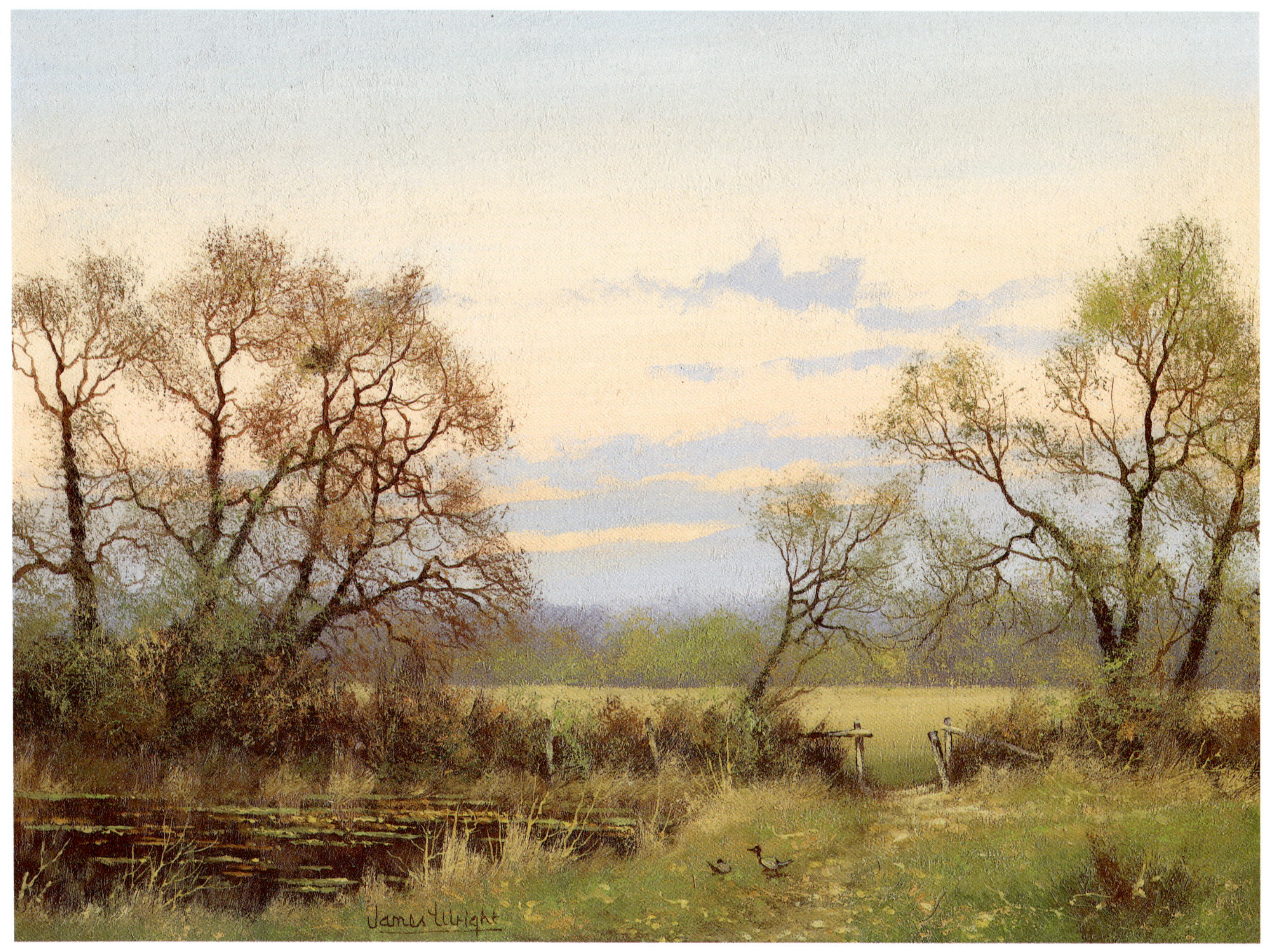

The End of the Day.

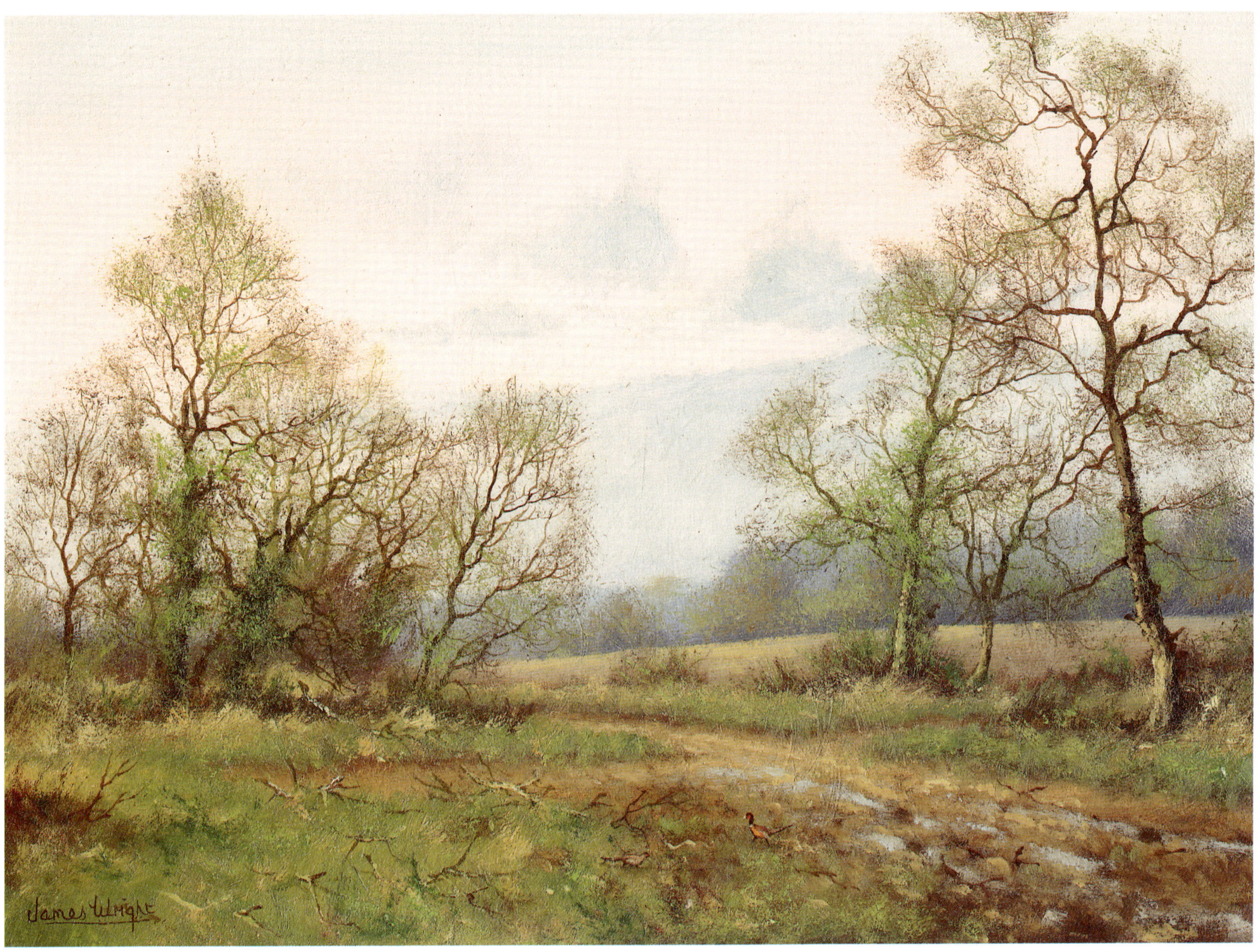

Fen Landscape.

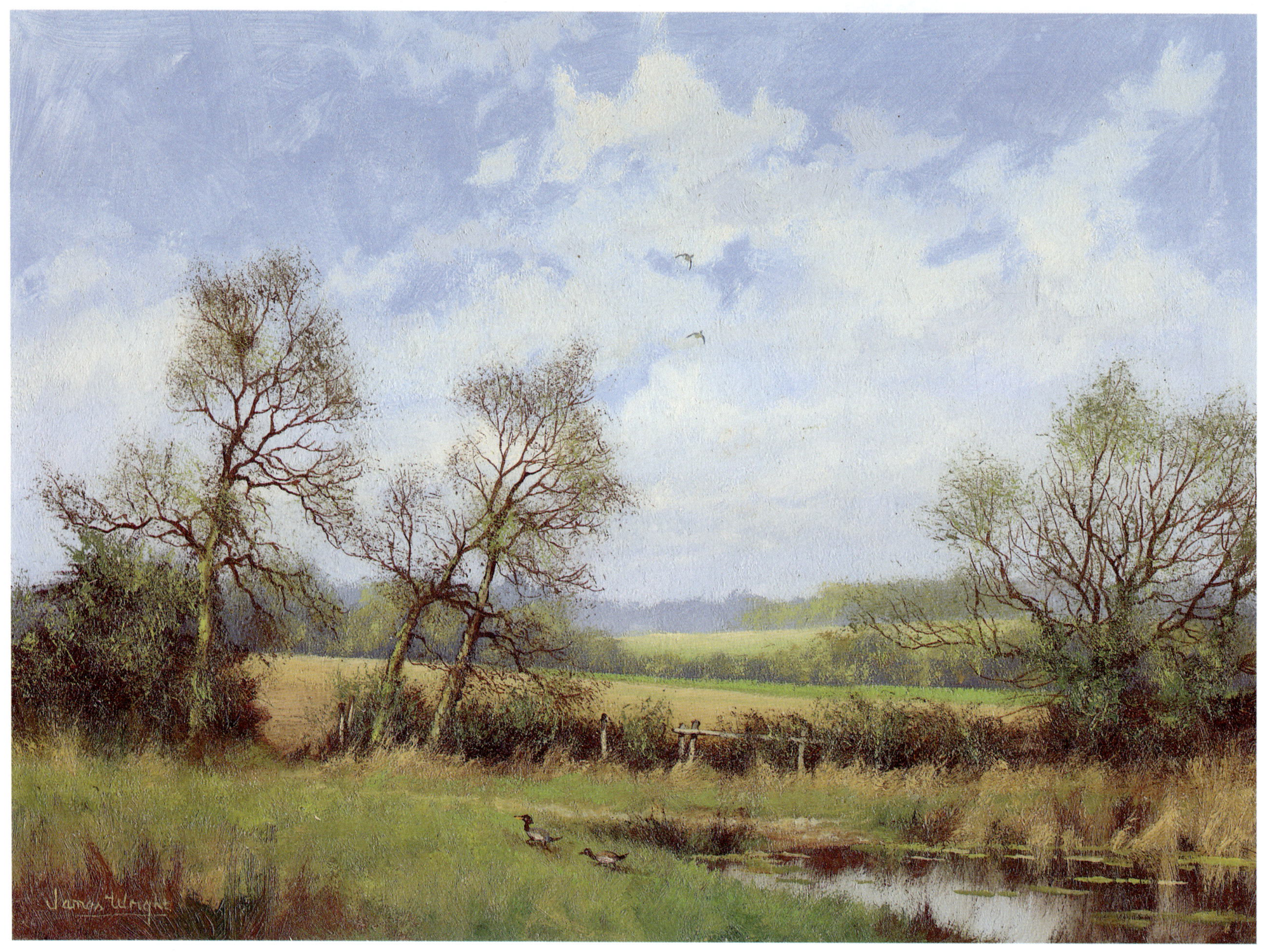

Norfolk Fields.

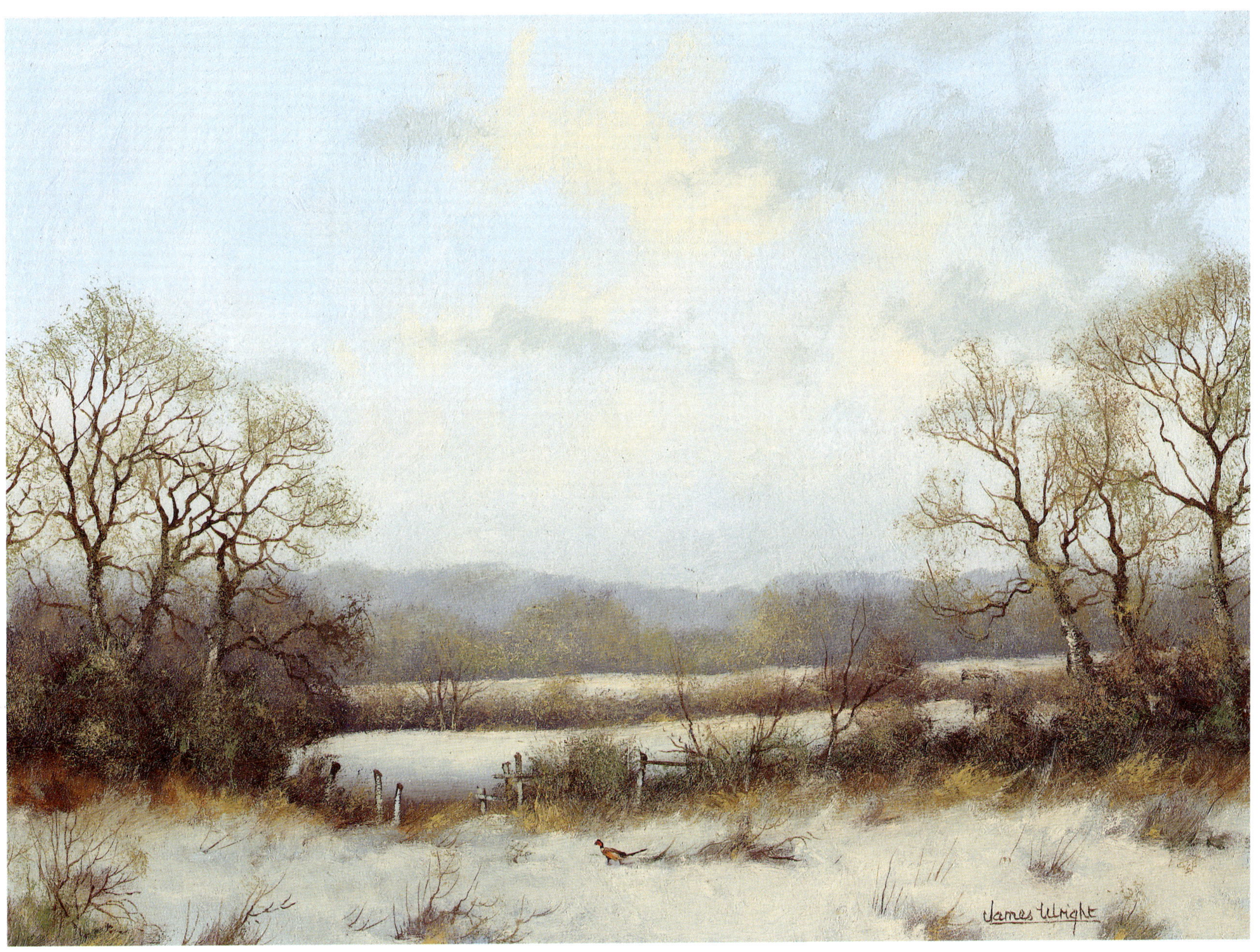

The First Snow.

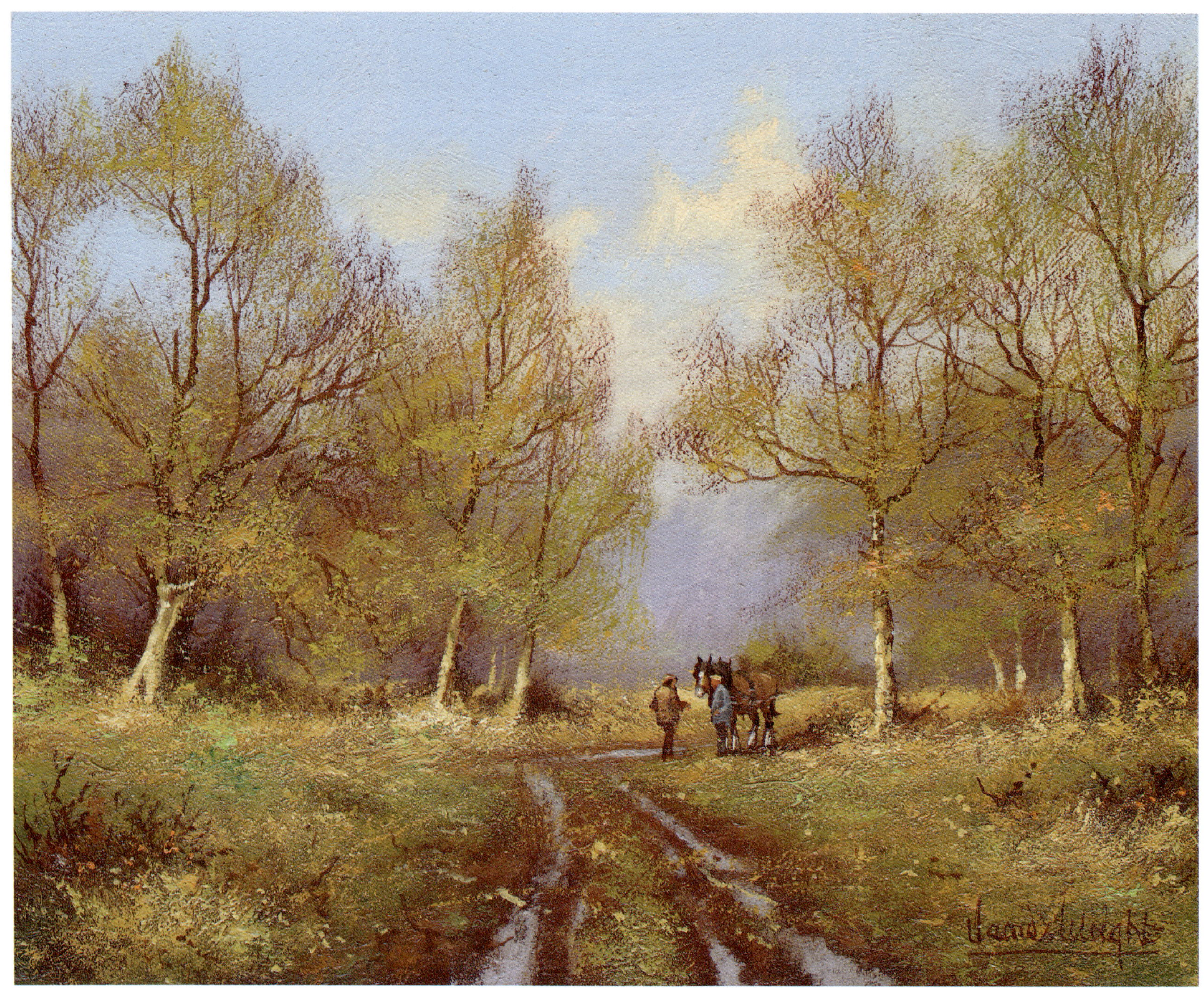

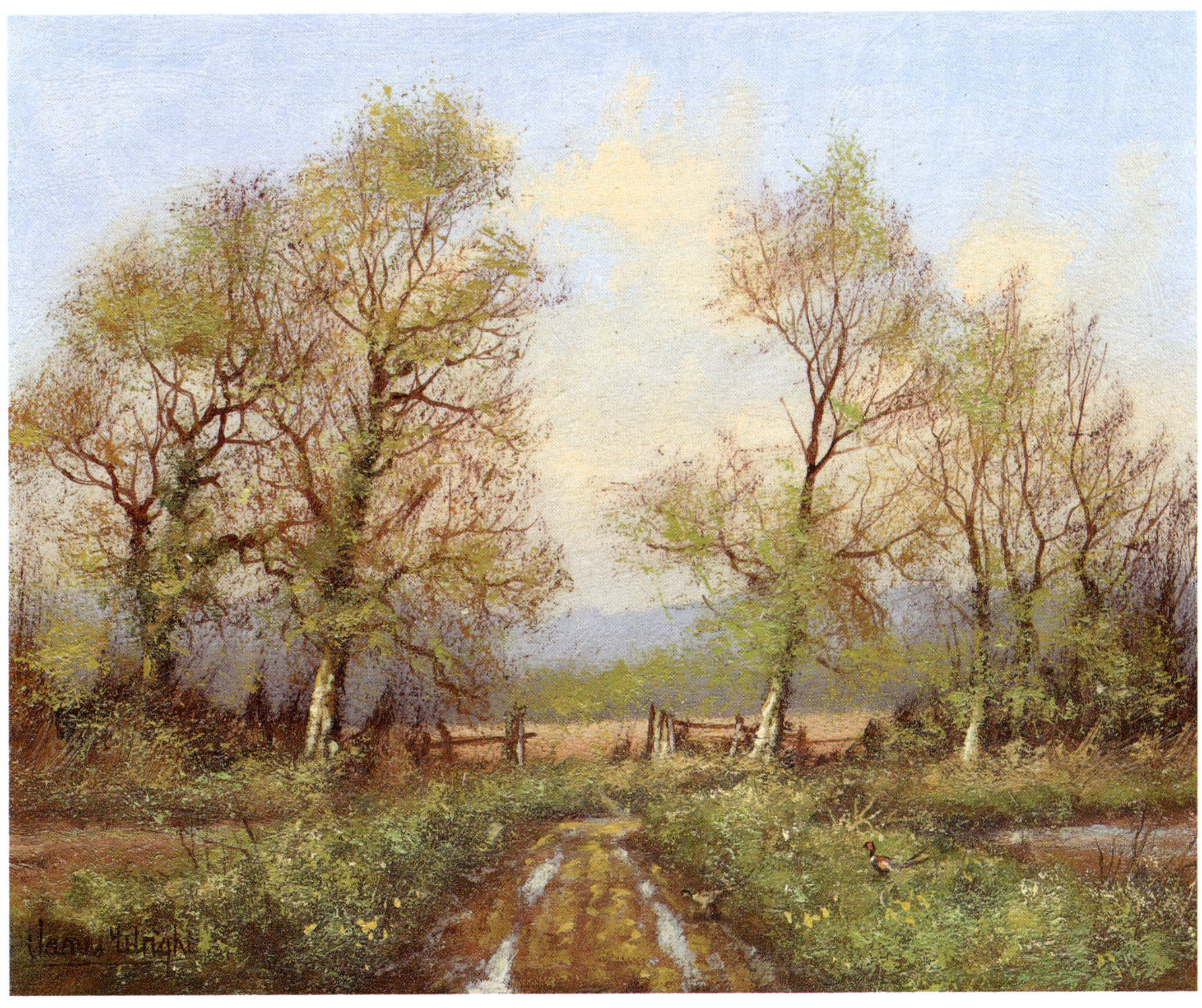

After the Rain.

Opposite: *Homeward Bound.*

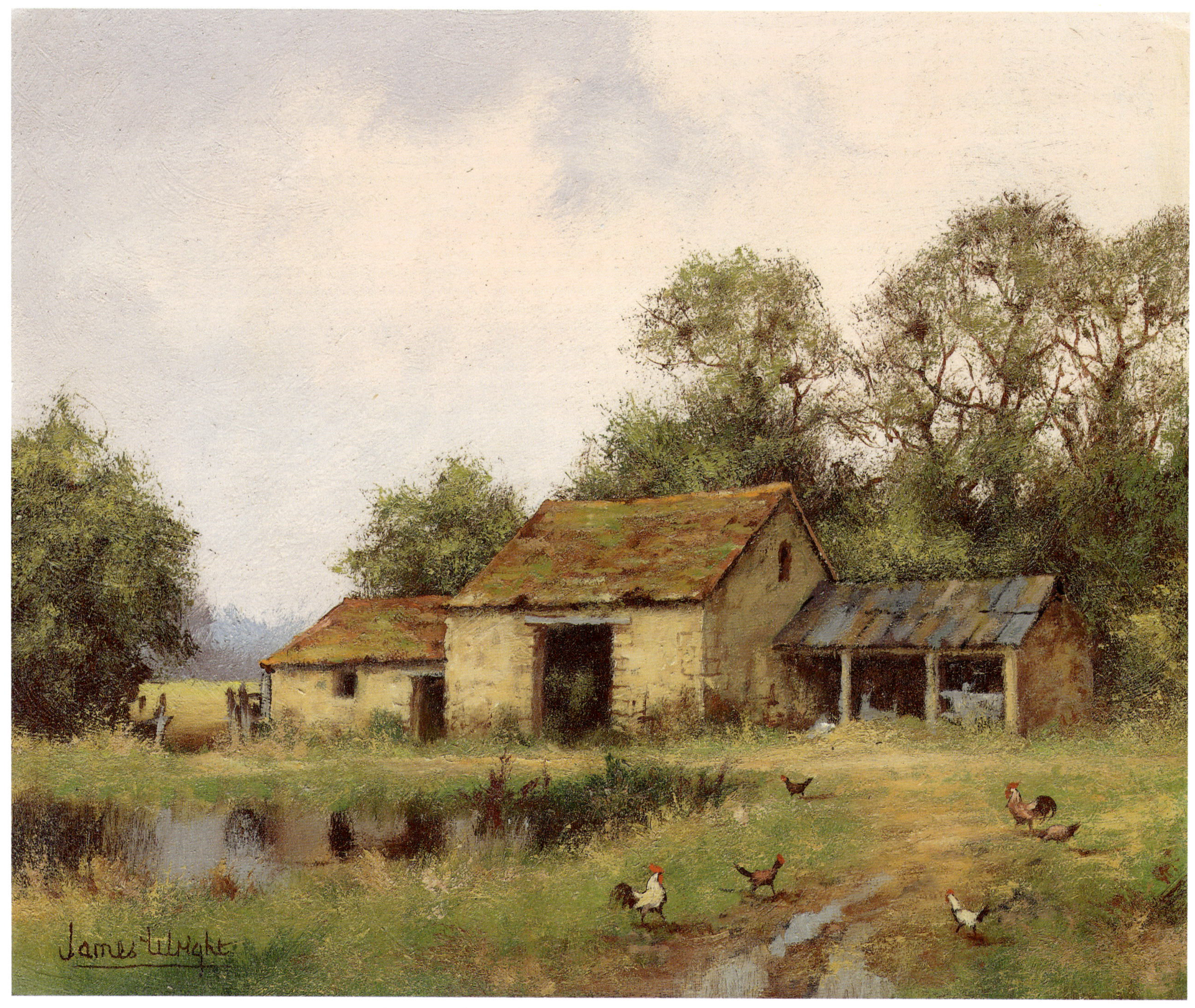

Barn, Pond and Chickens.

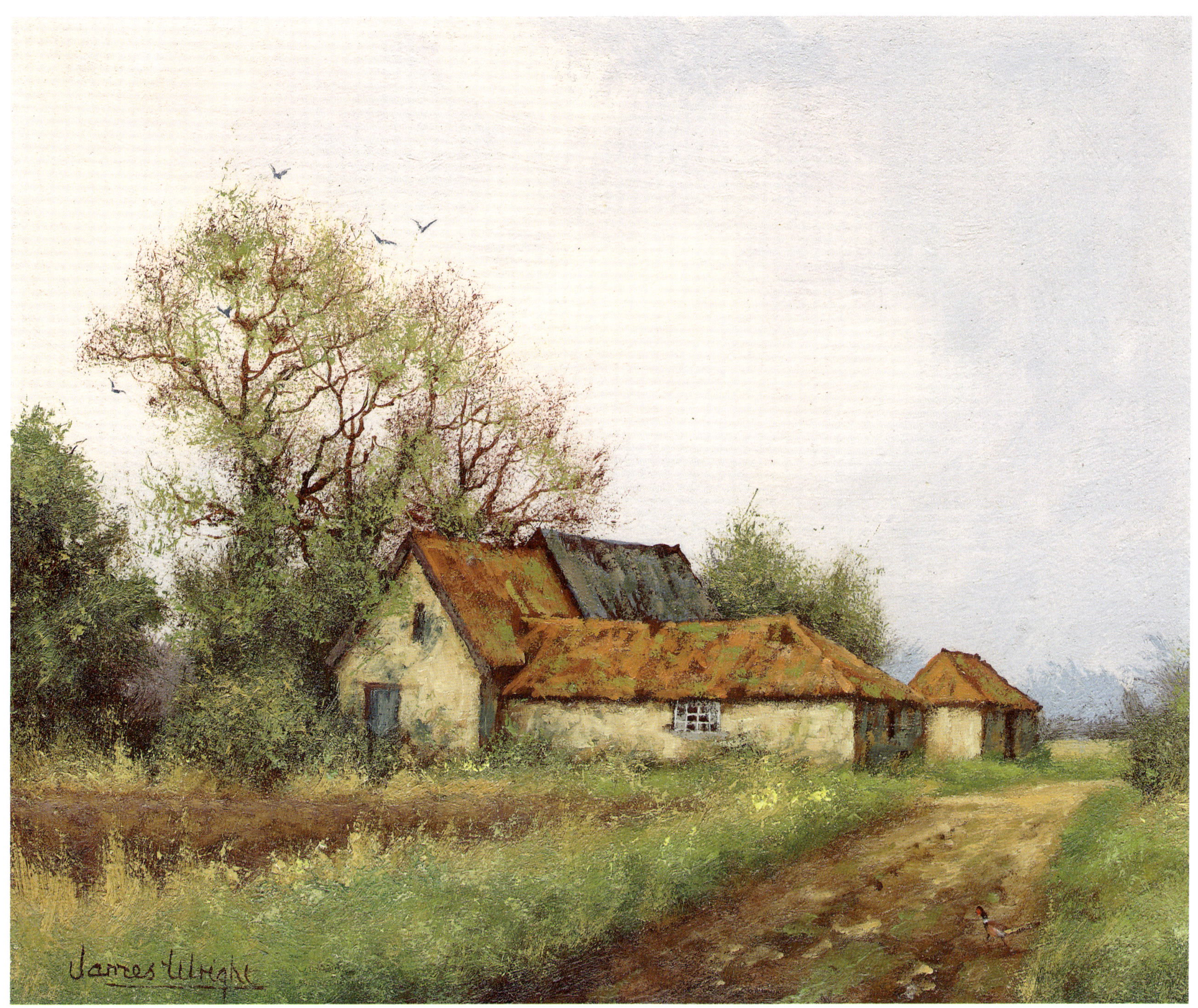

Barn near Woodbridge.

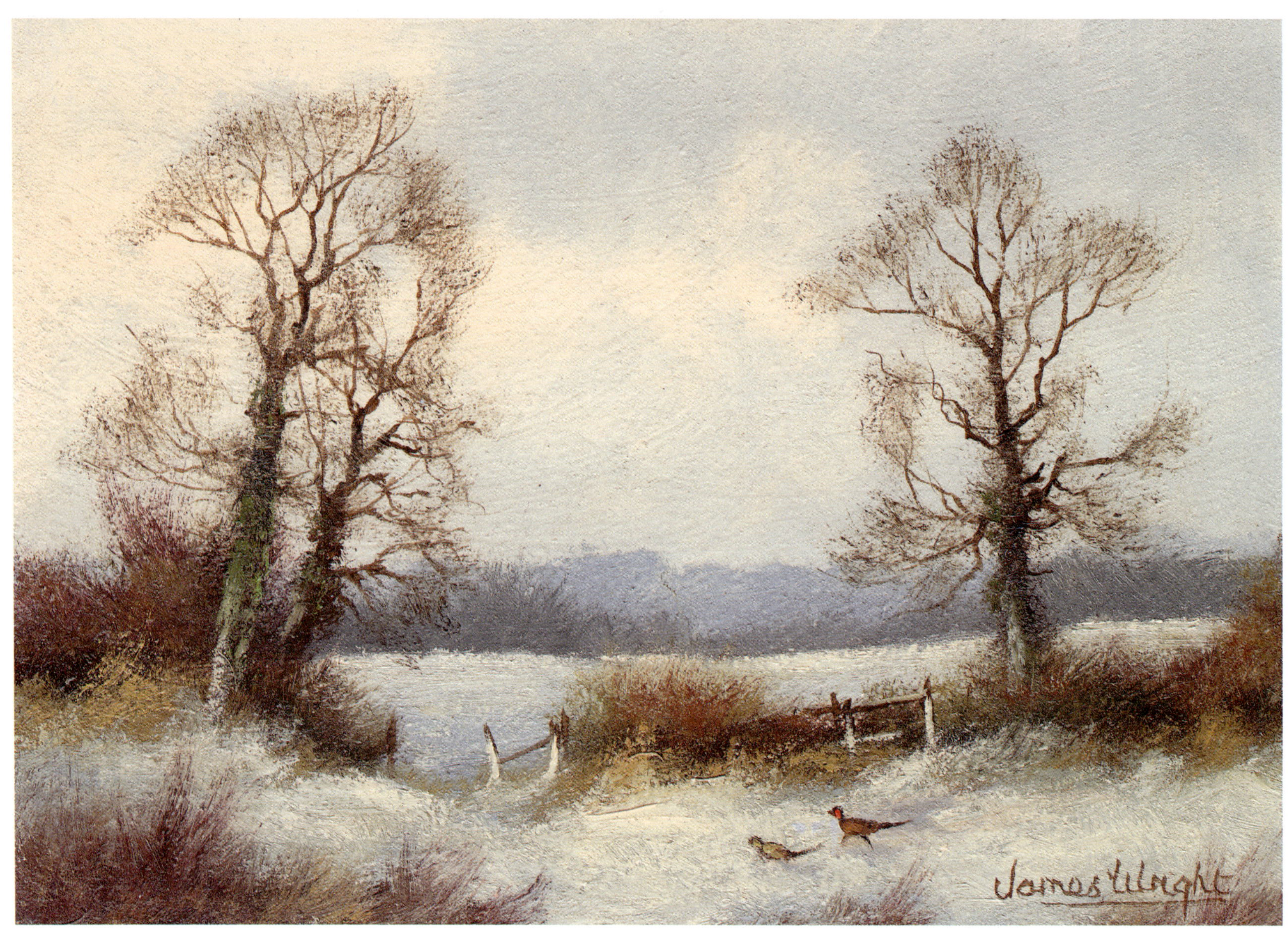

Hard Times.

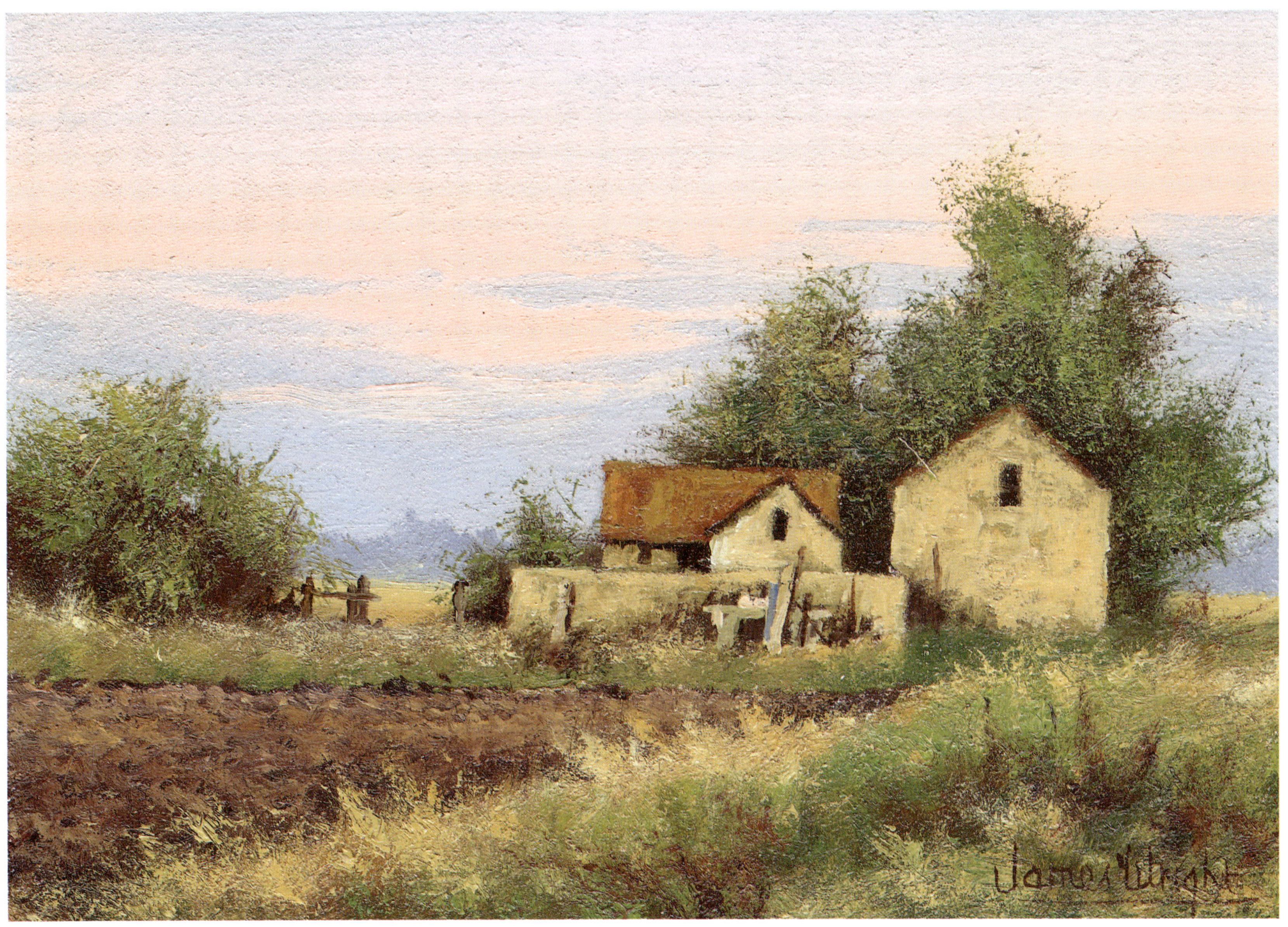

Farm Buildings, Moulton Chapel.

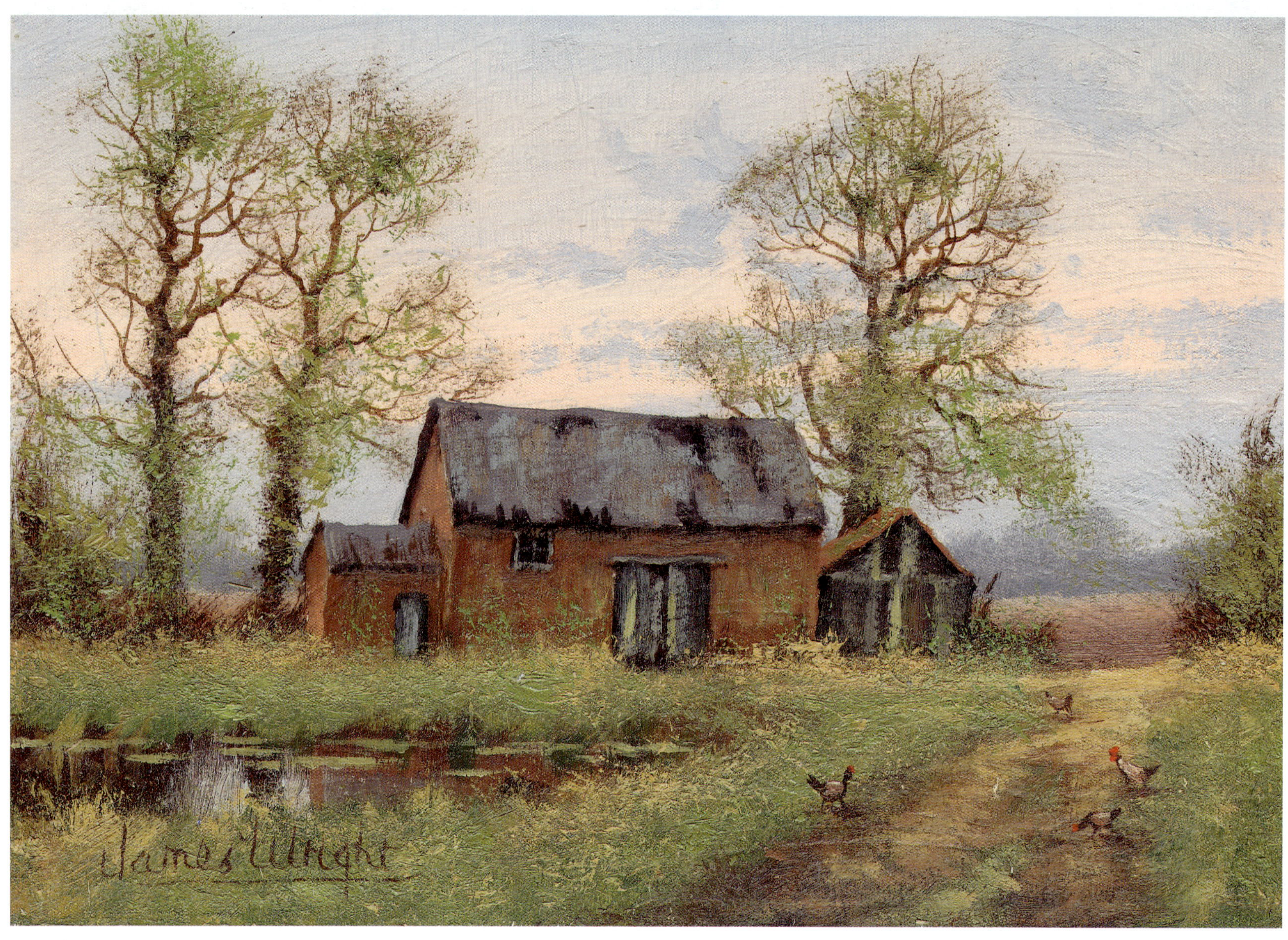

Barn and Pond.

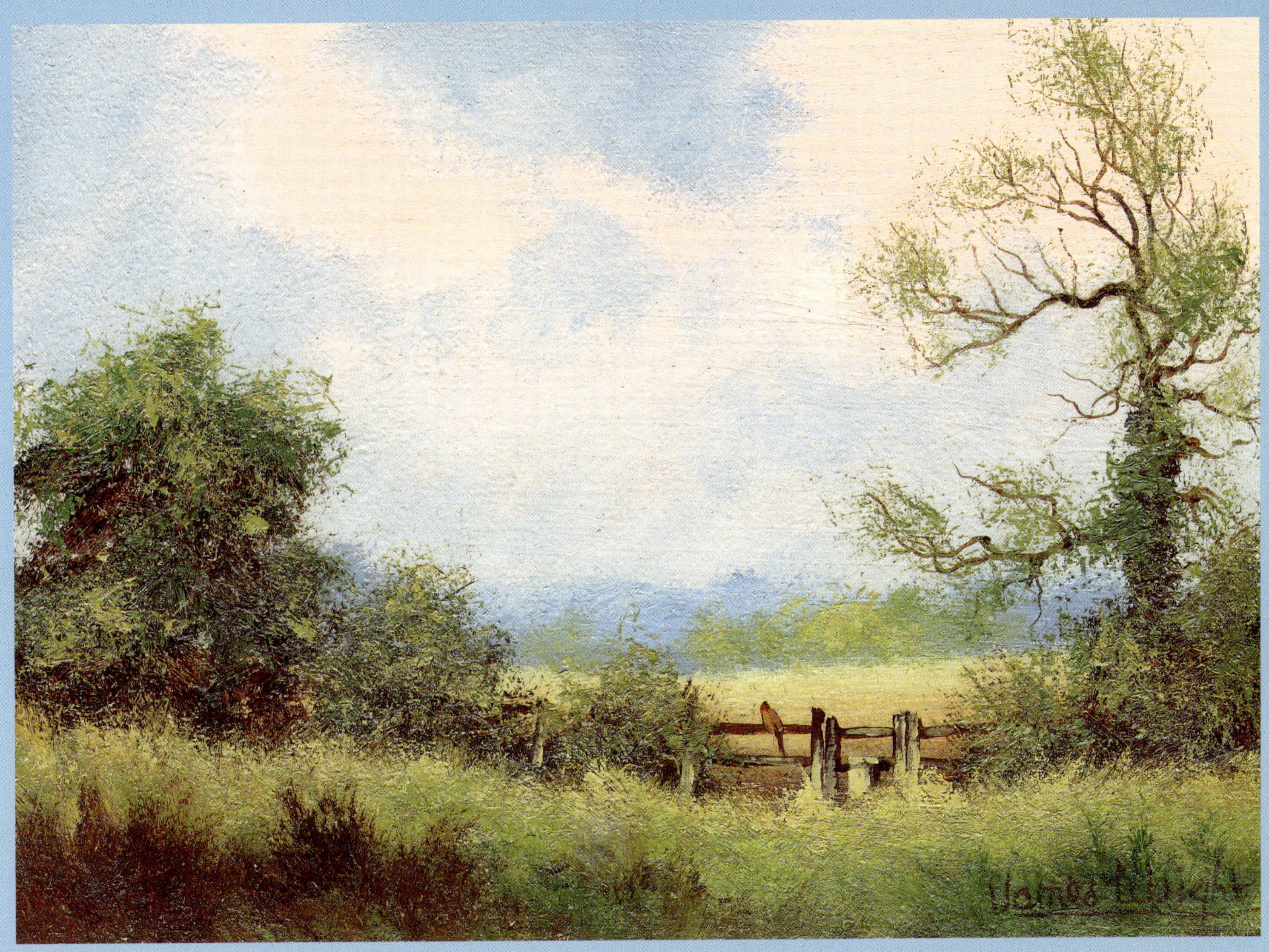

Sitting on the Fence.

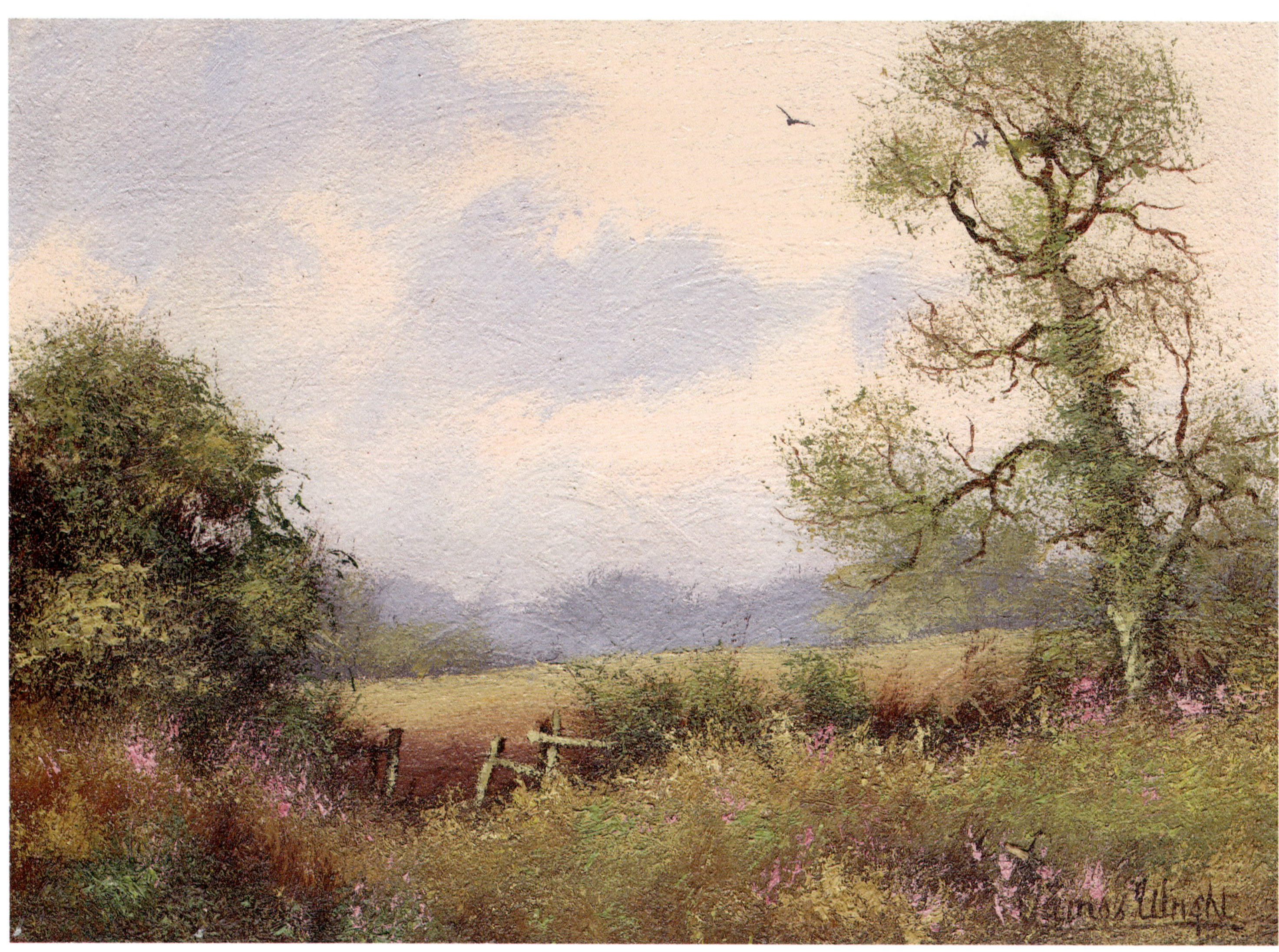

The Broken Stile.

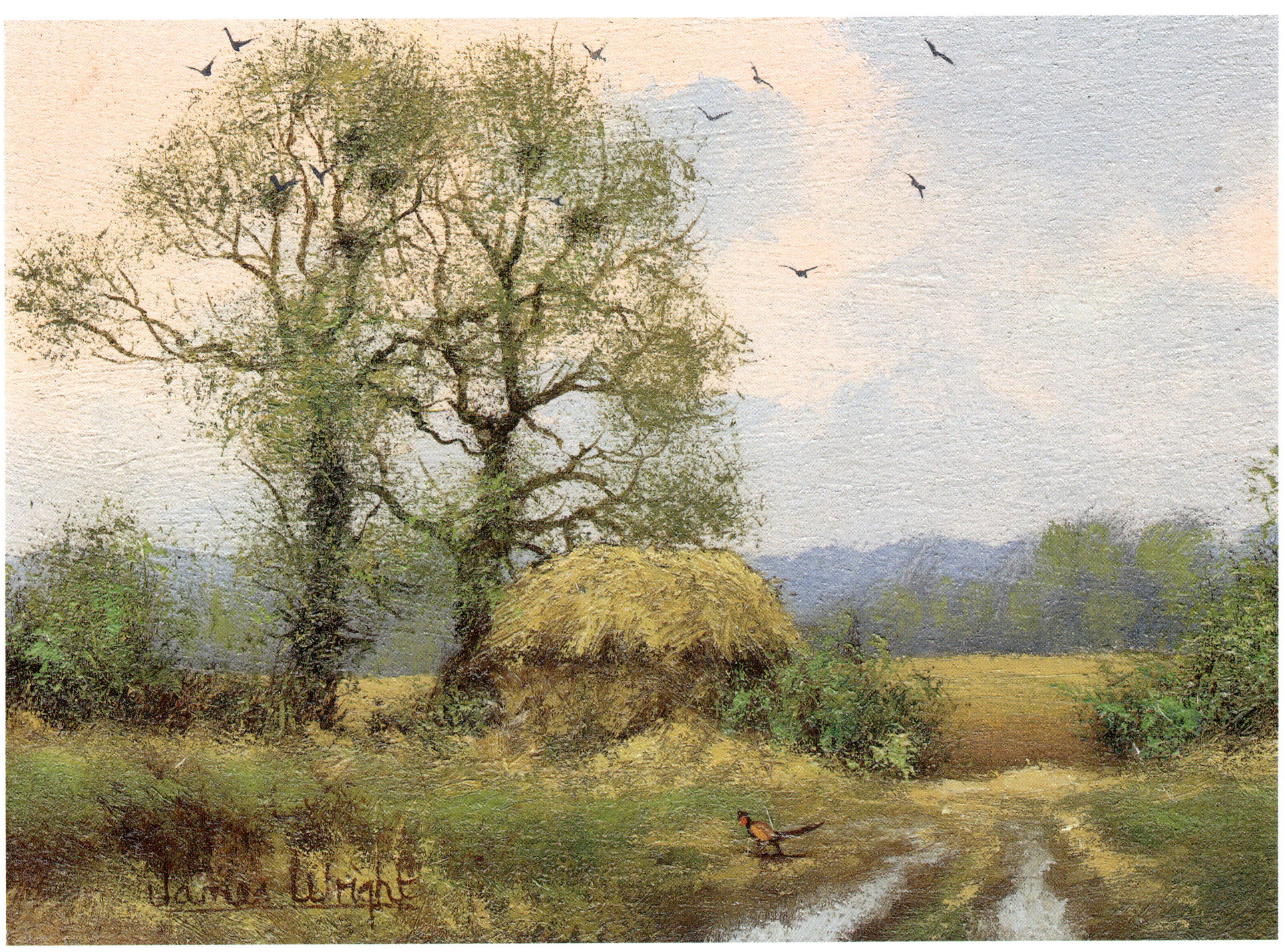

Signs of Spring.

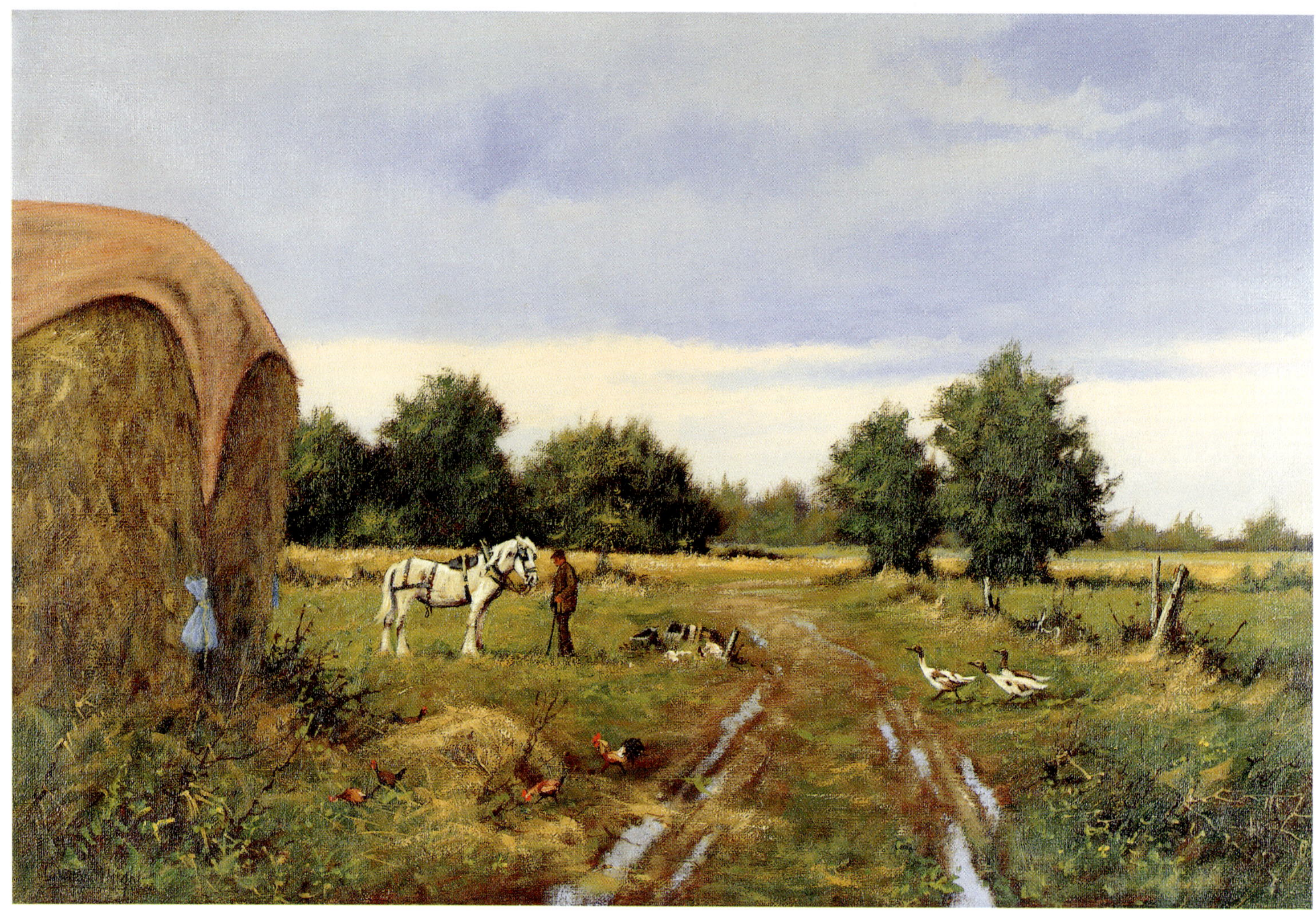

Horse, Geese and Haystack.

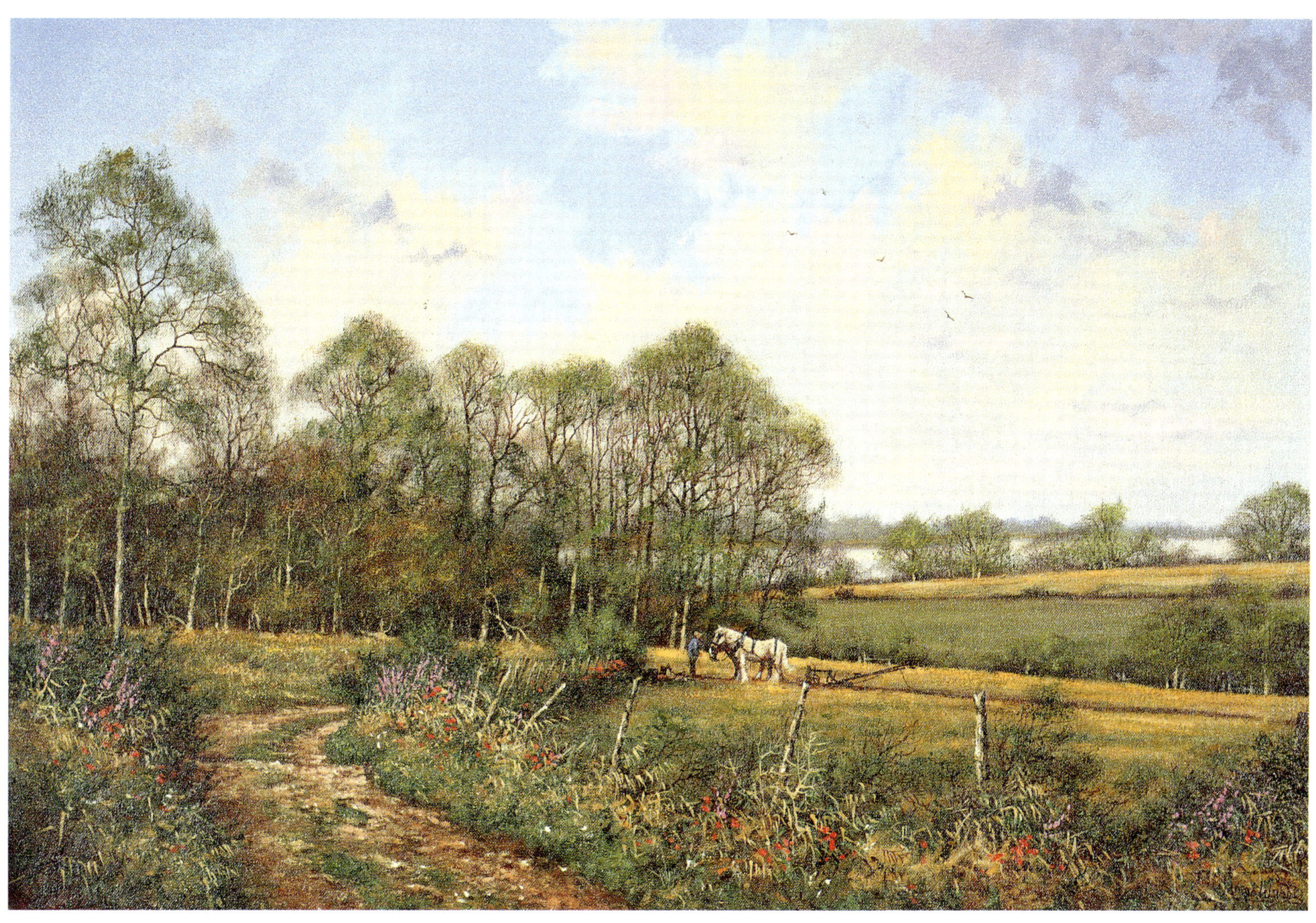

Ploughing.

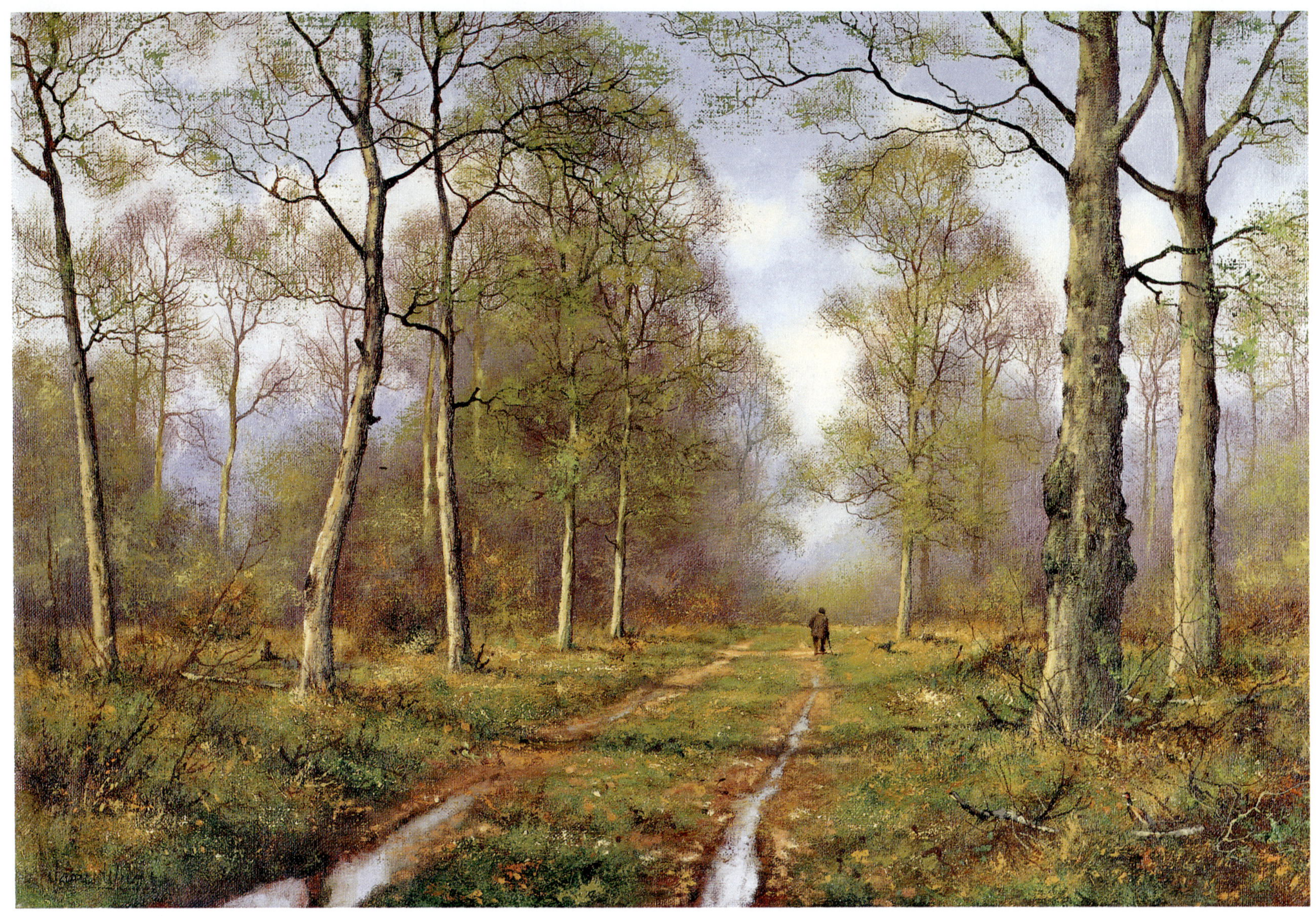

Short Wood.

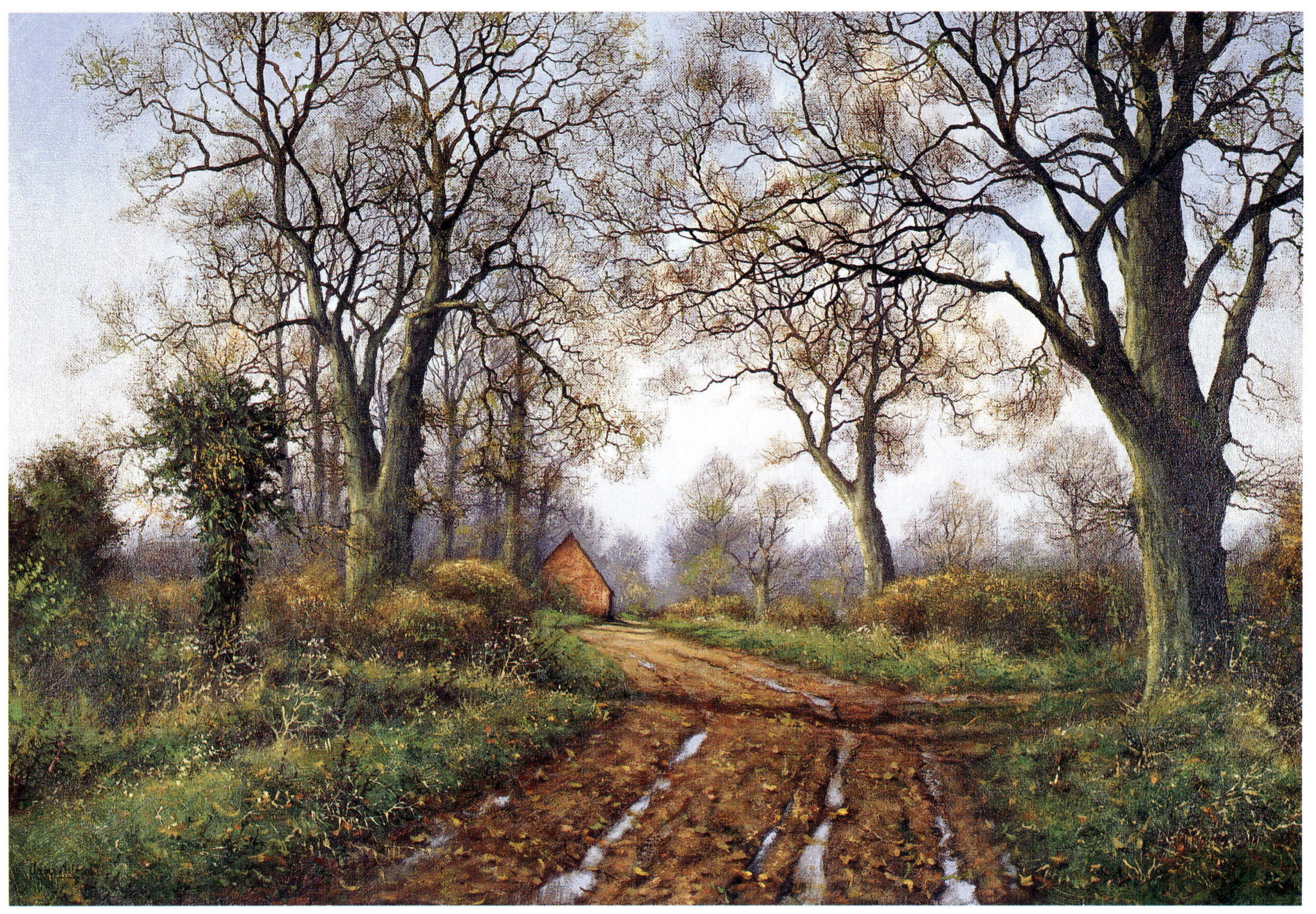

Woodbastwick.

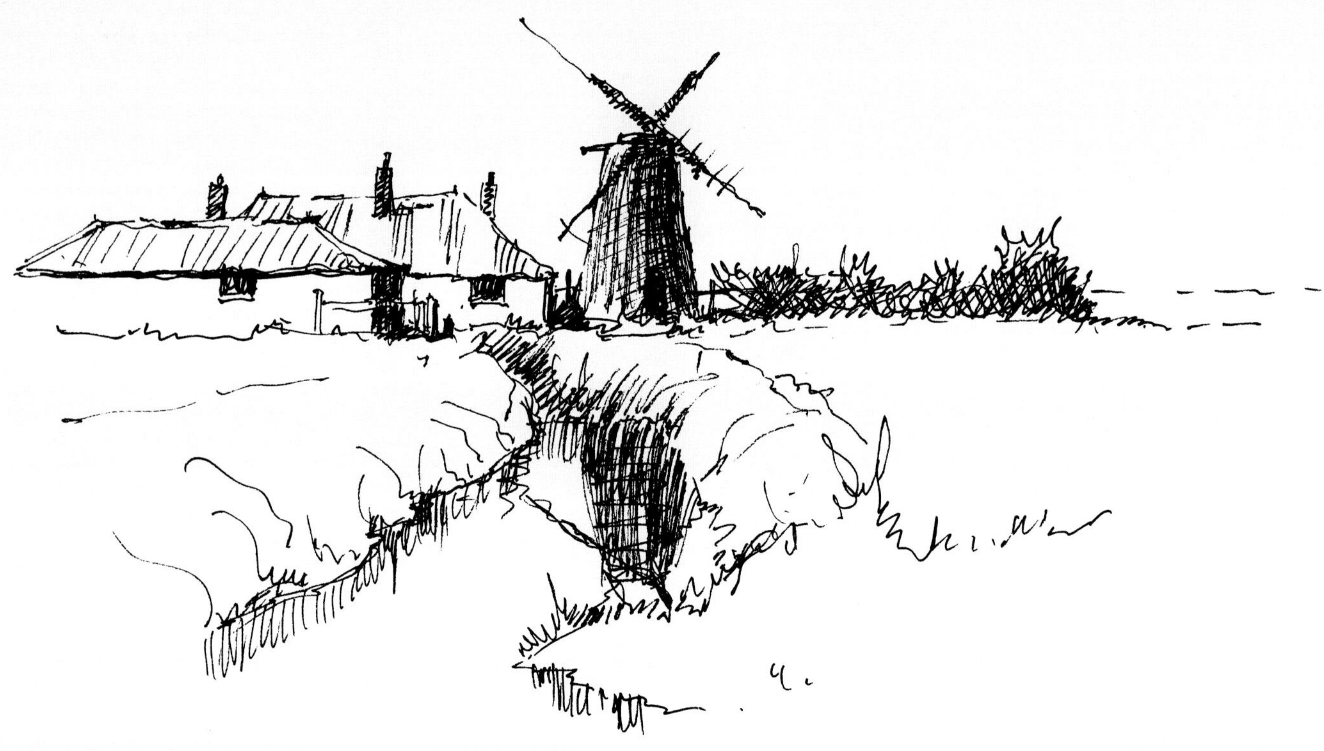